EMMETT DULANEY

MCSE
TRAINING GUIDE

INTERNET INFORMATION SERVER 4

New Riders

MCSE Training Guide: Internet Information Server 4

By Emmett Dulaney

Published by:
New Riders Publishing
201 West 103rd Street
Indianapolis, IN 46290 USA

Copyright© 1998 by Macmillan Publishing U.S.A./A Simon and Schuster Company. The Publishing Operation of Viacom, Inc.

Printed in the United States of America

Library of Congress Catalog No.: 98-84504

CIP data available upon request

ISBN: 0-56205-823-1

01 00 99 98   4 3 2 1

Interpretation of the printing code: the rightmost double-digit number is the year of the book's printing; the rightmost single-digit number, the number of the book's printing. For example, a printing code of 98-1 shows that the first printing of the book occurred in 1998.

Screen reproductions in this book were created using Collage Plus from Inner Media, Inc., Hollis, NH.

Executive Editor *Mary Foote*
Acquisitions Editor *Nancy Maragioglio*
Development Editor *Ami Frank*

Technical Editors
R. Andrew Brice
Robert Bogue

Managing Editor
Sarah Kearns

Project Editor
Tom Dinse

Copy Editors
Nancy Albright
Howard A. Jones

Indexer
Ginny Bess

Cover Designer
Karen Ruggles

Book Designer
Glenn Larsen

Production Team
Michael Henry
Linda Knose
Tim Osborn
Staci Somers
Mark Walchle

About the Author

Emmett Dulaney is an MCSE, MCP+Internet, CNE, and LAN Server Engineer. The coauthor of *Teach Yourself MCSE NT Workstation in 14 Days*, he is also the Certification Corner columnist for *NT Systems* Magazine, and an instructor for DataTech and Indiana University\Purdue University of Fort Wayne.

Acknowledgments

I would like to thank everyone who put in such hard work on this book to make it the best product they could: Nancy Maragioglio and Mary Foote, who together conceptualized the project and walked it through the channels. Chris Zahn added tremendous developmental value, while Rob Bogue and Andrew Brice looked at the technical side. I hope we can all work together again on another project in the near future.

Dedications

For Karen, Kristin, Evan and Spencer.

We'd Like to Hear from You!

As part of our continuing effort to produce books of the highest possible quality, MCP would like to hear your comments. To stay competitive, we really want you, as a computer book reader and user, to let us know what you like or dislike most about this book or other Macmillan products.

You can mail comments, ideas, or suggestions for improving future editions to the following address below or email us at `networking.mcp.com`. The address of our Internet site is `http://www.mcp.com` (World Wide Web).

Thanks in advance—your comments help us to continue publishing the best books available on computer topics in today's market.

Note Although we cannot provide general technical support, we're happy to help you resolve problems you encounter related to our books, disks, or other products. If you need such assistance, please contact our Tech Support department at 800-545-5914 ext. 3833.

Contents at a Glance

Table of Contents

Introduction

MCSE Training Guide: Internet Information Server 4 is designed for advanced end-users, service technicians, and network administrators, with the goal of certification as a Microsoft Certified Systems Engineer (MCSE), Microsoft Certified Systems Engineer with the +Internet credential (MCSE+Internet), or Microsoft Certified Professional with the +Internet specialization (MCP+Internet). The IIS 4 exam (Exam 70-087: "Implementing and Supporting Microsoft® Internet Information Server 4.0") measures your ability to implement, administer, and troubleshoot information systems that incorporate components of Internet Information Server, as well as your ability to provide technical support to users of IIS, Index Server, and related services.

Who Should Read This Book

This book is designed to help you meet these goals by preparing you for the "Implementing and Supporting Microsoft® Internet Information Server 4.0" (Exam 70-087).

This book is your one-stop shop. Everything you need to know to pass the exam is in here, and Microsoft has approved it as study material. You do not *need* to take a class in addition to buying this book to pass the exam. However, depending on your personal study habits or learning style, you may benefit from taking a class in addition to studying this book, or buying this book in addition to attending a class.

This book also can help advanced users and administrators who are not studying for the exam, but are looking for a single-volume reference on IIS 4.

How This Book Helps You

This book conducts you on a self-paced tour of all the areas covered by the IIS 4 exam and teaches you the specific skills you need to achieve your MCSE or MCP certification. You'll also find helpful hints, tips, real-world examples, exercises, and references to additional study materials. Specifically, this book is set up to help you in the following ways:

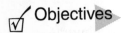 **Objectives**

▶ **Organization.** This book is organized by major exam topics and individual exam objectives. Every objective you need to know for the "Implementing and Supporting Microsoft® Internet Information Server 4.0" exam is covered in this book; we've included a margin icon, like the one in the margin here, to help you quickly locate these objectives as they are addressed in the chapters. This information is also conveniently condensed in the tear card at the front of this book.

▶ **Time-management advice.** Quizzes appear at the beginning of each chapter to test your knowledge of the objectives contained within that chapter. If you already know the answers to some or all of these questions, you can make a time-management decision accordingly, adjusting the amount of time you spend on a given topic.

▶ **Extensive practice test options.** Plenty of questions appear at the end of each chapter to test your comprehension of material covered within that chapter. An answer list follows the questions so you can check yourself. These review questions help you determine what you understand thoroughly and what topics require further review on your part.

You'll also get a chance to practice for the certification exams by using the TestPrep test engine on the accompanying CD-ROM. The questions on the CD-ROM provide a more thorough and comprehensive look at what the certification exams really are like.

Note   For a complete description of New Riders' newly developed test engine, please see Appendix I, "All About TestPrep."

For a complete description of what you can find on the CD-ROM, see Appendix H, "What's on the CD-ROM."

For more information about the exam or the certification process, contact Microsoft:

Microsoft Education: 800-636-7544

Internet: `ftp://ftp.microsoft.com/Services/MSEdCert`

World Wide Web: `http://www.microsoft.com/train_cert/default.htm`

CompuServe Forum: GO MSEDCERT

Understanding What the IIS 4 (#70-087) Exam Covers

The "Implementing and Supporting Microsoft® Internet Information Server 4.0" exam (#70-087) covers the IIS 4 main topic areas represented by the conceptual groupings of the test objectives. Each chapter represents one of these main topic areas. It focuses on determining your skill in seven major categories:

▶ Planning

▶ Installation and configuration

▶ Configuring and managing resource access

▶ Integration and interoperability

▶ Running applications

▶ Monitoring and optimization

▶ Troubleshooting

The "Implementing and Supporting Microsoft® Internet Information Server 4.0" certification exam uses these categories to measure your ability. Before taking this exam, you should be proficient in the job skills described in the following sections.

Planning

The Planning section is designed to make sure that you understand the hardware requirements of IIS, capabilities of the product, and its limitations. The knowledge needed here also requires the understanding of general networking concepts. The objectives are as follows:

- ▶ Choose a security strategy for various situations. Security considerations include

  - ▶ Controlling anonymous access

  - ▶ Controlling access to known users and groups

  - ▶ Controlling access by host or network

  - ▶ Configuring SSL to provide encryption and authentication schemes

  - ▶ Identifying the appropriate balance between security requirements and performance requirements

- ▶ Choose an implementation strategy for an Internet site or an intranet site for standalone servers, single-domain environments, and multiple-domain environments. Tasks include

  - ▶ Resolving host header name issues by using a HOSTS file or DNS, or both

  - ▶ Choosing the appropriate operating system on which to install IIS

- ▶ Choose the appropriate technology to resolve specified problems. Technology options include

  - ▶ WWW service

  - ▶ FTP service

- ▶ Microsoft Transaction Server

- ▶ Microsoft SMTP Service

- ▶ Microsoft NNTP Service

- ▶ Microsoft Index Server

- ▶ Microsoft Certificate Server

Installation and Configuration

The Installation and Configuration part of the IIS exam is the meat of the exam. You are tested on virtually every possible component of the protocol. The objectives are as follows:

- ▶ Install IIS. Tasks include

  - ▶ Configuring a Microsoft Windows NT Server 4.0 computer for the installation of IIS

  - ▶ Identifying differences to a Windows NT Server 4.0 computer made by the installation of IIS

- ▶ Configure IIS to support the FTP service. Tasks include

  - ▶ Setting bandwidth and user connections

  - ▶ Setting user logon requirements and authentication requirements

  - ▶ Modifying port settings

  - ▶ Setting directory listing style

  - ▶ Configuring virtual directories and servers

- ▶ Configure IIS to support the WWW service. Tasks include

  - ▶ Setting bandwidth and user connections

  - ▶ Setting user logon requirements and authentication requirements

  - ▶ Modifying port settings

► Setting default pages

► Setting HTTP 1.1 host header names to host multiple Web sites

► Enabling HTTP Keep-Alives

► Configure and save consoles by using Microsoft Management Console.

► Verify server settings by accessing the metabase.

► Choose the appropriate administration method.

► Install and configure Certificate Server.

► Install and configure Microsoft SMTP Service.

► Install and configure Microsoft NNTP Service.

► Customize the installation of Microsoft Site Server Express Analysis Content Analyzer.

► Customize the installation of Site Server Express Analysis Report Writer and Usage Import.

Configuring and Managing Resource Access

The Configuring and Managing Resource Access component of the "Implementing and Supporting Microsoft® Internet Information Server 4.0" certification exam concentrates on how to use the various sharing and authentication components of IIS:

► Create and share directories with appropriate permissions. Tasks include

► Setting directory-level permissions

► Setting file-level permissions

- ▶ Create and share local and remote virtual directories with appropriate permissions. Tasks include
    - ▶ Creating a virtual directory and assigning an alias
    - ▶ Setting directory-level permissions
    - ▶ Setting file-level permissions
- ▶ Create and share virtual servers with appropriate permissions. Tasks include assigning IP addresses.
- ▶ Write scripts to manage the FTP service or the WWW service.
- ▶ Manage a Web site by using Content Analyzer. Tasks include
    - ▶ Creating, customizing, and navigating WebMaps
    - ▶ Examining a Web site by using the various reports provided by Content Analyzer
    - ▶ Tracking links by using a WebMap
- ▶ Configure Microsoft SMTP Service to host personal mailboxes.
- ▶ Configure Microsoft NNTP Service to host a newsgroup.
- ▶ Configure Certificate Server to issue certificates.
- ▶ Configure Index Server to index a Web site.
- ▶ Manage MIME types.
- ▶ Manage the FTP service.
- ▶ Manage the WWW service.

Integration and Interoperability

The Integration and Interoperability component of the "Implementing and Supporting Microsoft® Internet Information Server

4.0" certification exam concentrates on configuring IIS to interact with databases:

▶ Configure IIS to connect to a database. Tasks include configuring ODBC.

▶ Configure IIS to integrate with Index Server. Tasks include

    ▶ Specifying query parameters by creating the .idq file

    ▶ Specifying how the query results are formatted and displayed to the user by creating the .htx file

Running Applications

The Running Applications component of the "Implementing and Supporting Microsoft® Internet Information Server 4.0" certification exam looks at scripting on IIS and the options available to do so. The objectives are as follows:

▶ Configure IIS to support server-side scripting.

▶ Configure IIS to run ISAPI applications.

▶ Configure IIS to support ADO associated with the WWW service.

Monitoring and Optimization

The Monitoring and Optimization component of the IIS exam covers how to monitor your site and optimize it for the greatest performance combination attainable:

▶ Maintain a log for fine-tuning and auditing purposes. Tasks include

    ▶ Importing log files into a Usage Import and Report Writer Database

    ▶ Configuring the logging features of the WWW service

> ▶ Configuring the logging features of the FTP service

> ▶ Configuring Usage Import and Report Writer to analyze logs created by the WWW service or the FTP service

> ▶ Automating the use of Report Writer and Usage Import

▶ Monitor performance of various functions by using Performance Monitor.

▶ Analyze performance. Performance issues include

> ▶ Identifying bottlenecks

> ▶ Identifying network-related performance issues

> ▶ Identifying disk-related performance issues

> ▶ Identifying CPU-related performance issues

▶ Optimize performance of IIS.

▶ Optimize performance of Index Server.

▶ Optimize performance of Microsoft SMTP Service.

▶ Optimize performance of Microsoft NNTP Service.

▶ Interpret performance data.

▶ Optimize a Web site by using Content Analyzer.

Troubleshooting

The Troubleshooting component of the IIS certification exam covers eight components running the entire gamut of troubleshooting. The objectives are as follows:

▶ Resolve IIS configuration problems.

▶ Resolve security problems.

▶ Resolve resource access problems.

▶ Resolve Index Server query problems.

▶ Resolve setup issues when installing IIS on a Windows NT Server 4.0 computer.

▶ Use a WebMap to find and repair broken links, hyperlink texts, headings, and titles.

▶ Resolve WWW service problems.

▶ Resolve FTP service problems.

Hardware and Software Recommended for Preparation

As a self-paced study guide, *MCSE Training Guide: Internet Information Server 4* is meant to help you review concepts with which you already have training and hands-on experience. To make the most of the review, you need to have as much background and experience as possible. The best way to do this is to combine studying with working on real networks, using the products on which you will be tested. This section gives you a description of the minimum computer requirements you need to build a solid practice environment.

Computers

The minimum computer requirements to ensure that you can study everything on which you'll be tested are one or more workstations running Windows 95 or NT Workstation and two or more servers running Windows NT Server, all connected by a network.

Workstations: Windows 95 and Windows NT

▶ Computer on the Microsoft Hardware Compatibility list

▶ 486DX 33MHz or better

▶ 16MB RAM

▶ 200MB hard disk

- 3.5-inch 1.44MB floppy drive

- VGA video adapter

- VGA monitor

- Mouse or equivalent pointing device

- Two-speed CD-ROM drive

- Network Interface Card (NIC)

- Presence on an existing network or use of a hub to create a test network

- Microsoft Windows 95 or NT Workstation 4.0

Servers: Windows NT Server

- Two computers on the Microsoft Hardware Compatibility List

- 486DX2 66MHz or better

- 32MB RAM

- 340MB hard disk

- 3.5-inch 1.44MB floppy drive

- VGA video adapter

- VGA monitor

- Mouse or equivalent pointing device

- Two-speed CD-ROM drive

- Network interface card (NIC)

- Presence on an existing network or use of a hub to create a test network

- Microsoft Windows NT Server 4.0

Tips for the Exam

Remember the following tips as you prepare for the certification exams:

▶ **Read all the material.** Microsoft has been known to include material not expressly specified in the objectives. This course has included additional information not required by the objectives in an effort to give you the best possible preparation for the examination and for the real-world network experiences to come.

▶ **Complete the exercises in each chapter.** They help you gain experience using the Microsoft product. All Microsoft exams are experienced-based and require you to have used the Microsoft product in a real networking environment. Exercises for each objective are placed at the end of each chapter.

▶ **Take each pre-chapter quiz to evaluate how well you know the topic of the chapter.** Each chapter opens with at least one short answer/essay question per exam objective covered in the chapter. At the end of the chapter you will find the quiz answers and pointers to where in the chapter that specific objective is covered.

▶ **Complete all the questions in the "Review Questions" sections.** Complete the questions at the end of each chapter—they help you remember key points. The questions are fairly simple, but be warned: Some questions require more than one answer.

▶ **Review the exam objectives.** Develop your own questions for each topic listed. If you can make and answer several questions for each topic, you should not find it difficult to pass the exam.

 Note Although this book is designed to prepare you to take and pass the "Implementing and Supporting Microsoft® Internet

Information Server 4.0" certification exam, there are no guarantees. Read this book, work through the questions and exercises, and when you feel confident, take a practice assessment exam using the TestPrep test engine. This should tell you whether you are ready for the real thing.

Also note that this exam is one of the first to use the new Computer Adaptive Testing (CAT) method. This is a new approach to testing that is less time-consuming. The exam also includes a number of simulation-based questions. For more information on these new methods, see Appendix G.

Remember, the primary object is not to pass the exam—it is to understand the material. After you understand the material, passing the exam should be simple. Knowledge is a pyramid; to build upward, you need a solid foundation. The Microsoft Certified Professional programs are designed to ensure that you have that solid foundation.

Good luck!

New Riders Publishing

The staff of New Riders Publishing is committed to bringing you the very best in computer reference material. Each New Riders book is the result of months of work by authors and staff who research and refine the information contained within its covers.

As part of this commitment to you, the NRP reader, New Riders invites your comments. Please let us know if you enjoy this book, if you have trouble with the information or examples presented, or if you have a suggestion for the next edition.

Please note, however, that New Riders staff cannot serve as a technical resource during your preparation for the Microsoft certification exams or for questions about software- or hardware-related problems. Please refer instead to the documentation that accompanies IIS 4 or to the applications' Help systems.

If you have a question or comment about any New Riders book, there are several ways to contact New Riders Publishing. We will respond to as many readers as we can. Your name, address, or phone number will never become part of a mailing list or be used for any purpose other than to help us continue to bring you the best books possible. You can write to us at the following address:

New Riders Publishing
Attn: Publisher
201 W. 103rd Street
Indianapolis, IN 46290

If you prefer, you can fax New Riders Publishing at 317-817-7448.

You also can send e-mail to New Riders at the following Internet address:

certification@mcp.com

NRP is an imprint of Macmillan Computer Publishing. To obtain a catalog or information, or to purchase any Macmillan Computer Publishing book, call 800-428-5331.

Thank you for selecting *MCSE Training Guide: Internet Information Server 4*!

Chapter 1

Planning

This chapter helps you prepare for the exam by covering the following objectives:

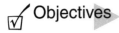 **Objectives**

- ▶ Choose a security strategy for various situations. Security considerations include the following:

    - ▶ Controlling anonymous access

    - ▶ Controlling access to known users and groups

    - ▶ Controlling access by a host or network

    - ▶ Configuring SSL to provide encryption and authentication schemes

    - ▶ Identifying the appropriate balance between security requirements and performance requirements

- ▶ Choose an implementation strategy for an Internet site or an intranet site for standalone servers, single-domain environments, and multiple-domain environments. Tasks include the following:

    - ▶ Resolving host header name issues by using a HOSTS file or DNS, or both

    - ▶ Choosing the appropriate operating system on which to install IIS

- ▶ Choose the appropriate technology to resolve specified problems. Technology options include the following:

    - ▶ WWW service

continues

- ▶ FTP Service

- ▶ Microsoft Transaction Server

- ▶ Microsoft SMTP Service

- ▶ Microsoft NNTP Service

- ▶ Microsoft Index Server

- ▶ Microsoft Certificate Server

**Test Yourself! Before reading this
chapter, test yourself to determine
how much study time you will
need to devote to this section.**

1. What is the name of the user account set up by default for the anonymous account to use?

2. DNS can be used for dynamic resolution of host names to IP addresses. If you want to use static name resolution, such as at a small site, you use the HOSTS file. The length of each entry in the HOSTS file is how many characters?

3. You are concerned about security at your site and implement the use of certificates. All of your clients are using Microsoft's Internet Explorer browser. What is the minimum version they can use now that certificates are employed at your site?

Answers are located at the end of the chapter...

The topics for this chapter simply reflect the Planning objectives. They include the following:

▶ Choosing a Security Strategy

▶ Implementation Strategies

▶ Choosing Appropriate Technologies

Choosing a Security Strategy

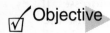 Microsoft Internet Information Server (IIS) 4.0 incorporates a number of security features into its service—and builds on Windows NT 4.0's security. There are five sub-objectives for this category:

▶ Controlling anonymous access

▶ Controlling access to known users and groups

▶ Controlling access by host or network

▶ Configuring SSL to provide encryption and authentication schemes

▶ Identifying the appropriate balance between security requirements and performance requirements

Each of these sub-objectives is examined in the following sections.

Controlling Anonymous Access

Anonymous access enables clients to access your servers (FTP or WWW) without giving a name, or using the name *anonymous*. Traditionally, WWW access has been completely anonymous. FTP began as a service requiring usernames, but later anonymous access was added. When a user has entered *anonymous* as his username, he can log on to your site by using his email address as his password.

IIS uses the default IUSR_*computername* account for all anonymous logons. This account, like all other user accounts, appears in the User Manager for Domains utility (shown in Figure 1.1) and can be administered from there.

Figure 1.1

The anonymous user account can be administered from User Manager for Domains.

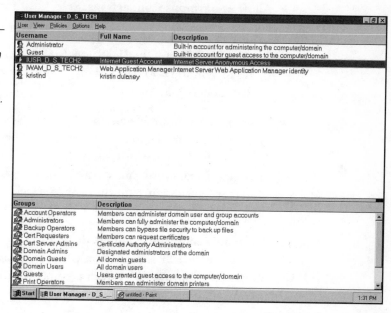

Permissions set up for this account determine an anonymous user's privileges. The default properties are shown in Figure 1.2, including the fact that the user cannot change the password and that the password does not expire.

Figure 1.2

The default anonymous user account properties.

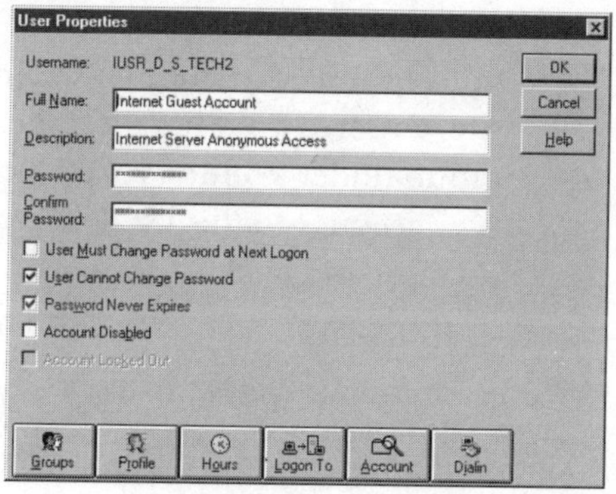

Anonymous FTP

On the FTP Accounts Security tab, you can configure the following options:

▶ **Allow Anonymous Connections.** Select this for anonymous connections.

▶ **Username.** Displays the IUSR_*computername* name as set up by IIS in Windows NT User Manager for Domains and in Internet Service Manager.

▶ **Password.** A randomly generated password was created by User Manager for Domains and Internet Service Manager. You must have a password; no blanks are allowed. If you change this password, make sure it matches the one in User Manager for Domains and Internet Service Manager for this user.

▶ **Allow only anonymous connections.** Click this option to limit access to your FTP server to only those who log on as anonymous. This restricts users from possibly logging on with an account that has administrative rights.

The Enable Automatic Password Synchronization option was added to eliminate accidental password inconsistencies between IIS 4 and User Manager.

▶ **Administrator.** Select those accounts that are allowed to administer this virtual FTP site. To administer a virtual FTP site, a user should first be a member of the Administrative group under Windows NT. Click the Add button to add a user account to this list. Remove an account by selecting the account and clicking Remove.

FTP passwords are ALWAYS transmitted as clear text, and because of that FTP should be limited to anonymous access only.

Anonymous WWW

IIS 4.0 can be set up to verify the identify of clients who access your Web site. On public Web sites on which non-critical or public domain information and applications are available, authentication of users connecting to your Web site may not be important. However, if you have secure data or want to restrict Web access to specific clients, logon and authentication requirements become very important.

Use the following steps to set authentication and logon requirements:

1. Open Internet Service Manager.

2. Right-click on a Web site, file (NTFS systems only), or directory you want to configure.

3. Click on Properties. The property sheet for that item is displayed, as shown in Figure 1.3.

Figure 1.3

The properties for a Web site are available through Internet Service Manager.

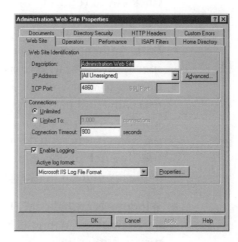

4. Click the Directory Security (or File Security if you want to set file-specific properties) tab.

5. Click the Edit button under Anonymous Access and Authentication Control. The Authentication Methods dialog box appears, as shown in Figure 1.4.

Figure 1.4

The authentica-
tion methods can
be defined for
each Web site.

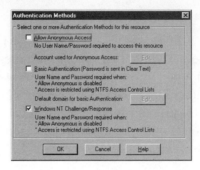

6. Select an authentication method from the following options:

▶ **Allow Anonymous Access**. Enables clients to connect to your Web site without requiring a username or password. Click the Edit button to select the Windows NT user account used to access your computer. By default the account IUSR_*computername* is used. This account is granted Log on Locally user rights by default and is necessary for anonymous logon access to your Web site. Click OK to return to the Authentication Methods dialog box.

▶ **Basic Authentication**. Use this method if you do not specify anonymous access and you want a client connecting to your Web site to enter a valid Windows NT username and password to log on. This sends a password in clear text format (the passwords are transmitted in an unencrypted format). Click the Edit button to specify a default logon domain for users who do not explicitly name a domain.

▶ **Windows NT Challenge/Response**. This setting is used if you want the Windows NT Challenge/Response feature to authenticate the client attempting to connect to your Web site. The only Web browsers that support this feature include Internet Explorer 2.0 and higher. During the challenge/response procedure, cryptographic information is exchanged between the client and server to authenticate the user.

Note   Basic Authentication transmits the username and password in encrypted text when using SSL.

7. Click OK.

Preventing Anonymous WWW Access

Normally, you want anonymous WWW access at most sites. This isn't the case, however, if you're dealing with sensitive data. In this situation, you can prevent the use of anonymous access by requiring IIS to authenticate users. Authentication can be done on the basis of known users and groups, by host or network, or by Secure Socket Layer authentication.

Authentication of users takes place only if you have disabled anonymous access, or anonymous access fails because there isn't an anonymous account with appropriate permissions in NTFS.

Controlling Access to Known Users and Groups

As opposed to the anonymous model, you can use NTFS (NT File System) permissions to limit access to your site to a defined set of users or groups. In this situation, all users must have a Windows NT account that is valid, and they must provide the user ID and password to establish the connection. When connected, the permissions set for the user govern what he can and cannot access.

NTFS permissions can be broken into five categories:

▶ **Change**—Assigns Read (R), Execute (X), Write (W), and Delete (D) permissions.

▶ **Full Control**—Assigns R, X, W, and D permissions (also includes the ability to change permissions and take ownership).

▶ **No Access**—No Access overrides all other permissions. It still enables users to connect, but nothing shows up except the message You do not have permission to access this directory.

▶ **Read**—Assigns only R and X permissions.

▶ **Special Access**—Whatever you define.

As with all Windows NT permissions, user and group permissions accumulate, with the exception of No Access, which instantly overrides all other permissions.

Controlling Access by Host or Network

In addition to limiting access to your site on the basis of users or groups, you also can limit it based upon the host or network the access is coming from. In so doing, there are two models you can operate under. The first is where you select a group of networks or hosts and grant them access. In so doing, you are saying that only they can come in, while everyone else is denied access.

The other model is to select a group of networks or hosts and deny them access. In so doing, you are saying that this group is not allowed access, while everyone else is. The solution to your situation is dependent upon your individual site and needs.

To grant access to only a few, do the following:

1. Start Internet Service Manager, select the Web site (or file or directory), and open the properties.

2. Choose either Directory Security or File Security, based upon which one you want to assign access for, as shown in Figure 1.5.

Figure 1.5

*The Directory
Security property
choices for the
Web site.*

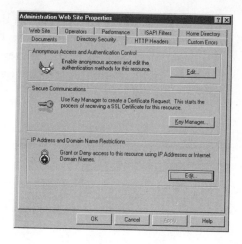

3. Click Edit under IP Address and Domain Name Restrictions.

4. Select Denied Access from the IP Address and Domain Name Restrictions dialog box.

5. Click Add.

6. Select either Single Computer, Group of Computers, or Domain Name from the Grant Access On dialog box, shown in Figure 1.6.

Figure 1.6

The three methods of denying access to a Web site.

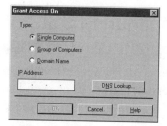

7. Type in the IP address of those to whom you're giving access, or click the DNS Lookup button to browse for them by name.

8. Click OK twice.

Exercise 1 illustrates the opposite of this action and shows how to deny access to a select group of hosts or networks. To pass this exam, you must memorize the subnet mask table shown in Table 1.1. Pay particular attention to the number of hosts available with each subnet.

Table 1.1

Valid Subnet Range Values	
Last Digits of Subnet Address	Number of Addresses in Range
128	128
192	64
224	32
240	16
248	8
252	4
254	2
255	1 (not used)

Configuring SSL

Secure Sockets Layer—or SSL—enables you to protect communications over a network whether that network be an intranet or the Internet. It does so by establishing a private (and encrypted) communication link between the user and the server.

As an interesting aside, SSL can be used to authenticate not only specific users, but also the anonymous user. If SSL is enabled and a user attempts anonymous access, the Web server looks for a valid certificate on the client and rejects those lacking such.

Note   Never use SSL on a server with a processor that cannot afford the extra load. The processor impact of SSL is substantial because everything must be encrypted.

To enable SSL on your server, implement the following steps:

1. Start Internet Service Manager and click the Key Manager icon. The Key Manager utility is displayed, as shown in Figure 1.7.

Figure 1.7

The Key Manager utility enables you to generate certificate requests.

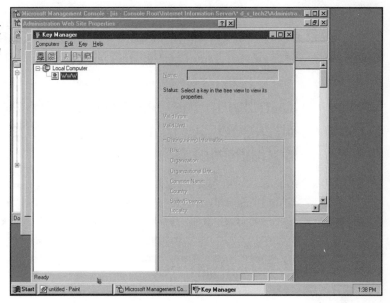

2. Use Key Manager to generate a certificate request file by choosing Create New Key.

3. Submit the request for a certificate to an online authority and obtain their approval (which can take between days and months).

4. Save the certificate, which is returned as an ASCII file.

5. Start Internet Service Manager once more and click on Key Manager. Select the key from the window and choose Install Key Certificate. You have now completed this part and must assign it to a Web site.

6. Select a Web site in Internet Service Manager and open the properties.

7. Go to Advanced under Web Site Identification.

8. Assign the Web site IP address to port 443 under the Multiple SSL identities of this Web Site dialog box.

9. Click Edit on the Secure Communications option of the property sheet. This opens the Secure Communications dialog box.

10. On the Secure Communications dialog box, set the Web server to require a secure channel and enable the Web server's SSL client certificate authentication.

Identifying the Appropriate Balance Between Security and Performance Requirements

In the absence of security, users can access resources without any difficulties. In the presence of absolute security, users cannot access resources at all. Somewhere between the two extremes lies the security-to-usability equilibrium you are striving for. Determining where that equilibrium rests at each site is the responsibility of the administrator.

Common sense plays a large part in the decision on how much security to implement. For example, security should be tighter at any financial institution or site conducting financial transactions than at a user's home page. Likewise, site security should be tighter at any site involving medical or employment information than one containing sports scores.

For an intranet, you should consider creating a group of users who need to access your documents and assigning the Log on Locally right to the group. Use Windows NT Challenge Response for authentication, and make certain that only the selected group has permission to read and access the documents.

For a public Web site, consider using Microsoft Certificate Server in combination with Secure Sockets Layer (SSL).

Understanding Implementation Strategies

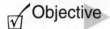 Objective

When implementing IIS, there are several factors to consider: the environment, the method of host name resolution, and the operating system. One of the following sections examines the host name issues, while another looks at operating system possibilities. The following paragraphs concentrate on the issues of environment.

There are three possibilities for IIS environments in the Windows NT world: on a standalone server, in a single-domain environment, and in a multiple-domain environment.

On a standalone server, it is important that IIS be able to interact with the LAN, WAN, or other network architecture that you're seeking. Confining IIS to a standalone server adds a level of security in that users who penetrate the security of the server are able to access only that server and nothing more. At the same time, in a single-domain environment, placing IIS on the PDC can add a considerable (additional) load on an already busy server. The balance must be weighed at each site, and it may indeed be more beneficial to place IIS on a Windows NT Server that has been installed as a Server Role instead of a Domain Controller. This would allow the server to be a member of the domain, for security, while not taxing it with authentication duties.

In a single-domain environment, IIS is often installed on the Primary Domain Controller. In so doing, IIS is able to capitalize upon the security of the PDC and user/resource authentication there.

In a multiple-domain environment, it is important that IIS be accessible to all of the domains. Bandwidth becomes extremely important as the server faces the limitations of the "wire." Thought should be given to using the best (fastest) Network Interface Card possible, with an ample amount of RAM and a fast processor to service all of the traffic the IIS server will face.

Resolving Host Name Issues with HOSTS or DNS

There are two methods of resolving host names in a Windows NT environment—with static HOSTS files and with dynamic DNS. This section looks at both solutions.

Understanding HOSTS

The HOSTS file is an ASCII text file that statically maps local and remote host names and IP addresses. It is located in *systemroot*\System32\Drivers\etc.

In most operating systems (such as UNIX) and prior to Windows NT version 4.0, HOSTS is case sensitive. Regardless of operating system, the file is limited to 255 characters per entry. It is used by PING and other utilities that need it to resolve host names locally and remotely. One HOSTS file must reside on each host, and the file is read from top to bottom. As soon as a match is found for a host name, the file stops being read. For that reason, when there are duplicate entries, the latter ones are always ignored, and the most commonly used names should be near the top of the file.

An example of the default HOSTS file is shown in the following code listing:

```
# Copyright (c) 1993-1995 Microsoft Corp.
#
# This is a sample HOSTS file used by Microsoft TCP/IP for
# Windows NT.
#
# This file contains the mappings of IP addresses to host names.
# Each entry should be kept on an individual line. The IP address
# should be placed in the first column followed by the
# corresponding host name. The IP address and the host name
# should be separated by at least one space.
#
# Additionally, comments (such as these) may be inserted on
# individual lines or following the machine name denoted by a '#'
# symbol.
```

```
#
# For example:
#
#      102.54.94.97      rhino.acme.com        # source server
#       38.25.63.10      x.acme.com            # x client host

127.0.0.1        localhost
```

There are several things to notice in this file. The first is that the pound sign (#) indicates a comment. When the file is read by the system, every line beginning with a comment is ignored. When a # appears in the middle of a line, the line is only read up to the sign. If this were in use on a live system, the first 17 lines should be deleted or moved to the end of the file to keep them from being read every time the file is referenced.

The second thing to note is the following entry:

```
127.0.0.1        localhost
```

This is a *loopback* address in every host. It references the internal card, regardless of the actual host address, and can be used for diagnostics to verify that things are working properly internally, before testing that they are working properly down the wire.

Within the HOSTS file, fields are separated by white space that can be either tabs or spaces. As mentioned earlier, a host can be referred to by more than one name—to do so, separate the entries on the same line with white space, as shown in the following example:

```
127.0.0.1        me loopback localhost
199.9.200.7      SALES7 victor
199.9.200.4      SALES4 nikki
199.9.200.3      SALES3 cole
199.9.200.2      SALES2 victoria
199.9.200.1      SALES1 nicholas
199.9.200.5      SALES5 jack
199.9.200.11     ACCT1
199.9.200.12     ACCT2
```

```
199.9.200.13    ACCT3
199.9.200.14    ACCT4
199.9.200.15    ACCT5
199.9.200.17    ACCT7
```

The aliases are other names by which the system can be referenced. Here, me and loopback do the same as localhost, while nicholas is the same as SALES1. If an alias is used more than once, the search stops at the first match because the file is searched sequentially.

Understanding DNS

The Domain Name System is one way to resolve host names in a TCP/IP environment. In non-Microsoft environments, host names are typically resolved through HOSTS files or DNS. In a Microsoft environment, WINS and broadcasts are also used. DNS is the primary system used to resolve host names on the Internet. In fact, DNS had its beginning in the early days of the Internet.

In its early days, the Internet was a small network established by the Department of Defense for research purposes. This network linked computers at several government agencies with a few universities. The host names of the computers in this network were registered in a single HOSTS file located on a centrally administered server. Each site that needed to resolve host names downloaded this file. Few computers were being added to this network, so the HOSTS file wasn't updated too often, and the different sites only had to download this file periodically to update their own copies.

As the number of hosts on the Internet grew, it became more and more difficult to manage all the names through a central HOSTS file. The number of entries was increasing rapidly, changes were being made frequently, and the server with the central HOSTS file was being accessed more and more often by the different Internet sites trying to download a new copy.

DNS was introduced in 1984 as a way to resolve host names without relying on one central HOSTS file. With DNS, the host names reside in a database that can be distributed among multiple servers, decreasing the load on any one server and also allowing more than one point of administration for this naming system. The name system is based on hierarchical names in a tree-type directory structure. DNS enables more types of registration than the simple host-name-to-TCP/IP-address mapping used in HOSTS files and enables room for future defined types.

Because the database is distributed, it can support a much larger database than can be stored in a single HOSTS file. In fact, the database size is virtually unlimited because more servers can be added to handle additional parts of the database. The Domain Name System was first introduced in 1984.

History of Microsoft DNS

DNS was first introduced in the Microsoft environment as part of the Resource Kit for Windows NT Server 3.51. It wasn't available as part of the Windows NT distribution files. With version 4.0, DNS is now integrated with the Windows NT source files. Although DNS is not installed by default as part of a Windows NT 4.0 Server installation, you can specify DNS to be included as part of a Windows NT installation or you can add DNS later, just as you would any other networking service that's part of Windows NT.

Microsoft DNS is based on RFCs (Requests for Comments) 974, 1034, and 1035. A popular implementation of DNS is called BIND (Berkeley Internet Name Domain), developed at UC Berkeley for its version of UNIX. However BIND isn't totally compliant with the DNS RFCs. Microsoft's DNS does support some features of BIND, but Microsoft DNS is based on the RFCs, not on BIND.

 Note   You can read these RFCs, or any other RFC, by going to the InterNIC Web site at `http://ds.internic.net/ds/rfc-index.html`.

The Structure of DNS

Some host-name systems, like NetBIOS names, use a flat database. With a flat database, all names exist at the same level, so there can't be any duplicate names. These names are like Social Security numbers: Every participant in the Social Security program must have a unique number. The Social Security system is a national system that encompasses all workers in the United States, so it must use an identification system to distinguish between all the individuals in the United States.

DNS names are located in a hierarchical path, like a directory structure. You can have a file called TEST.TXT in C:\ and another file called TEST.TXT in C:\ASCII. In a network using DNS, you can have more than one server with the same name, as long as each is located in a different path.

Because of DNS's hierarchical structure, there can be two hosts with the same name, so long as they're not at the same place in the hierarchy. For instance, there's a server named (or probably aliased) at microsoft.com, and one at compaq.com, but because they're at different places in the domain tree they're still unique.

DNS Domains

The Internet Network Information Center (InterNIC) controls the top-level domains. These have names like com (for businesses), edu (for educational institutions like universities), gov (for government organizations), and org (for non-profit organizations). There are also domains for countries. You can visit the InterNIC Web site at http://www.internic.com/. Table 1.2 summarizes common Internet domains.

Table 1.2

Common Internet Domains

Name	Type of Organization
com	Commercial organizations
edu	Educational institutions
org	Non-profit organizations
net	Networks (the backbone of the Internet)
gov	Non-military government organizations

Name	Type of Organization
mil	Military government organizations
num	Phone numbers
arpa	Reverse DNS
xx	Two-letter country code

DNS Host Names

To refer to a host in a domain, use a fully qualified domain name (FQDN), which completely specifies the location of the host. An FQDN specifies the host name, the domain or subdomain the host belongs to, and any domains above that in the hierarchy until the root domain in the organization is specified. On the Internet, the root domain in the path is something like com, but on a private network the top-level domains may be named according to some internal naming convention. The FQDN is read from left to right, and each host name or domain name is specified by a period. The syntax of an FQDN follows:

```
host name.subdomain. … .domain
```

An example of an FQDN is www.microsoft.com, which refers to a server called www located in the subdomain called microsoft in the domain called com. Referring to a host by its FQDN is similar to referring to a file by its complete directory path. However, a complete filename goes from general to specific, with the filename at the rightmost part of the path. An FQDN goes from specific to general, with the host name at the leftmost part of the name.

Fully qualified domain names are more like addresses. An address starts with the most specific information: who is to receive the letter. Then the address specifies the house number in which the recipient lives, the street on which the house is located, the city where the street is located, and finally the most general location, the state where that city is located.

Zone Files

The DNS database is stored in files called *zones*. It's possible, even desirable, to break the DNS database into a number of zones. Breaking the DNS database into zones was part of the original design goal of DNS. With multiple zones, the load of providing access to the database is spread between a number of servers. Also, the administrative burden of managing the database is spread out, because different administrators manage only the parts of the DNS database stored in their own zones. A zone can be any portion of the domain name space; it doesn't have to contain all the subdomains for that part of the DNS tree. Zones can be copied to other name servers through replication. With multiple zones, smaller amounts of information are copied when zone files are replicated than would be if the entire domain was located in one zone file.

 Note Splitting a DNS database into zones doesn't always guarantee that it will be distributed. Another approach to this is with subdomains being handled by separate DNS servers.

Reverse Lookup

Looking up an IP address to find the host name is exactly the same as the process of looking up an FQDN using a DNS Server (only backwards). An FQDN starts with the specific host and then the domain; an IP address starts with the network ID and then the host ID. Because you want to use DNS to handle the mapping, both must go the same way, so the octets of the IP address are reversed. That is, 148.53.66.7 in the inverse address resolution is 7.66.53.148.

 Note In actuality, the final octet of the IP address is rarely reversed into an Inarpa address.

Once the IP address is reversed, it is going the same way as an FQDN. Now you can resolve the address using DNS. Just as with resolving www.scrimtech.com, you need to create a zone. This zone must have a particular name. To find the name, take the assigned portion of the address—for example, in 148.53.66.7 the portion that was assigned is 148.53, and for 204.12.25.3 it is 204.12.25. Now, create a zone in which these numbers are reversed and to which you add in-addr.arpa—that is, 53.148.in-addr.arpa or 25.12.204.in-addr.arpa, respectively.

Choosing an Appropriate Operating System

There are three operating systems that Internet Information Server 4.0 will run on: Windows NT Server, Windows NT Workstation, and Windows 95.

Note

IIS runs as itself only on Windows NT Server. On Windows 95 and Windows NT Workstation, it runs as Peer Web Services, a chopped up/scaled down version of IIS.

Windows 95 should not be considered a practical choice for a production environment because it—in and of itself—is not a server operating system. Windows 95 is limited to only one connection at a time and has no built-in method of true, secure, user authentication. Windows 95, however, is an excellent platform for a mobile development workforce to use on laptops while fine-tuning IIS applications that aren't yet live.

Windows NT Workstation 4.0 includes Peer Web Services, a limited version of IIS 2.0. Windows NT Workstation can be used with IIS for a very small intranet implementation. The number of concurrent connections Workstation can support is limited to 10, and that makes the product less than minimal for an Internet Server service. Like Windows 95, it is ideal for a laptop operating system that a mobile development workforce can use for tuning applications.

Windows NT Server 4.0 supports an unlimited number of concurrent connections, up to 256 phone connections (RAS), and is fine-tuned for a production server environment. As such, there is no better operating system on which to run IIS, and this should be the one used in all production Internet environments.

Choosing Appropriate Technologies

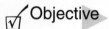 There are a number of servers and services that come with the basic Internet Information Server 4.0 product. Many of these have been with IIS since version 2.0 or before, while several are new to this release. Choosing the right server or service to add can only be accomplished by understanding the purpose behind each.

WWW

While the World Wide Web is often used synonymously with the term Internet, the World Wide Web is but one of the Internet's components. The Internet has been in existence for years but never gained fame with the masses until the World Wide Web was created to place a graphical service on it.

Use the World Wide Web if you want to include HTML (Hypertext Markup Language) documents on your site, as illustrated in Figure 1.8, and allow remote clients and browsers to reach them.

FTP

An FTP (File Transport Protocol) server enables clients attaching to your server to transmit files to and from the server, as illustrated in Figure 1.9.

Although FTP is one of the oldest Internet services, it is still one of the most popular ways to transfer files over the Internet.

Figure 1.8

An example of a WWW site.

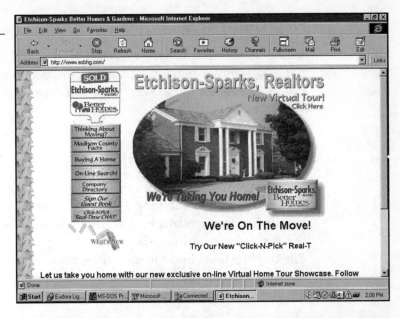

Figure 1.9

An example of an FTP site.

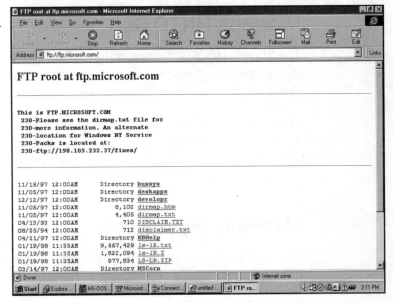

Microsoft Transaction Server

Microsoft Transaction Server—acronymed as MTS—is a transaction processing system for managing and developing server applications. It enables you to keep track of transactions that occur on the server.

Microsoft SMTP Service

Microsoft SMTP Service uses the Simple Mail Transfer Protocol to send and receive email using TCP port 25 for operations. Once installed, it can be managed and administered through Internet Service Manager or Internet Service Manager for SMTP Service. The two function almost identically, with the difference being that the latter enables you to administer SMTP through HTML, while the former requires administration from the server.

Microsoft NNTP Service

The Microsoft NNTP Service supports the Network News Transport Protocol and enables clients to access newsgroups. You can reach and interact with existing newsgroups or create new ones.

Microsoft NNTP supports MIME, HTML, GIF, and JPEG. Like SMTP, when installed it can be managed and administered through Internet Service Manager or Internet Service Manager for SMTP Service.

Microsoft Index Server

Microsoft Index Server indexes Web content at your Internet or intranet site to enable clients to quickly find information through queries. It includes a query engine that can find the results and has the ability to format the results to meet specifications you define.

Index Server can work with HTML documents as well as Excel and Word documents.

Microsoft Certificate Server

Microsoft Certificate Server enables you to increase the security of your site by issuing certificates (digital identifiers) that use public-key encryption. Certificates enable you to verify that you have secure communication across the network, whether that network is an intranet or the Internet. The server certificates are issued from a third-party organization and contain information about the organization and the public key.

With public-key encryption, there are actually two keys involved, forming a key pair. The first is the public key, which is a known value and the one used to establish a secure HTTP connection. The second key is a private key, known only by the user. The two are mathematical opposites of each other and are used to negotiate a secure TCP/IP connection.

When the connection is established, a session key (typically 40-bits in length) is used between the server and client to encrypt and decrypt the transmissions.

Certificate Server is an integral component of the Microsoft Internet Security Framework (ISF) model. This integration means that Windows NT users and groups can be mapped to certificates, and the users still receive the benefit of a single logon to the network.

Requests for certificates come into Microsoft Certificate Server across HTTP, email, or as Remote Procedure Calls. Every request is verified against a policy before being responded to in X.509 format (used for authentication with the SSL protocol). Different policies can be in place for different groups of users, and policy modules can be written in Microsoft Visual Basic, C++, or Java.

The browser that requests the certificates must be Microsoft Internet Explorer 3.0 or greater or Netscape Navigator 3.0 or greater.

Exercises

Exercise 1.1: Denying Access to a Select Group of Hosts or Networks

To deny access to only a few networks or hosts, do the following:

1. Start Internet Service Manager, select the Web site (or file or directory) and open the properties.

2. Choose either Directory Security or File Security, based upon which you want to assign access for.

3. Click Edit under TCP/IP and Domain Name Restrictions.

4. Select Granted Access from the IP Address and Domain Name Restrictions dialog box.

5. Click Add.

6. Select either Single Computer, Group of Computers, or Domain Name from the Deny Access On dialog box.

7. Type in the IP address of those to whom you're denying access, or click the DNS Lookup button to browse for them by name.

8. Click OK twice.

Exercise 1.2: Find the Local Host Name and Test It

The following exercise steps show you how to find the local host name and verify that you can ping it:

1. From the Start menu, choose Programs, MS-DOS prompt.

2. Type **HOSTNAME** to see the local host's name.

3. Type **PING {HOSTNAME}** (the {HOSTNAME} is the value returned in step two).

Exercise 1.3: Edit the HOSTS File

The following exercise steps show you how to find and edit the HOSTS file on a Windows NT Server machine.

1. From the Start menu, choose Programs, MS-DOS prompt.

2. Change the directory to the appropriate location by typing:

   cd*systemroot*\\System32\\Drivers\\etc

   (*systemroot* is your Windows NT directory.)

3. Type **PING ME** and notice the error that comes back because the host isn't found.

4. Type **EDIT HOSTS**.

   The last line of the file should read:

   127.0.0.1localhost

5. Move one space to the right of the last character and enter

   ME

   so the line now reads:

   127.0.0.1localhost ME

6. Exit the editor and save the changes.

7. Type **PING ME** and notice the successful results.

Exercise 1.4: Viewing Internet Explorer Certificates

To view the certificates presently in Internet Explorer 4.0, do the following:

1. In Explorer, select Internet Options from the View menu.

2. Select the Content tab, and click Personal.

continues

Exercise 1.4: Continued

3. If any certificates are there, they will be displayed in the list box. You can then select one and click the button marked View Certificates.

4. Select each Field to view the details in the Details box.

Exercise 1.5: Turning on Windows NT Challenge/Response

To turn on the Windows NT Challenge/Response authentication, do the following:

1. Choose a Web site in Internet Service Manager and choose the property sheet.

2. Click Edit under Anonymous Access and Authentication Control.

3. Choose Windows NT Challenge/Response from the Authentication Methods dialog box.

Review Questions

1. The Internet Information Server provides you with the ability to share information with any type of computer that can use the TCP/IP protocol. IIS includes which servers?

    A. FTP

    B. SNMP

    C. TCP/IP

    D. WWW

2. Zachary wants to create a Web site to which the public is not allowed access. Instead, only the internal hosts that fall within a specified IP address range can get to it. He sets the IP and Domain Name Restriction specifications to an IP address of 192.2.2.0 and the subnet mask to 255.255.255.240. Which host addresses can access Zachary's site?

    A. 192.2.2.0 through 192.2.2.3

    B. 192.2.2.0 through 192.2.2.7

    C. 192.2.2.0 through 192.2.2.15

    D. 192.2.2.0 through 192.2.2.31

    E. 192.2.2.0 through 192.2.2.61

3. Which service resolves host names to IP addresses?

    A. DNS

    B. DHCP

    C. WINS

    D. BDC

4. Your organization currently uses a UNIX server for DNS. The server is fully configured using BIND files. In what two ways can you configure your Microsoft DNS Server so that you won't need to re-enter any information?

    A. Set up Microsoft DNS as the primary and transfer the zone to the UNIX system

    B. Set up Microsoft DNS as the secondary and transfer the zone from the UNIX system

    C. Configure the Microsoft DNS server as an IP Forwarder

    D. Configure the Microsoft DNS server as a Caching Only server

5. Which of the following is *not* part of a Fully Qualified Domain Name? (Choose all options that apply.)

    A. Type of organization

    B. Host name

    C. Company name

    D. CPU type

6. What are the benefits of DNS? (Select all options that apply.)

    A. It allows a distributed database that can be administered by a number of administrators.

    B. It allows host names that specify where a host is located.

    C. It allows WINS clients to register with the WINS server.

    D. It allows queries to other servers to resolve host names.

7. With what non-Microsoft DNS platforms is Microsoft DNS compatible?

    A. Only UNIX DNS servers that are based on BIND

    B. Only UNIX DNS servers that are based on the DNS RFCs

    C. UNIX DNS servers that are either BIND-based or RFC-based

    D. Only other Microsoft DNS servers

8. In the DNS name www.microsoft.com, what does microsoft represent?

    A. The last name of the host

    B. The domain in which the host is located

    C. The IP address of the building in which the host is located

    D. The directory in which the host name file is located

9. Evan wants to install a service or server on his IIS system that will enable users to upload files to his site. Which server/service should he consider?

    A. WWW

    B. FTP

    C. Microsoft Transaction Server

    D. SMTP

    E. NNTP

10. Kristin wants to install a service or server on her IIS system that will enable users to upload files to newsgroups. Which server/service should she consider?

    A. WWW

    B. FTP

    C. Microsoft Transaction Server

    D. SMTP

    E. NNTP

11. Spencer wants to install a service or server on his IIS system that will enable users to send email to the Internet. Which server/service should he consider?

   A. WWW

   B. FTP

   C. Microsoft Transaction Server

   D. SMTP

   E. NNTP

12. Microsoft NNTP supports which of the following file types?

   A. MIME

   B. UUENCODE

   C. HTML

   D. GIF

   E. PDF

Review Answers

1. **A,D**. Of those listed, IIS includes FTP and WWW servers.

2. **C**. Setting an IP address of 192.2.2.0 and subnet mask to 255.255.255.240 will make the valid host range 192.2.2.0 through 192.2.2.15.

3. **A**. The DNS server resolves host names to IP addresses.

4. **B,D**. Set up DNS as the secondary and transfer the zone from the UNIX system and configure the DNS server as a Caching Only server.

5. **D**. CPU type is not a component of an FQDN.

6. **A,B,D**. Although DNS on a Windows NT server can be configured to query the WINS server for a name resolution, WINS clients do not register themselves directly with the DNS server.

7. **C**. Windows NT DNS is based on the RFCs for DNS, but it is designed to be compatible with DNS servers based on BIND as well.

8. **B**. The path specifies a host named www in a domain microsoft. The domain microsoft is located in the top-level domain com.

9. **B**. FTP is used to enable clients to upload and download files.

10. **E**. NNTP is used to communicate with newsgroups.

11. **D**. SMTP is used to send email to the Internet.

12. **A,C,D**. NNTP accepts HTML, MIME, JPEG, and GIF.

Answers to Test Yourself Questions at Beginning of Chapter

1. IUSR_computername is the name of the anonymous account automatically created during the installation of IIS. See "Controlling Anonymous Access."

2. Each line in the HOSTS file is limited to 255 characters in length. See "Understanding HOSTS."

3. Internet Explorer 3.0 is the earliest version of that browser that will work with certificates. See "Microsoft Certificate Server."

Installation and Configuration

2

This chapter helps you prepare for the exam by covering the following objectives:

Objectives

▶ Install IIS. Tasks include

  ▶ Configuring a Microsoft Windows NT Server 4.0 computer for the installation of IIS

  ▶ Identifying differences to a Windows NT Server 4.0 computer made by the installation of IIS

▶ Configure IIS to support the FTP service. Tasks include

  ▶ Setting bandwidth and user connections

  ▶ Setting user logon requirements and authentication requirements

  ▶ Modifying port settings

  ▶ Setting directory listing style

  ▶ Configuring virtual directories and servers

▶ Configure IIS to support the WWW service:

  ▶ Setting bandwidth and user connections

  ▶ Setting user logon requirements and authentication requirements

continues

> ▸ Modifying port settings
>
> ▸ Setting default pages
>
> ▸ Setting HTTP 1.1 host header names to host multiple Web sites
>
> ▸ Enabling HTTP Keep-alives

▸ Configure and save consoles by using Microsoft Management Console.

▸ Verify server settings by accessing the metabase.

▸ Choose the appropriate administration method.

▸ Install and configure Certificate Server.

▸ Install and configure Microsoft SMTP Service.

▸ Install and configure Microsoft NNTP Service.

▸ Customize the installation of Microsoft Site Server Express Content Analyzer.

▸ Customize the installation of Microsoft Site Server Express Usage Import and Report Writer.

Test Yourself! Before reading this chapter, test yourself to determine how much study time you will need to devote to this section.

1. As an IIS consultant, a client asks you to outline the features of IIS 4 that should be installed for search documents, providing digital certificates and newsgroup capabilities. What features should you install with IIS?

2. You are setting up an IIS installation in your client's office. The client wants to have Basic Authentication enabled. What two conditions must be met for Basic Authentication to work?

3. After setting up IIS on your client's server, the client wants to know how he should administer IIS. What do you say?

4. To keep inactive connections or slow connections from consuming network resources, describe the technique you should use to limit this resource problem.

5. You've set up the FTP Service on a client's IIS server. What is the default authentication method used by the FTP Service?

6. What is the metabase, and why is it used by IIS?

7. You're asked by another administrator in your office to provide a copy of your MMC console of your Web site. Can you do this? If so, how?

Answers are located at the end of the chapter...

Microsoft makes it fairly easy to install Internet Information Server 4.0 (IIS) under Windows NT Server 4.0. During installation, setup wizards walk you through the process. Although you don't need to know a whole lot about IIS before jumping into the IIS setup, you should know the requirements of IIS and how your Windows NT Server 4.0 system should be set up. This chapter covers these points.

After you install IIS, you need to know how to configure its World Wide Web and FTP services, along with setting up Microsoft Management Console (MMC) consoles and how to choose the appropriate administration method. You learn how in this chapter. The following topics are covered:

▶ Installing IIS

▶ Configuring IIS to support the FTP service

▶ Configuring IIS to support the WWW service

▶ Configuring and saving consoles by using Microsoft Management Console

▶ Verifying server settings by accessing the metabase

▶ Choosing the appropriate administration method

▶ Customizing the Installation of Microsoft Site Server Express Analysis Content Analyzer

▶ Customizing the Installation of Microsoft Site Server Analysis Report Writer and Usage Import

Note

The Microsoft Certificate Server, Microsoft SMTP Service, and Microsoft NNTP Service can be automatically installed when you install IIS 4. The following section covers how to install these three services, along with any configuration concerns for the services. Because the installation is automatic, separate sections for the objectives "Install and Configure Certificate Server," "Install and Configure Microsoft SMTP Service," and "Install and Configure Microsoft NNTP Service" are not included in this chapter.

Installing IIS

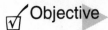

Microsoft Internet Information Server (IIS) 4 is the newest Internet and Web server designed to run under Windows NT Server 4.0. Setting up and configuring IIS is the first step in setting up an Internet or intranet site.

IIS 4 includes the following features:

- ▶ Authentication Server
- ▶ SMTP Mail Server
- ▶ Microsoft Management Console
- ▶ NNTP News Server
- ▶ Script Debugger
- ▶ Site Analyst
- ▶ Transaction Server
- ▶ Usage Analyst
- ▶ Web Publishing Wizard
- ▶ Windows Scripting Host
- ▶ FrontPage Server Administrator

After you install IIS 4, you can add Hypertext Markup Language (HTML) files to your server for users to connect to and view.

Configuring a Microsoft Windows NT Server 4 Computer for the Installation of IIS

IIS 4 is available only as part of the Windows NT 4.0 Option Pack. Currently, IIS 4 is available on CD-ROM from Microsoft or as a large download from Microsoft's Web site. You can download it as

part of the Windows NT 4.0 Option Pack from Microsoft at the
following address:

```
http://www.microsoft.com/downtrial/optionpack.asp
```

You also can order an Option Pack CD-ROM from Microsoft from
the same site. With this download, you're provided with IIS 4,
Microsoft Site Server Express 2.0, Transaction Server 2.0, Microsoft Message Queue Server 1.0, Certificate Server 1.0, Index
Server Express, Internet Explorer 4.0, remote-access services for
virtual networking, and Windows NT Service Pack 3.

 Note   The version of IIS provided with Windows NT 4.0 Server is IIS
2.0. This book covers how to install IIS 4.

Before you set up IIS 4, your system must meet or exceed the
hardware requirements summarized in Tables 2.1 and 2.2. Table
2.1 shows requirements for a system running an Intel $x86$ processor. Table 2.2 lists requirements for a system running a DEC Alpha
processor.

Table 2.1

IIS 4 hardware requirements for an Intel system.	
Hardware Device	Requirements
CPU	Minimum of a 90MHz 486DX processor. For better performance, you need a Pentium 133-or-higher processor.
Hard disk space	Minimum of 50MB, but it is recommended you have at least 120MB. This does not include storage needed for files you plan to distribute via IIS.
Memory	Minimum of 32MB. For Web site on which you will store multimedia files or expect a great deal of traffic, 48MB is the recommended minimum.
Monitor	Super VGA monitor with 800×600 resolution.

Table 2.2

IIS 4 hardware requirements for an Alpha system.

Hardware Device	Requirements
CPU	Minimum of 150MHz processor.
Hard disk space	Minimum of 120MB, but you should allocate up to 200MB for best performance.
Memory	Minimum of 48MB. For better performance, have at least 64MB.
Monitor	Super VGA monitor with 800×600 resolution.

Tip

If you install all the components that ship with IIS 4, you need over 355MB of hard disk space.

Before you install IIS 4, remove any installations of a previous version of IIS. You also should disable other versions of FTP, Gopher, or World Wide Web services you have installed under Windows NT Server 4.0. This includes the Windows Academic Centre (EMWAC) service included with the Windows NT Resource Kit.

You also should have the following software installed:

▶ Windows NT Server 4.0

▶ Service Pack 3 for Windows NT Server 4.0

▶ Internet Explorer 4.01 or higher

You also must be logged on to the Windows NT Server computer with Administrator privileges.

Another consideration before installing IIS 4 is to install TCP/IP (Transmission Control Protocol/Internet Protocol) on your Windows NT 4.0 computer. TCP/IP is used to provide Internet connectivity to retrieve data from the Internet.

For systems in which file-level security is needed, configure Windows NT Server with the NT File System (NTFS). NTFS enables you to limit access to files and directories. Systems running FAT do not allow you to limit access at the file level, only the directory level.

Finally, you should consider installing DHCP (Dynamic Host Configuration Protocol) if you plan to run IIS 4 on an Intranet. DHCP automatically assigns IP (Internet Protocol) addresses to computers connecting to the server and those that are set up to use DHCP. For systems connecting to the Internet, you need to acquire a TCP/IP address from the InterNIC or from an Internet Service Provider (ISP).

 Note

For load balancing purposes, it is recommended that you install DHCP on a different server within your intranet than the one IIS is running on.

 Tip

To help secure your IIS installation, you should perform the following tasks in addition to the tasks described previously:

▶ Turn on auditing (which requires NT to be running on NTFS and not FAT for files and directories).

▶ Limit the Guest account and other accounts to specific directories on the server.

▶ Limit who has membership to the administrators group.

▶ Start only those services and protocols required by your system.

▶ Use complex password schemes.

▶ Review network share permissions.

 Note

Disable NetBIOS over TCP/IP for additional security.

Installing IIS 4

After you get Windows NT Server 4.0 set up to receive IIS 4, you're ready to start the IIS 4 setup program. Make sure you are connected to the Internet or to your intranet before installing IIS.

 Tip

If you decide you don't want to install IIS 4 and you've already started the IIS 4 setup program, don't cancel it. This will leave files on your system that the uninstall program cannot remove. Finish the entire installation process, then uninstall IIS 4 if you don't want it on your system.

To start IIS 4 setup, insert the Option Pack CD-ROM and locate the Setup icon in Explorer. Double-click the Setup icon. Or, if you downloaded IIS 4 from the Internet, double-click the setup file.

 Note

IIS 4 relies on Internet Explorer 4.0 for many of its management and configuration tasks. If you do not already have IE 4.0 installed, you'll be prompted to install it when you start the IIS 4 setup routine. Be sure to click Yes if prompted to install IE 4.0. Windows NT will need to shut down and restart before continuing with the IIS installation.

Next, perform the following steps:

1. Click Next on the Welcome to the Windows NT 4.0 Option dialog box. The End User License Agreement screen appears.

2. Click Accept.

3. Click Custom. A dialog box with components will appear. You also can click Minimum or Typical, but these steps assume you want to have control over the components that are installed.

4. Click the component you want to install. If you want to change the specific options (called *subcomponents*) that install with the components, click the Show Subcomponents button. This displays a dialog box with the specific options that fall under a component heading. Selected components and subcomponents have check marks next to them.

Specific components and their subcomponents are listed in Table 2.3.

Table 2.3

IIS 4 setup options.

Component	Subcomponents	Description
Certificate Server	Certificate Server Certificate Authority	Enables you to create Certificate Authority on the IIS server to issue digital certificates to users accessing your Web.
	Certificate Server Documentation	Documents to help you install and configure Certificate Authorities.
	Certificate Server Web Client	Enables you to post Web pages on your server to submit requests and retrieve certificates from a Certificate Authority.
FrontPage 98 Server Extensions	FrontPage Server Extensions files	Enables you to author Web pages and administer Web sites using Microsoft FrontPage and Visual InterDev.
Visual InterDev RAD	Visual InterDev RAD Remote Deployment Support	Enables you to deploy applications remotely on the Web server.

Component	Subcomponents	Description
Internet Information Server (IIS)	Common Program Files	Files used by several IIS components.
	Documentation	Product documentation for IIS.
	File Transfer Protocol(FTP) Server	Provides FTP support to set up an FTP site to allow users to upload and download files from your site.
	Internet News Server	Installs the Microsoft Internet News Server for NNTP news.
	Internet Service Manager	Provides a snap-in for the Microsoft Management Console (MMC) to administer IIS.
	Internet Service Manager (HTML)	Provides an HTML-based administrative tool for IIS. You use IE 4.0 with this manager to administer IIS.
	SMTP Server	Installs the SMTP (Simple Mail Transfer Protocol) Server for email.
	World Wide Web samples	Installs sample IIS Web sites and other samples.
	World Wide Web Server	Installs the Web server so clients can access your Web site.
Microsoft Data Access Components 1.5 (MDAC, ADO, ODBC, and OLE)	ActiveX Data Objects (ADO) 1.5	Installs the ActiveX Data Objects and other OLE DB and ODBC files.

continues

Table 2.3 Continued

Component	Subcomponents	Description
	Data Sources	Installs the drivers and providers to access common data sources, including Jet and Access (ODBC), Oracle, and SQL Server data sources.
	Remote Data Service 1.5 (RDS/ADC)	Installs Remote Data Service. Click the Show Subcomponents button to see options for this subcomponent.
Microsoft Index Server	Index Server System Files	Installs the files for the the Index Server system.
	Language Resources	Installs Index Server language resources. Click the Show Subcomponents button to see a list of these languages. US English Language is the default setting.
	Online Documentation	Installs Index Server documentation.
	Sample Files	Installs sample files on how to use the Index Server.
Microsoft Message Queue (MSMQ)	Administration Guide	Installs the MSMQ Administration Guide.
	Administration Tools	Enables you to control and monitor your message queuing enterprise.
	Microsoft Message Queue Server	Installs the required MSMQ files.

Component	Subcomponents	Description
	Software Development Kit	Installs the MSMQ SDK for creating MSMQ applications with C or C++ APIs or with ActiveX components.
Microsoft Script Debugger	Microsoft Script Debugger	Installs the Microsoft Script Debugger to debug Active Server Pages scripts and applications.
Microsoft Site Server Express 2.0	Analysis—Content	Enables you to analyze your site with content, site visualization, link management, and reporting tool.
	Analysis—Usage	Enables you to analyze your site usage.
	Publishing— Posting Acceptor 1.01	Enables IIS to receive files uploaded to it using the HTTP POST protocol.
	Publishing— Web Publishing Wizard 1.52	Automatically uploads new or revised content to Web servers.
Internet Connection Services for RAS (Remote Services)	Connection Manager Admin- istration Kit	Sets up dial-up profiles in Access Connection Manager.
	Connection Point Services	Provides administration and services to phonebooks.
	Internet Authentication Services	Installs the Internet Authentication Service.
	Product Documentation	Installs documentation for Remote Access Services.

continues

Table 2.3 Continued

Component	Subcomponents	Description
Transaction Server	Microsoft Management Console	Installs MMC, which is an interface for systems management applications.
	Transaction Server (MTS) Core Components	Installs MTS files.
	Transaction Server Core Documentation	Installs MTS product documentation.
	Transaction Server Deployment	Installs headers, libraries, and samples to help you create transaction components.
Windows Scripting Host	Windows Scripting Host Files	Installs executable files for the Windows Scripting Host.
	Windows Scripting Host Sample Scripts	Provides sample scripts.

The following steps assume all components and subcomponents are selected. Depending on your choices, you may not see all the dialog boxes shown in these steps.

5. Click Next. A dialog box showing the default publishing folders appears. The following list summarizes these folders:

▶ Web services are installed in the `C:\Inetpub\wwwroot` folder.

▶ FTP services are installed in the `C:\Inetpub\ftproot` folder.

▶ Applications are installed in the `C:\Program Files` folder.

You can change any of these default folders by typing over them or clicking the Browse button next to them.

6. Click Next. The Transaction Server dialog box displays. The MTS Install Folder field shows where Transaction Server will be installed. By default, this folder is named C:\Program Files\Mts. You can change this folder if you like.

7. Click Next. A dialog box to set remote administration features displays. You can choose to administer IIS from a Local account, in which no other account information is needed, or from a Remote account on another machine, which requires the Administrator Account name and its password. You can click the Browse button to locate the Administrator Account.

8. Click Next. The Index Server dialog box displays the default folder for the index. This default directory is C:\Inetpub. You can change this folder if you like.

9. Click Next. The Mail Server dialog box displays the default folder for the mailroot directory. Other folders (mail queue, mailbox, and badmail) will be created under this folder. The default for this folder is C:\Inetpub\Mailroot.

10. Click Next. The News Server dialog box displays the default folder for the nntpfile directory. Articles and data files used by the news server will be stored under this folder. The default for this folder is C:\Inetpub\nntpfile.

11. Click Next. Select from one of the following types of MSMQ servers:

   ▶ **Primary Enterprise Controller (PEC).** Installs only one PEC on the network and contains the master copy of the MSMQ Information Store. This PEC will act as the Primary Site Controller for one site. You must have SQL Server installed to choose this option.

   ▶ **Primary Site Controller (PSC).** Installs one PSC for each site, which is a physical set of computers communicating with each other, usually paralleling the physical location of the computers. You must have SQL Server installed to choose this option.

- ▶ **Backup Site Controller (BSC).** BSCs provide a backup of the PSC in case the PSC fails. You must have SQL Server installed to choose this option.

- ▶ **Routing Server.** Provides routing services, remote message store, and store-and-forward services. These servers are spread across the network to enable messages to reach a target queue via different paths. Each PEC, PSC, and BSC also acts as a Routing Server.

12. Click Next. The Microsoft Certificate Server Setup—Introduction dialog box displays. This wizard shows how to create a new Certificate Authority.

13. Click Next. In the Certificate Server—Choose Storage Location dialog box, enter the location to store configuration files and certificate files. Unless the Windows NT domain controller is available for use, enter a shared folder.

14. Click Next. Fill in your identification information, including name, state, country, locality, and other items.

15. Click Next. In the Choose Key Storage Location dialog box, enter the names you want for the System Store and Container for your keys.

16. Click Next. In the Choose Database Location dialog box, you are shown the default folder in which the certificate information will be stored.

17. Click Next. The Choose CSP and Hashing dialog box shows the Cryptographic Services Providers (CSP) you can select. You also can choose the hash algorithms from the Hash list.

18. Click Next. The Choose Certificate Output File Names dialog box shows the signature and key exchange certificate names. You can change these if necessary; however, the default names should suffice for most installations.

19. Click Next. You can enter a comment to identify the certificate later.

20. Click Next. Setup now completes the installation process and installs the IIS files on your hard disk. This process may take a long time to complete.

21. Click Finish when all the files are installed to your system.

22. Click Yes when prompted to restart your computer.

Identifying Changes to a Windows NT Server 4.0 Computer Made by the Installation of IIS

When you install IIS 4, your Windows NT Server 4.0 computer will include some new components:

▶ Microsoft Management Console (MMC) is the host for the Internet Service Manager. Internet Service Manager is IIS's administrative program.

▶ Registry changes can be viewed by selecting Start | Programs | Windows NT 4.0 Option Pack | Microsoft Site Server Express 2.0 | Documentation. Expand the Microsoft Internet Information Server option and click Administrator's Reference in the left pane (see Figure 2.1) and click Registry. Click the topic you want to read, such as WWW Service Registry Entries.

▶ New services include the FTP Publishing Service, IIS Administration Service, Content Index, and World Wide Web Publishing Service.

Note

The three services added during IIS 4 installation—FTP Publishing Service, IIS Administration Service, and World Wide Web Publishing Service—are set to start when you start Windows NT Server. You can change the default settings for each service from the Services dialog box.

Figure 2.1

You can view the different Registry changes from the Windows NT 4.0 Option Pack Documentation.

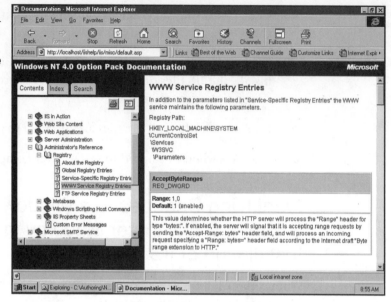

▶ User Manager for Domains lists a new username in the list of user accounts. This username is IUSR_*computername* and allows anonymous access to Internet services on your computer.

▶ Performance Monitor can now be used to track several IIS services, including Content Index, Content Index Filter, FTP Service, HTTP Content Index, HTTP Service, and Internet Information Services Global. Some of the over 75 counters added to Performance Monitor enable you to track connections, bytes transferred, and cache information.

Configuring IIS to Support the FTP Service

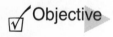 Objective

An FTP (File Transport Protocol) server provides clients attaching to your server the capability of transmitting files to and from the server. Although FTP is one of the oldest Internet services, it is still one of the most popular ways to transfer files over the Internet.

Before you go live with your IIS 4 server, you may want to configure some of the settings relating to FTP. These include

- ▶ Setting bandwidth and user connections

- ▶ Setting user logon requirements and authentication requirements

- ▶ Modifying port settings

- ▶ Setting directory listing style

- ▶ Configuring virtual directories and servers

Setting User Connections

To conserve bandwidth for other clients accessing your FTP site, consider limiting the number of connections that can be made to your FTP server. When connection limits are maxed out, those attempting to connect to your server will be rejected and must try again later. Another task you should consider for your FTP site is to limit the bandwidth used by the WWW server. You are shown how to do this in the "Setting Bandwidth and User Connections" section later in this chapter. This will provide more bandwidth for your FTP service.

To set user connections, perform the following steps:

1. Select Start | Programs | Windows NT 4.0 Option Pack | Microsoft Internet Information Server | Internet Service Manager.

2. Expand the Internet Information Server folder.

3. Expand the FTP server that you want to modify.

4. Right-click the Default FTP Site entry. Your Web site may be named something different.

5. Click Properties. The FTP Site Properties sheet appears.

6. On the FTP Site tab, click the Limited To option (see Figure 2.2.

Figure 2.2

Use the FTP Site tab to set the number of simultaneous connections to your site.

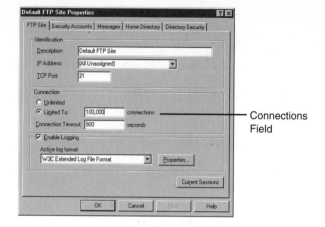

Connections Field

7. Enter a value in the connections field. The default is 100,000, but you may want to lower this if your resources are limited.

8. In the Connection Timeout field, enter a value for the amount of time your server should automatically disconnect an idle session. The default is 15 minutes (900 seconds), but an average setting is five minutes (300 seconds). For an infinite amount of time, enter all 9s in this field.

Note

Even if a connection is lost or a client stops working, your site will continue to process data until the timeout value is reached. Setting an appropriate timeout value will limit the loss of resources due to these lost connections.

9. Click OK, or keep open if you want to continue changing FTP site settings.

Setting User Logon Requirements and Authentication Requirements

To enable clients to access your FTP server, you need to set up user logon and authentication requirements. If you want to allow all users access to your FTP server, you must allow anonymous connections. Users with the name *anonymous* can then log into your site by using their email address as their password.

IIS uses the default IUSR_computername account for all anonymous logons. Permissions set up for this account determine an anonymous user's privileges.

On the FTP Site Properties sheet, Security Accounts tab, you can configure the following options:

▶ **Allow Anonymous Connections.** Select this for anonymous connections.

▶ **Username.** Displays the IUSR_computername name as set up by IIS in the Windows NT User Manager for Domains and in the Internet Service Manager.

▶ **Password.** A randomly generated password was created by User Manager for Domains and Internet Service Manager. You must have a password here; no blanks are allowed. If you change this password, make sure it matches the one in the User Manager for Domains and Internet Service Manager for this user.

▶ **Allow only Anonymous Connections.** Click this option to limit access to your FTP server to only those who log on as anonymous. This restricts users from logging on with an account that has administrative rights.

▶ **Administrator.** Select those accounts who are allowed to administer this virtual FTP site. Click the Add button to add a user account to this list. Remove an account by selecting the account and clicking Remove.

▶ **Enable Automatic Password Synchronization.** Select this option to automatically synchronize the IUSR_Computername account password seen here with the IUSR_computername account password contained in the Windows NT User Account database.

Modifying Port Settings

Port settings are used by clients to connect to your FTP site. By default, the FTP server is set up with a port setting of 21. You can change this setting to a unique TCP port number, but you must announce this setting to all clients who want to access your server.

Perform the following steps to change the port number:

1. Choose the following: Start | Programs | Windows NT 4.0 Option Pack | Microsoft Internet Information Server | Internet Service Manager.

Tip

You can use the HTML version of Internet Service Manager if you want to administer IIS from Internet Explorer 4.0. The procedures shown in this chapter, however, show how to use the Microsoft Management Console (MMC) to run the Internet Service Manager.

2. Expand the Internet Information Server folder.

3. Expand the server in which you want to modify the port value (see Figure 2.3).

Figure 2.3

The Microsoft Management Console provides access to the Internet Service Manager to administer your FTP site.

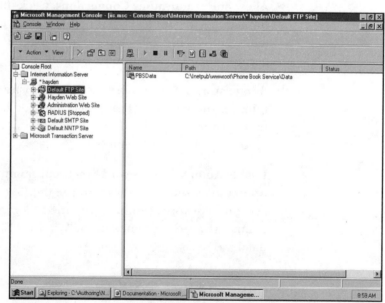

4. Right-click the Default FTP Site entry. Your FTP site may be named something different.

5. Click Properties. The FTP Site Properties sheet displays (see Figure 2.4).

Figure 2.4

Use the FTP Site Properties sheet to change the port setting.

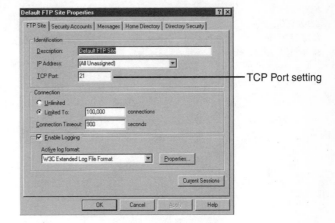

TCP Port setting

6. Change the TCP Port value to a new setting.

7. Click OK.

Setting Directory Listing Style

A directory listing style is the way in which your server will display a directory listing. Because Windows NT Server uses a listing style similar to DOS (such as C:\folder\subfolder), you can change this to display in UNIX format. UNIX format (such as /c/directory/subdirectory/) is commonly found on the Internet and is expected by most Web browsers. Use UNIX format for the greatest compatibility on the Internet.

To change your server's directory listing style, perform the following steps:

1. From the FTP Site Properties sheet (see the preceding section), click the Home Directory tab (see Figure 2.5).

2. Under Directory Listing Style, select UNIX. The default is MS-DOS.

3. Click OK, or keep open if you want to continue changing FTP settings.

Figure 2.5

The Home Directory tab includes settings for changing the directory listing style, as well as other default FTP directory settings.

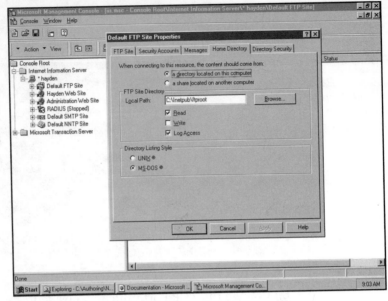

Figure 2.5

The Home Directory tab includes settings for changing the directory listing style, as well as other default FTP directory settings.

Configuring FTP Home Directory

IIS 4 enables you to change the home directory for your virtual server. When you install the FTP service, IIS 4 creates a default home directory called \inetpub\ftproot. This directory, which has no name and is indicated by a slash (/) in a URL, is the primary location for FTP files.

You place files in the home directory and its subdirectories to enable clients to access them (the files).

To change your home directories, perform the following steps:

1. From the FTP Site Properties sheet (see the preceding section), make sure the Home Directory tab appears (refer to Figure 2.5).

2. In the When connecting to this resource, the content should come from area, select one of the following paths:

    ▶ **A Directory Located on This Computer.** Select this option to specify a local directory.

▶ **A Share Located on Another Computer.** Select this option to specify a directory on another computer on the network.

3. In the Local Path field (or Network Share if you select the second option from the preceding list), enter the path to the directory you want to specify as the home directory. For local directories, use standard syntax, such as C:\directory\subdirectory. However, network paths must follow the Universal Naming Convention (UNC), such as *computername**sharename*. For shares, enter the username and password to access that computer, if prompted.

4. Set the home directory access controls from the following options:

   ▶ **Read.** Lets clients read and download files you store in the home directory or in virtual directories. You must select Read permissions for FTP directories, or every request for a file stored in the home directory will result in an error message being returned to the client. By default, this option is selected.

   ▶ **Write.** Lets clients upload files to the home directory on your FTP server. This option should be selected only for FTP servers in which users must upload files. By default, this option is not selected.

Note

Directory settings for home directories set up on NTFS drives must match NTFS settings. If settings do not match, IIS uses the most restrictive settings.

   ▶ **Log Access.** Provides a record of visitors to the home directory. By default, this option is selected.

5. Click OK.

IIS 4 also enables you to create Virtual Directories, which enable you to set up directories located on other servers for your visitors to access. You set up Virtual Directories from Internet Service

Manager. Perform the following steps to create Virtual Directories for your FTP service:

1. Right-click on the FTP server and select New|Virtual Directory. The New Virtual Directory Wizard displays (see Figure 2.6).

Figure 2.6

Assign a name to your new Virtual Directory.

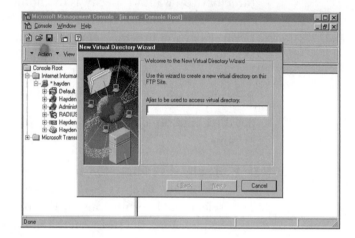

2. Enter a name for the Virtual Directory. The name you enter here will be the name placed in the URL to access this directory.

3. Click Next. Enter the path to the directory to which you want the Virtual Directory to point. Use UNC notation for directories on another system.

4. Click Next. Set the following permissions to the Virtual Directory:

   ▶ **Allow Read Access.** Enables visitors to read files on the Virtual Directory.

   ▶ **Allow Write Access.** Enables visitors to write files to the Virtual Directory.

5. Click Finish.

Configuring IIS to Support the WWW Service

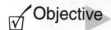 **Objective** ▶   After you install IIS 4, you can configure the WWW service for your Web site. The configuration changes you can make include the following:

▶ Setting bandwidth and user connections

▶ Setting user logon requirements and authentication requirements

▶ Modifying port settings

▶ Setting default pages

▶ Setting HTTP 1.1 host header names to host multiple Web sites

▶ Enabling HTTP keep-alives

Setting Bandwidth and User Connections

In order to conserve bandwidth for other clients accessing your Web site, consider limiting the number of connections that can connect to your site. When connection limits are maxed out, those attempting to connect to your server will be rejected and must try again later. You can limit the number of connections to your Web site, email, or news servers.

Another task you should consider for your Web site is to limit the bandwidth used by the Web server. This leaves bandwidth available for other services, such as email or news services. Limiting bandwidth is known as *throttling bandwidth,* and it limits only the bandwidth used by static HTML files. If you have multiple sites set up, you can throttle the bandwidth used by each site.

Tip

If you want to view your Web site's connection activity, open Windows NT Performance Monitor and set it to view FTP Service or Web Service from the Object list. You then can view Anonymous Users/sec, Bytes Received/sec, and other counters. Use this information to help you set the bandwidth and user connections.

To set user connections and set bandwidth throttling, follow Exercise 2.2 at the end of the chapter.

Setting User Logon Requirements and Authentication Requirements

IIS 4 can be set up to verify the identity of clients who access your Web site. On public Web sites on which noncritical or public domain information and applications are available, authentication of users connecting to your Web site may not be important. However, if you have secure data or want to restrict Web access to specific clients, logon and authentication requirements become very important.

Perform the following steps to set authentication and logon requirements:

1. Open Internet Service Manager.

2. Right-click a Web site, file (NTFS systems only), or directory you want to configure.

3. Click Properties. The property sheet for that item will appear.

4. Click the Directory Security (or File Security if you want to set file-specific properties) tab (see Figure 2.7).

5. Click the Edit button under Anonymous Access and Authentication Control. The Authentication Methods dialog box appears (see Figure 2.8)

Figure 2.7

You can set logon and authentica- tion requirements from the Directory Security tab.

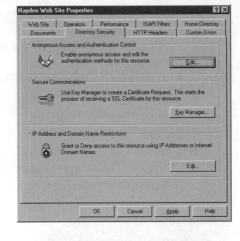

Figure 2.8

Select one or more authentica- tion methods from the Authentica- tion Methods dialog box.

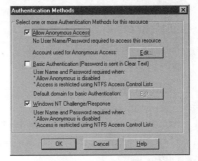

6. Select an authentication method from the following options:

   ▶ **Allow Anonymous Access.** This option enables clients to connect to your Web site without requiring a username or password. Click the Edit button to select the Win- dows NT user account used to access your computer. The default account IUSR_*computername* is used. This account is granted Log on Locally user rights by default and is necessary for anonymous logon access to your Web site. Click OK to return to the Authentication Methods dialog box.

   ▶ **Basic Authentication.** Use this method if you do not specify anonymous access and you want a client con- necting to your Web site to enter a valid Windows NT username and password to logon. This sends a pass- word in clear text format with the passwords being transmitted in an unencrypted format. Click the Edit button to specify a default logon domain for users who do not explicitly name a domain.

▶ **Windows NT Challenge/Response.** This setting is used if you want the Windows NT Challenge/Response feature to authenticate the client attempting to connect to your Web site. The only Web browsers that support this feature include Internet Explorer 2.0 and higher. During the challenge/response procedure, encrytped information is exchanged between the client and server to authenticate the user.

 Tip

IIS 4 uses the Basic and Windows NT Challenge/Response to authenticate users if anonymous access is denied either through the dialog box or via NTFS permissions.

7. Click OK.

If you have a server certificate installed, you also can use the Secure Sockets Layer (SSL) to authenticate users logging on to your Web site.

Modifying Port Settings

In a process similar to setting the port for FTP sites, you can change the default port setting for your Web site to any unique TCP port number. If you do this, however, you must let all clients know of your port setting before they can connect to your Web site. For a port setting other than the default, which is 80, the user must enter the port value as part of the URL.

To set the port setting, perform the following steps:

1. In the Web Site Properties dialog box, click the Web Site tab (see Figure 2.9).

2. In the TCP Port field, enter a new value for the port address. This must be a unique TCP value for your server.

Figure 2.9

The default port setting is usually the best for public Web sites, but you can change it by modifying the TCP Port setting on the Web Site tab.

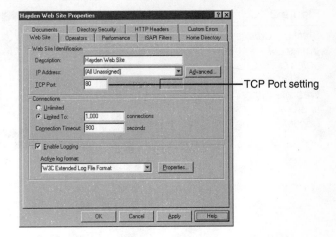

TCP Port setting

3. Click OK, or keep open if you want to continue changing Web site settings.

Setting Default Pages

If you have any experience browsing the Web, you know that for many sites you do not have to enter a specific document name (such as index.html) when accessing the Web site's home page. You can set IIS 4 to display a default page when clients access your site without a specified document in the URL. From this default page (usually your home page or index page), you can direct users to other documents or resources on your site.

IIS 4 enables you to specify more than one default document and list the documents in order of preference. When a client connects to your site, IIS searches for the topdocument and displays it if found. If it can't be found—for example, it is being updated or edited—the next default document is displayed.

To set default pages, perform the following:

1. From the Web Site Properties sheet, click the Documents tab (see Figure 2.10).

2. Select the Enable Default Document button. This option is enabled by default.

Figure 2.10

Setting a default document enables users to connect to your Web site without specifying a document name.

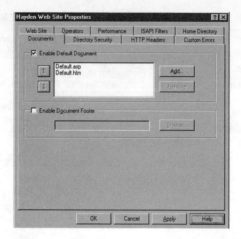

3. Click the Add button to specify a different default document.

4. In the Add Default Document dialog box, specify a new default document. An example of one that many Web sites use is index.htm.

5. Click OK.

6. Click the up or down arrows on the Documents tab to modify the search order for the default documents.

7. Click the Enable Document Footer option if you want IIS to insert an HTML file (which is really a short HTML document with formatting tags for footer content) to the bottom of your Web documents.

8. Enter the path and filename for the footer file.

9. Click OK, or keep open if you want to continue changing Web site settings.

Setting HTTP 1.1 Host Header Names to Host Multiple Web Sites

IIS 4 provides support for HTTP 1.1 host headers to allow multiple host names to be associated with one IP address. With this feature, a separate IP address is not needed for every virtual server you support. Microsoft Internet Explorer 3.0-and-later and Netscape Navigator 2.0-and-later support this feature, but many other browsers do not.

To set host header names for multiple Web sites, perform the following steps:

1. From the Web Site Properties sheet, click the Web Site tab.

2. Click the Advanced button. The Advanced Multiple Web Site Configuration dialog box displays (see Figure 2.11).

Figure 2.11

Add multiple host header names for hosting multiple Web sites.

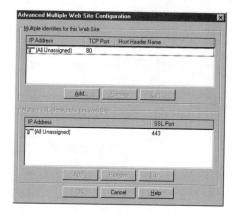

3. Click the Add button. The Advanced Web Site Identification dialog box displays (see Figure 2.12).

Figure 2.12

Fill in the information to identify the multiple host name.

4. Fill in the IP Address, TCP Port, and Host Header Name fields. The IP Address field must include an IP address that has already been defined by the DHCP Server. The Host Header Name field must include a registered DNS value.

5. Click OK.

6. Click OK to close the Advanced Multiple Web Site Configuration dialog box, or click Add to continue adding new multiple host header names to this site.

7. Click OK to close the Web Site Properties sheet.

Enabling HTTP Keep-Alives

You can enable IIS 4's Keep-Alive feature to enable clients to maintain open connections. This way a client does not need to re-establish connections for each request. By enabling Keep-Alive, you decrease the amount of time a client waits to connect to another document or application on your site. But you also increase the amount of resources devoted to this client.

To enable HTTP keep-alives, perform the following steps:

1. From the Web Site Properties sheet, click the Performance tab (see Figure 2.13).

Figure 2.13

Enable the HTTP keep-alive setting on the Performance tab.

HTTP Keep-Alive setting ——

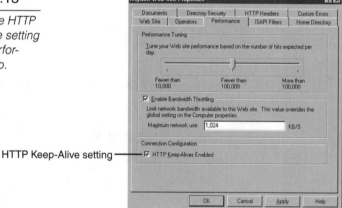

2. Select HTTP Keep-Alives Enabled. This option is enabled by default. If a checkmark already appears in this checkbox, no changes are needed.

3. Click OK.

Configuring and Saving Consoles by Using Microsoft Management Console

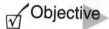 **Objective**

Microsoft Management Console (MMC) is used to organize and perform management tasks for IIS 4. MMC does not actually administer any part of IIS or your network; rather, it provides a framework for other applications (called *snap-ins*) to administer parts of the network. Internet Service Manager, for instance, is a snap-in. When Internet Service Manager starts (not the HTML version), an MMC console appears with the Internet Service Manager displayed as a snap-in.

In the future, Microsoft BackOffice and Windows NT will offer MMC snap-in administration tools. Other vendors are expected to provide snap-ins as well.

When you start a snap-in in MMC, a console displays. Consoles have one or more windows. The Internet Service Manager, for instance, includes two windows. On the left side, called the *scope pane,* a tree view is shown. The right pane, which shows the results of selecting something on the left page, is called the *results pane.*

You can view multiple windows in a console and then save that view for later. You might, for instance, create one window to show a snap-in for changing settings and another window to display a Web page with program updates. You can then display that window view or share it with other users via email, floppy disk, or network.

Verifying Server Settings by Accessing the Metabase

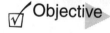 **Objective**

The *metabase* is a memory-resident data storage area that stores your IIS 4 configuration values. The metabase is analogous to, but not identical to, the Windows NT Registry. It is also faster and more flexible than the Registry. The metabase has keys that correspond to IIS elements; each key has properties that affect the configuration of that element. The hierarchy of the NNTP service keys, for example, is shown in Figure 2.14.

Figure 2.14

The hierarchy of the NNTP service keys.

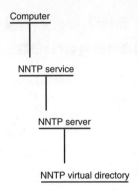

You can use the IIS Administration Objects to configure your IIS 4 installation, as well as change settings that affect the operation of your IIS Web server, FTP site, virtual directories, and other components. One application that uses the IIS Administration in Objects is the Internet Service Manager (HTML) that you use in Internet Explorer 4.0 (see Figure 2.15).

Figure 2.15

The HTML version of Internet Service Manager uses IIS Administration Objects to configure IIS components.

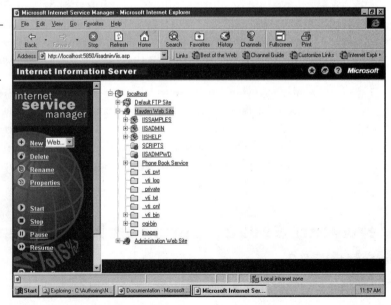

Choosing the Appropriate Administration Method

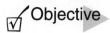 **Objective**

IIS 4 provides two main ways to administer your IIS installation. You still must use the common Windows NT administration tools to set file and directory rights and user accounts, and to view performance measurements. But to administer IIS 4, you use Internet Service Manager, either as a snap-in to MMC or as an HTML application in Internet Explorer 4.0.

With Internet Service Manager (HTML), you can manage your Web site remotely using a standard Web browser (IE 4.0 is recommended). This makes it convenient for administrators to manage a Web site when physically away from the Web site. An administrator, for instance, may be located in a different building than where the Web server is housed. By using Internet Service Manager (HTML), the administrator can connect to the server and administer it from the remote location.

Internet Service Manager (HTML) can be customized using Active Server Pages and the IIS Administration Objects. By customizing Internet Service Manager (HTML), or by creating new HTML-based administration tools, ISPs and administrators can create pages for customers or users to modify settings on the Web.

For administration tasks on the server, administrators can use familiar Windows NT Server administration tools, including the following:

▶ **User Manager for Domains.** Create a new user for your system to access file, print, and Web services.

▶ **Event Viewer.** Monitor systems events and log application and security events used by the Web server. Event Viewer also can be used to audit access to secure files.

▶ **Performance Monitor.** Monitor the performance of IIS 4, including FTP and Web services, including HTTP and indexing counters. Use Performance Monitor to get a view of server load.

Customizing the Installation of Microsoft Site Server Express Analysis Content Analyzer

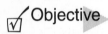
Objective

The Site Server Express Analysis Content Analyzer (Content Analyzer for short) enables you to create WebMaps to give you a view of your Web site, helping you manage your Web site. WebMaps are graphical representations of resources on your site. These resources can include HTML documents, audio and video files, Java applets, FTP resources, and applications.

Content Analyzer also enables you to manage your links. You can ensure links are included in the resources and that they all work correctly.

When you install IIS 4, you have the option of installing all or part of the Microsoft Site Server Express 2.0 tool. If you choose the Content Analyzer option (refer to Table 2.3), the Analysis-Content subcomponent should be selected if you want to install the Content Analyzer.

The system requirements and recommendations for installing Content Analyzer are shown in Table 2.4.

Table 2.4

Content Analyzer system requirements.

Component	Requirement	Recommendation
CPU	Intel 486 66MHz	120MHz Pentium
RAM	16MB	32MB
Hard disk space	14MB	
Internet connection	Modem	Direct
Browser	IE 3.0 or above Netscape Navigator 3.0 or above	IE 4.0
Authoring tools	Not required	Recommended
Multimedia applications	Not required	Recommended

After IIS 4 is installed, you start Content Analyzer by selecting Start | Programs | Windows NT 4.0 Option Pack | Site Server Express 2.0 | Content Analyzer. Click the Open WebMap button to display WebMaps in Content Analyzer. A sample WebMap is included, named SAMPLE.WMP. The Content Analyzer displays as shown in Figure 2.16. This screen shows an example of a WebMap created by Content Analyzer and displayed in tree and Cyberbolic views.

Figure 2.16

Most Web site administrators use the tree and Cyberbolic views to view WebMaps.

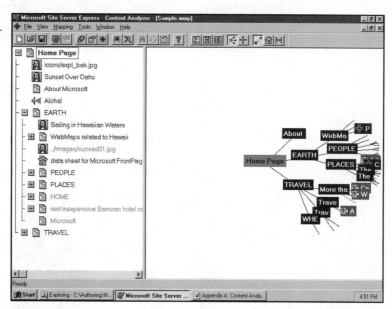

Customizing the Installation of Microsoft Site Server Analysis Report Writer and Usage Import

Site Server Express includes two types of usage components: the Usage Import (see Figure 2.17) and Report Writer (see Figure 2.18). These tools enable you to gather and review IIS 4 log files from a server. With the data you collect from nine different reports, you can chart and identify trends on the usage of your IIS server.

Figure 2.17

Usage Import enables you to log data about your IIS 4 site.

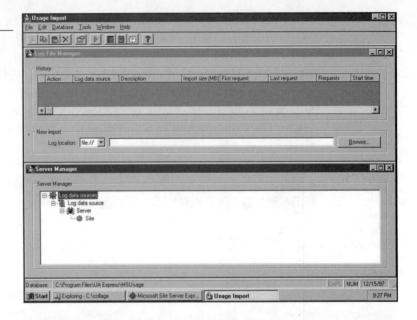

Figure 2.18

Report Writer is used to create reports from site data collected by Usage Import and saved in a database.

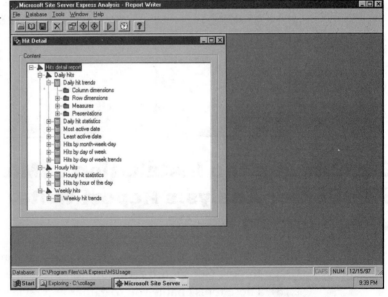

When you plan to use Usage Import and Report Writer, you should also install a relational database. The database is used to store imported log file data so each of the Site Server Express components can interact with the database to process, organize, and analyze the data. Usage Import is used to filter and configure the data in the database. Report Writer then uses that information to create reports based on the activity on your IIS site.

You can install Report Writer if you select to install the Site Server Analysis Usage Import component. The system requirements and recommendations for installing Usage Import and Report Writer are shown in Table 2.5.

Table 2.5

Usage Import and Report Writer system requirements.

Component	Requirement	Recommendation
CPU	90MHz Pentium	133MHz Pentium
RAM	16MB	32MB
Hard disk space	15MB	Additional space for log files needed
Internet connection	Modem	Direct
Browser	HTML 2-compatible browser that supports tables	IE 4.0

 Tip

You can use the Internet connection to resolve IP addresses, run Whois inquiries, and conduct HTML title lookups.

You also may want to install the following optional reporting applications:

▶ Microsoft Word version 7 (or later) to create Word reports

▶ Microsoft Excel version 7 (or later) to create spreadsheet reports

▶ Microsoft Access or the Access runtime version

▶ Microsoft SQL Server if the total size of your databases are more than 75MB per month

▶ Precompiled DLL for Microsoft ISAPI

▶ Source code for Apache and Netscape NSAPI server extensions

 Note When Access is used with Usage Import and Report Writer, a default database by the name of ANALYST.MDB is created by the installation program. A compressed copy of ANALYST.MDB in its original format (no Internet sites or log file data are contained in this file) is created in a zip file called TEMPLATE.ZIP. Use this file if you need to create a new database.

Exercises

Exercise 2.1: Installing IIS

The following exercise walks you through a simple installation of IIS:

1. Insert the Option Pack CD-ROM and locate the Setup icon in Explorer. Double-click on the Setup icon. If you downloaded IIS 4 from the Internet, double-click on the setup file.

2. Click Next on the Welcome to the Windows NT 4.0 Option dialog box. The End User License Agreement screen appears.

3. Click Accept.

4. Click Custom.

5. Click the components you want to install. Click Next. A dialog box showing the default publishing folders appears. A list summarizing folder locations appears.

6. Click Next. Walk through the dialog boxes adding the components you selected in step 5.

7. After installing the components, click Next. Setup now completes the installation process and installs the IIS files on your hard disk.

8. Click Finish when all the files are installed to your system.

9. Click Yes when prompted to restart your computer.

Exercise 2.2: Setting User Connections and Bandwidth Throttling

The following exercise walks you through setting user connections and setting bandwidth throttling:

1. Select Start | Programs | Windows NT 4.0 Option Pack | Microsoft Internet Information Server | Internet Service Manager.

2. Expand the Internet Information Server folder.

3. Expand the server that you want to modify.

4. Right-click the Default Web Site entry. Your Web site may be named something different.

5. Click Properties. The Web Site Properties sheet appears.

6. On the Web Site tab, click the Limited To option (see Figure 2.19).

Figure 2.19

Use the Web Site tab to set the number of simultaneous connections to your site.

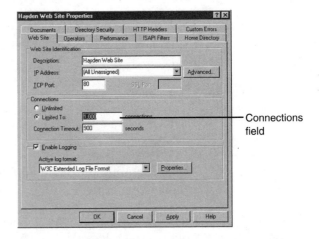

— Connections field

7. Enter a value in the connections field. The default is 1,000, but you may want to lower this if your resources are limited.

8. In the Connection Timeout field, enter a value for the amount of time your server should automatically disconnect an idle session. The default is 15 minutes (900 seconds), but an average setting is five minutes (300 seconds). For an infinite amount of time, enter all 9s in this field.

 Note

Even if a connection is lost or a browser stops working, your site will continue to process data until the timeout value is reached. Setting an appropriate timeout value will limit the loss of resources due to these lost connections.

9. Click the Performance tab (see Figure 2.20).

Figure 2.20

Set the band-width throttling value to limit the bandwidth available to your Web site.

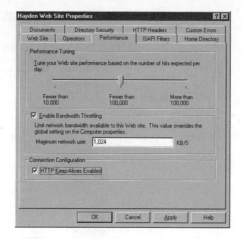

10. Click the Enable Bandwidth Throttling option.

11. In the Maximum network use field, enter a value for the amount of bandwidth (measured in KB/S) you want IIS to use.

 Tip

The value you set on the Performance tab overrides settings for bandwidth throttling set on the Computer Properties sheet. This is true even if the value on the Performance tab is set higher than that on the Computer Properties sheet.

12. Click OK, or keep open if you want to continue changing Web site settings.

Exercise 2.3: Configuring Views

The following exercise shows you how to copy a window view, create a view with a different root, and close the scope pane:

1. Select Start | Programs | Windows NT 4.0 Option Pack | Microsoft Internet Information Server | Internet Service Manager. MMC displays with Internet Service Manager (see Figure 2.21).

2. Select Window | New Window. A copy of the window displays.

Figure 2.21

*MMC with
Internet Service
Manager snap-in
displayed.*

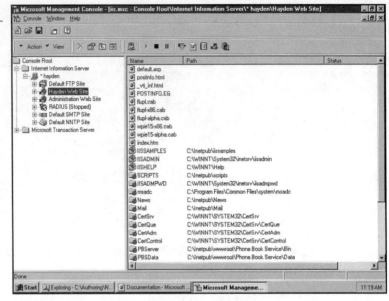

3. To create a view with a different root, click the node you want to view as the root.

4. Click the Action menu.

5. Click New window from here. A new window will appear with the node you select as the root node (see Figure 2.22).

Figure 2.22

*A node selected
as the root node.*

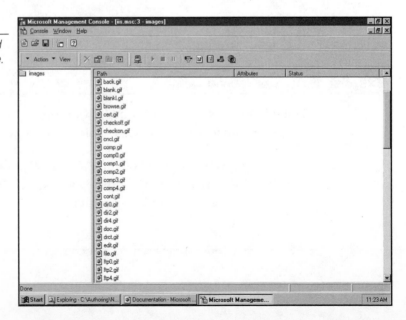

6. To view only the results pane, click the Action menu.

7. Click the Scope Pane option. The scope pane (the left pane) is removed so only the results pane shows.

8. To save this console, select Console | Save As.

9. Fill out the Save As dialog box. Consoles have an MSC extension.

10. Click Save.

Review Questions

1. As an IIS consultant, you're asked to install IIS on an intranet in your client's company. From the following choices, what are two changes to Windows NT you should make before installing IIS?

   A. Install TCP/IP and WINS

   B. Install DHCP and NTFS

   C. Install FAT32 and WINS

   D. None of the above

2. IIS 4 introduces the Microsoft Management Console (MMC) for managing and administering IIS tasks and resources. What types of applications can you run in MMC?

   A. DHTML pages

   B. Plug-ins

   C. Snap-ins

   D. All of the above

3. You are the administrator for an Internet site in a small publishing firm. The firm wants visitors to be able to enter the firm's domain name without a specific document to access the home page. What must you enable in IIS to allow this?

   A. A default page

   B. An index page

   C. home.html

   D. A virtual server with index.html

4. You are the administrator of your company's Internet and intranet site. You are away from the office and must access the IIS server for administration concerns. What is the best administration method for this situation?

   A. Connect to your FTP server as administrator.

   B. Use Internet Explorer 4.0 to access the default page.

   C. Use Internet Service Manager (HTML) to connect to the server via the Internet.

   D. All of the above.

5. You are an IIS consultant. A client wants to install ISS to support email, Web and FTP services, and database access. What are the minimum components that you must install?

   A. SMTP Service, WWW Service, FTP Service, Site Server Express, Index Server

   B. Full install

   C. NNTP Service, Web and FTP Services, ODBC support

   D. SMTP Service, WWW Service, FTP Service, Microsoft Data Access Components 1.5 with Data Sources

6. You're hired by a client to install IIS. The client wants to ensure that the WWW service is as secure as possible. Pick three choices from the following that will help provide a secure environment for IIS:

   A. Limit the Guest account and other accounts to specific directories on the server.

   B. Turn off auditing.

   C. Review network share permissions.

   D. Limit who has membership to the administrators group.

7. As the administrator of your company's intranet site, you need to connect to the server remotely for administration concerns. You plan to use Internet Service Manager (HTML). What privileges are required to do this?

   A. Guest rights

   B. Local user rights

   C. Administrator rights

   D. None of the above

8. You are an IIS administrator in an accounting firm. You are asked to install IIS on a server and you start the installation process. During the IIS Setup routine, you decide to end the installation to start it again the following day. What is your best course of action?

   A. Click the Cancel button to stop Setup.

   B. Finish Setup and then uninstall IIS.

   C. Shut down and restart Windows NT Server 4.0 and edit the Metabase.

   D. None of the above.

9. You are using Internet Service Manager and want to hide the scope pane. Select the correct sequence of steps from the following answers to complete this task:

   A. Select Console | Hide Scope Pane.

   B. Select Window | Panes | Hide Scope Pane.

   C. Select View | List.

   D. Select Action | Scope Pane.

10. As an IIS consultant, you're requested to set up IIS in a manufacturing firm. The firm would like IIS to be set up so Internet users must log in using a username and password. The firm wants the Windows NT Challenge/Response authentication feature to be used to authenticate the user. Which of the following answers is the best for this situation?

    A. The user must use an HTML 3.2–compatible browser.

    B. The user must use Internet Explorer 2.0 or later.

    C. The user must invoke Challenge/Response authentication on his/her client.

    D. None of the above.

11. When setting up the FTP Service in IIS, you want to enable anonymous users to upload files to the FTP server. What permission is needed to do this?

    A. Write Only

    B. Execute

    C. Read

    D. Both A and C

12. You are an IIS administrator and need to install IIS on a new server. During IIS installation, what services can be installed? (Choose three.)

    A. Certificate Server

    B. Transaction Server

    C. Message Queue

    D. Gopher

13. You've installed IIS on your Windows NT Server 4.0 server. What are two changes that have been made to this server after IIS has been installed?

    A. You'll no longer be able to use IE 4.0 as a client application.

    B. Performance Monitor will have Web Service objects available.

    C. User Manager for Domains lists a new username in the list of user accounts.

    D. The Metabase replaces the Windows NT Registry.

14. You are an Internet administrator in a small foam packaging firm. You've set up IIS to run an Internet site. What is the name of the new user created by IIS during installation? (computername is the computer name on which IIS is installed)

    A. IISR_computername

    B. anon_computername

    C. IWAM_computername

    D. IUSR_computername

15. You use Performance Monitor to monitor activity on your IIS server. Pick three counters that you can add to Performance Monitor to track the Web Service object:

    A. Anonymous Users/sec

    B. Bytes Created/sec

    C. Files/sec

    D. Total Head Requests

Review Answers

1. **B**. For systems in which file-level security is needed, config-
    ure NTFS so you can limit access to files and directories.
    Also, you should consider installing DHCP if you plan to run
    IIS 4 on an Intranet.

2. **C**. MMC does not actually administer any part of IIS or your
    network; rather, it provides a framework for other applica-
    tions (called snap-ins) to administer parts of the network.
    Internet Service Manager, for instance, is a snap-in. When
    Internet Service Manager starts (not the HTML version), an
    MMC console appears with the Internet Service Manager
    displayed as a snap-in.

3. **A**. You can set IIS 4 to display a default page when clients
    access your site without a specified document in the URL.
    From this default page (usually your home page or index
    page), you can direct users to other documents or resources
    on your site.

4. **C**. With Internet Service Manager (HTML), you can manage
    your Web site remotely using a standard Web browser, such
    as IE 4.0. This makes it convenient for administrators to
    manage a Web site when physically away from the Web site.
    An administrator, for instance, may be located in a different
    building than where the Web server is housed.

5. **D**. Table 2.3 describes the different services and components
    you can install with IIS 4.

6. **A, C, D**. To help secure your IIS installation, you should per-
    form the following tasks:

    ▶ Turn on auditing.

    ▶ Limit the Guest account and other accounts to specific
    directories on the server.

    ▶ Limit who has membership to the administrators
    group.

> ▶ Start only those services and protocols required by your system.

> ▶ Use complex password schemes.

> ▶ Review network share permissions.

7. **C**. By using Internet Service Manager (HTML), the administrator can connect to the server and administer it from the remote location.

8. **B**. If you decide you don't want to install IIS 4 and you've already started the IIS 4 setup program, don't cancel it. This will leave files on your system that the uninstall program cannot remove. Finish the entire installation process, then uninstall IIS 4 if you don't want it on your system.

9. **D**. To view only the results pane, click the Action menu and click the Scope Pane option. The scope pane (the left pane) is removed, so only the results pane shows.

10. **B**. Windows NT Challenge/Response feature authenticates the client attempting to connect to your Web site. The only Web browsers that support this feature include Internet Explorer 2.0 and higher. During the challenge/response procedure, encrypted information is exchanged between the client and server to authenticate the user.

11. **A**. Write enables clients to upload files to the home directory on your FTP server. This option should be selected only for FTP servers in which users must upload files. By default, this option is not selected.

12. **A, B, C**. Table 2.3 describes the different services and components you can install with IIS 4.

13. **B, C**. When you install IIS 4, your Windows NT Server 4.0 compute will change. The following are the changes that occur:

> ▶ Microsoft Management Console (MMC) is the host for the Internet Service Manager. Internet Service Manager is IIS's administrative program.

▶ Registry changes can be viewed by selecting Start | Programs | Windows NT 4.0 Option Pack | Microsoft Site Server Express 2.0 | Documentation. Click on Administrator's Reference in the left pane and click Registry. Click on the topic you want to read, such as WWW Service Registry Entries.

▶ New services include the FTP Publishing Service, IIS Administration Service, Content Index, and World Wide Web Publishing Service.

▶ User Manager for Domains lists a new username in the list of user accounts. This username is IUSR_computername and allows anonymous access to Internet services on your computer.

▶ Performance Monitor can now be used to track several IIS services, including Content Index, Content Index Filter, FTP Service, HTTP Content Index, HTTP Service, and Internet Information Services Global. Some of the over 75 counters added to Performance Monitor enable you to track connections, bytes transferred, and cache information.

14. **D**. User Manager for Domains lists a new username in the list of user accounts. This username is IUSR_computername and allows anonymous access to Internet services on your computer.

15. **A, C, D**. Performance Monitor can now be used to track HTTP Services. Some of the over 75 counters added to Performance Monitor enable you to track connections, bytes transferred, and cache information. Chapter 6 discusses Performance Monitor in more detail.

Answers to Test Yourself Questions at Beginning of Chapter

1. Microsoft Index Server 3.0, Microsoft Certificate Server, and Internet News Server. See "Installing IIS 4."

2. Anonymous access must be disabled, and anonymous access is denied because Windows NT permissions are set requiring the user to log on with a username and password. See "Setting User Logon Requirements and Authentication Requirements."

3. The client can use standard Windows NT Server administration tools, including Performance Monitor and User Manager for Domains. In addition, Internet Service Manager can be used as a snap-in to the Microsoft Management Console (MMC). For remote administration, Internet Service Manager (HTML) can be used in Internet Explorer 4.0. See "Choosing the Appropriate Administration Method."

4. Set the connection timeout period to a reasonable amount. See "Setting Bandwidth and User Connections."

5. Anonymous authentication. See "Setting User Logon Requirements and Authentication Requirements."

6. The metabase is a hierarchical database that stores IIS 4 settings. The metabase has keys that correspond to IIS elements; each key has properties that affect the configuration of that element. It is analogous to the Windows NT Registry, but it is much faster and more flexible then the Registry. See "Verifying Server Settings by Accessing the Metabase."

7. Yes, you can. Create a console view of the Web server you want to share and select Action I New Window From Here. When the new window displays, select Console I Save As and save the console with an MSC extension. Send the file to the other administrator. See "Configuring and Saving Consoles By Using Microsoft Management Console."

C h a p t e r

3

Configuring and
Managing Resource Access

This chapter helps you prepare for the exam by covering the following objectives:

 **Objectives**

> ▶ Create and share directories with appropriate permissions.
> Tasks include the following:
>
> > ▶ Setting directory-level permissions
> >
> > ▶ Setting file-level permission
>
> ▶ Create and share local and remote virtual directories with
> appropriate permissions. Tasks include the following:
>
> > ▶ Creating a virtual directory and assigning an alias
> >
> > ▶ Setting directory-level permissions
> >
> > ▶ Setting file-level permissions
>
> ▶ Create and share virtual servers with appropriate permis-
> sions. Tasks include the following:
>
> > ▶ Assigning IP addresses
>
> ▶ Write scripts to manage the FTP service or the WWW service
>
> ▶ Manage a web site by using Content Analyzer. Tasks include
> the following:
>
> > ▶ Creating, customizing, and navigating WebMaps

continues

▶ Examining a Web site by using the various reports provided by Content Analyzer

▶ Tracking links by using a WebMap

▶ Configure Microsoft SMTP Service to host personal mailboxes

▶ Configure Microsoft NNTP Service to host a newsgroup

▶ Configure Certificate Server to issue certificates

▶ Configure Index Server to index a web site

▶ Manage MIME types

▶ Manage the FTP service

▶ Manage the WWW service

Test Yourself! Before reading this chapter, test yourself to determine how much study time you will need to devote to this section.

1. What is the default port used for the WWW service?

2. Where should virtual directories always be stored?

3. Virtual servers allow one server to alias multiple what?

4. What utility included with the Windows NT Resource Kit can be used to count the number of lines in a log file?

5. What are two views that can be seen of a web site with Web-Maps?

6. What is the default port used for the SMTP service?

7. By default, and in the absence of SSL, what is the TCP port that the NNTP service uses?

8. After using Key Manager to generate a digital certificate request file for use with SSL, what must you do next?

9. With Index Server, what percentage of disk space does the data require?

10. MIME is an acronym for what?

11. In terms of increments of time, FTP log files can be created on what basis?

12. What is the process used to make a WWW site hidden?

Answers are located at the end of the chapter....

This chapter is a broad collection of assorted topics, many of which are addressed elsewhere in this book, but not in the context of configuration and management. Much of the configuration and management of services is done during the initial planning, installation, or troubleshooting phases. This chapter looks at the topics from a fine-tuning standpoint and accentuate what has already been addressed.

The topics covered in this chapter include the following:

▶ Creating and Sharing Directories

▶ Creating and Sharing Virtual Directories

▶ Creating and Sharing Virtual Servers

▶ Writing Scripts for Service Management

▶ Using Content Analyzer

▶ Configuring SMTP

▶ Configuring NNTP

▶ Configuring Certificate Server

▶ Configuring Index Server

▶ Managing MIME Types

▶ Managing the FTP Service

▶ Managing the WWW Service

Creating and Sharing Directories

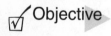 To create and share a new WWW or FTP directory, start the Internet Service Manager and select the server on which you want to create the directory. After that, implement the following steps:

1. Right-click and select New. This brings up the choice of creating an FTP or WWW site. Make the appropriate selection and the corresponding wizard starts. (WWW is used for the rest of this discussion.)

2. Enter the Web site description and select Next.

3. Select or verify the IP address to use. If you are creating a new site, make certain you use an address that is not currently being used, or it will create a conflict with the current one.

4. The TCP port defaults to 80. This is the default used for all WWW services. If you want to offer the service but hide it from most browsers, choose another port.

5. If SSL is to be used, enter the appropriate port for it (default is 443), and click Next.

6. Enter the path for what will appear as the home directory (you also can use the Browse button to specify).

7. By default, the checkbox appears, allowing anonymous access to the Web site (see Figure 3.1). If you do not want anonymous access, remove the check. Choose Next.

8. Select the access permissions for the directory. Choices include the following:

   ▶ Allow Read Access—Assigned by default

   ▶ Allow Script Access—Assigned by default

   ▶ Allow Execute Access—Includes Script access

   ▶ Allow Write Access

   ▶ Allow Directory Browsing

9. Choose Finish.

Figure 3.1

Selecting the home directory path and whether or not anonymous access is allowed.

Choosing the Access Rights

The five rights that you can select for IIS access work in conjunction with all other rights. Like share rights, the IIS rights are *in addition to* NTFS rights and of greatest value when you are using anonymous access. Allowing Read access lets a user view a file if their NTFS permissions also allow it. Taking away Read, however, prevents the user from viewing the file regardless of what NTFS permissions are set.

As listed previously, the names of the rights are pretty self-explanatory. The only caveats to note are that Read and Script access are assigned by default, and Execute is a superset of Script access.

Note

> The Execute permission allows for CGI & ISAPI scripts to execute, while Script is sufficient for IDC, IDQ, and ASP. These topics are explored further in Chapter Four, "Integration and Interoperability," and Chapter Five, "Running Applications."

Changing Permissions and Access for Directories

After the wizard has been run and the directory is configured for site access, you can change permissions and access for individual directories by selecting the directory in Internet Service Manager, right-clicking, and choosing Properties.

Figure 3.2 shows the properties for a directory. Notice that access permissions have now been set to read and write, or any combination thereof, and permissions are now None, Script, or Execute (which includes script).

Click the Directory Security tab of the directories properties and you see that you have three items that you can configure:

▶ Anonymous Access and Authentication Control

▶ Secure Communications

▶ IP Address and Domain Name restrictions

Figure 3.2

*The properties for
a WWW directory.*

The latter two options are discussed later in this chapter. Selecting
Edit on the enabling anonymous access portion brings up the
screen shown in Figure 3.3. From this screen you can choose to
allow or disallow anonymous access, and (by choosing Edit) the
name of the anonymous access account (which defaults to
IUSR_{computername}).

Figure 3.3

*The Authentica-
tion methods
dialog box for the
WWW anony-
mous user.*

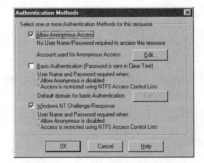

Changing Permissions and Access for Files

You also can control the permissions for specific files in a similar
manner. First, select the file and choose its properties. A screen
similar to Figure 3.4 is displayed. Choosing the File Security tab,
you can set the same options for the file as were illustrated in Figure 3.3 for the directory.

Figure 3.4

The properties for a WWW file.

Creating and Sharing Virtual Directories

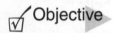 As the name implies, virtual directories are entities that do not exist, but give you the ability to reference relative file locations to make it appear as if they are in a directory. By so doing, you can get around issues such as disk space and determining where best to store files.

 If you are uncertain as to why you would want to create an additional shared directory, think of the example of an Internet Service Provider giving their clients the ability to have their own web page. Their personal Web site, in some cases, is added to the host's domain name. (For example `http://www.flash.net/~andrew.`)

The disadvantage to using virtual directories is a slight decrease in performance if they reside on a different server because files must be retrieved from the LAN. The only other downside is that virtual directories are not visible in directory listings and must be accessed through explicit links within HTML files.

Virtual directories must exist on servers that all reside within the same NT domain and within the domain in which the IIS server resides. Aside from this restriction, the directories can be either local or remote.

Creating a Virtual Directory

If you choose to create the virtual directory on a local computer, the Internet Service Manager can be used to assign an alias to it. To do so, implement the following steps:

1. Start the Internet Service Manager from the Programs portion of the Start menu.

2. Open a web site, right-click the left pane, and choose New.

3. Select Virtual Directory (as shown in Figure 3.5). This starts the New Virtual Directory Wizard.

Figure 3.5

Select Virtual Directory from the New menu.

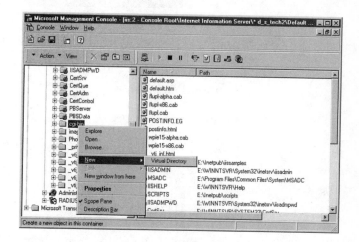

4. Enter an alias to be used for the virtual directory name, and click Next (as shown if Figure 3.6).

Figure 3.6

Enter an alias to be used for the virtual directory.

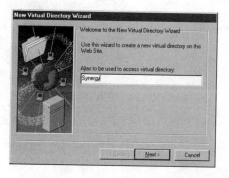

5. Enter the physical path to the virtual directory, as shown in Figure 3.7 (you also can select the Browse button), and click Next.

Figure 3.7

Enter the physical path for the virtual directory to use.

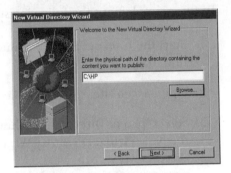

6. Select the access permissions for the virtual directory. Choices include the following:

- ▶ Allow Read Access

- ▶ Allow Script Access

- ▶ Allow Execute Access

- ▶ Allow Write Access

- ▶ Allow Directory Browsing

The choices, and defaults, are shown in Figure 3.8.

Figure 3.8

Selecting Access rights for the new virtual directory.

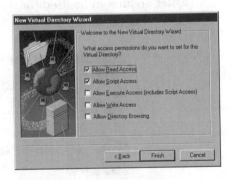

7. Select Finish.

Making Changes After Setup

After the wizard has been run and the virtual directory is configured for site access, you can change permissions and access for individual directories or files by selecting the directory\file in Internet Service Manager, right-clicking, and choosing Properties.

Creating and Sharing Virtual Servers

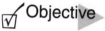 Objective

The major benefit of virtual servers is that they enable you to expand your site beyond the limitations of a single site per server. You can combine a number of different sites (domain names) on a single server through the implementation of virtual servers.

Also known as multi-homed hosts, multi-homed servers, or just plain multi-homing, virtual servers enable one host to respond to requests for the following totally three different sites:

```
http://www.synergy.com

http://www.synergy_technology.com

http://www.st.com
```

All of the previous domain names are Fully Qualified Domain Names (FQDNs). A fully qualified domain name completely specifies the location of the host. An FQDN specifies the host name, the domain or subdomain the host belongs to, and any domains above in the hierarchy until the root domain in the organization is specified. On the Internet, the root domain in the path is something like com, but on a private network the top-level domains may be named according to some internal naming convention. The FQDN is read from left to right, with each host name or domain name specified by a period. The syntax of an FQDN follows:

```
host name.subdomain. ... .domain
```

An example of an FQDN is www.microsoft.com, which refers to a server called www located in the subdomain called microsoft in the domain called com. Referring to a host by its FQDN is similar to referring to a file by its complete directory path. However, a complete file name goes from general to specific, with the file name at the rightmost part of the path.

An FQDN goes from specific to general, with the host name at the leftmost part of the name. Fully qualified domain names are more like addresses. An address starts with the most specific information: who is to receive the letter. The address specifies the house number in which the recipient lives, the street on which the house is located, the city where the street is located, and finally the most general location, the state where that city is located.

Assigning an IP Address

Each site is specified by a unique IP address, and the absence of a unique IP address makes the site visible to all virtual servers.

Creating a Virtual Server

To create a virtual server, you must first have created a directory to publish (local or virtual). Then implement the following steps:

1. Start Internet Service Manager.

2. From the Action menu, select New, and then WWW Site (see Figure 3.9).

Figure 3.9

Creating a virtual server begins with choosing to create a new site.

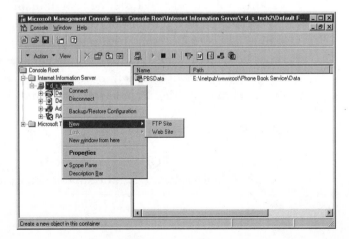

3. Enter an IP address to use for the site and the TCP port, as shown in Figure 3.10. Click on Next.

Figure 3.10

Enter the IP ad-dress and port for the virtual server.

4. Enter the path for the home directory and whether or not anonymous access is allowed. Click Next.

5. Configure the appropriate rights and click Finish.

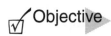 **Note**   Permissions for directories and sites on virtual servers can be configured the same as in the previous sections.

Writing Scripts for Service Management

 Objective

New to IIS 4.0 is the MicrosoftScript Debugger. It can be used to debug scripts written in Jscript, Visual Basic Scripting Edition (VBScript), and a number of other languages. If you know one of these languages, you can simply manage administrative tasks by writing scripts to manage your services (FTP or WWW).

Management tasks to automate should include the inspection of log files (described in the sections "Managing the FTP Service" and "Managing the WWW Service" later in this chapter). The log files can be examined for statistical information such as the number of hits, errors, and so on.

One way of exploring the log files is with the large number of UNIX-type utilities (all POSIX-compliant) found in the Windows

NT Resource Kit. These utilities also can be useful in creating scripts to examine the log files. The utilities include the following:

▶ find—Enables you to find a file according to specified criteria, such as date, size, and so on.

▶ grep—Enables you to locate an entry within a file. Possibly the most powerful search tool ever written; parameters enable you to search according to case (default is yes), count the entries, find only those that do not match, and more.

▶ touch—Enables you to change the extended attributes of a file, such as the date and time associated with the file, without ever opening it.

▶ wc—Enables you to count the entries in a file in terms of lines, words, or characters. This is most useful when trying to determine the number of entries in a file.

Using Content Analyzer

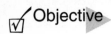 Content Analyzer is a new method of managing your Web site in a simplified manner. It enables you to create WebMaps, as shown in Figure 3.11, that let you see a graphical representation of your entire site.

The graphical representation includes all HTML pages, audio and video files, as well as graphic images and links to other services. The left side of the WebMap display (as shown in Figure 3.11) is a tree view of the site, while the right pane shows Cyberbolic view. You can choose to see either of the two or both—whichever is most convenient for you.

In addition to the graphical representation, Content Analyzer can be used to create a set of links to your site in a report that you can use for troubleshooting. You also can save the maps of your site (to a database, spreadsheet, or HTML file) for comparison at later points in time to see what has changed as time has progressed.

Figure 3.11

The WebMap view available in Content Analyzer.

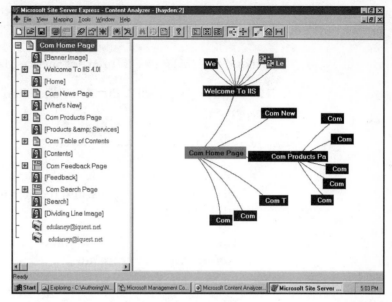

Configuring SMTP

SMTP, an acronym for Simple Mail Transfer Protocol, enables you to send mail to others on your network as well as to the Internet. The SMTP Site property sheet is used to set the basic connection parameters, such as the port to use (default port is 25), number of simultaneous connections (default is 1000), and length of inactivity before disconnect (default is 60 seconds).

Another great use for the SMTP service is to link its abilities to a web page. In other words, if you have a web site that requires some type of response by the visitor, then you can provide a resource for them to use to send you e-mail, without the visitor needing a mail client on their end. So, you've given the visitor the power to e-mail you something without requiring them to have an e-mail client, such as Outlook, installed on their machine.

Regardless of its size, each site has only one Microsoft SMTP site for the service. You cannot create additional sites or delete existing ones. To display the SMTP property sheets, implement the following steps:

1. Expand the SMTP tree in Internet Service Manager.

2. Highlight and right-click the SMTP site, then choose Properties.

3. The following five tabs are displayed:

   ▶ The SMTP Site tab enables you to determine how this server connects to, sends, and receives messages with other servers.

   ▶ The Operators tab enables you to determine which groups have operator status.

   ▶ The Messages tab lets you configure limits on message size and decide what to do with undeliverable mail; you also can specify a maximum number of recipients who can receive a single message (the default is 100).

   ▶ The Delivery tab specifies how many messages should be sent per connections, the route to use, and so on.

   ▶ The Directory Security tab enables you to specify other servers to accept only, or restrict only.

Configuring NNTP

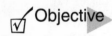 Objective ▶ NNTP, an acronym for Network News Transport Protocol, enables you to configure a server for clients to read newsgroups. The Microsoft NNTP Service included with IIS 4.0 is the server side of the operation, whereas Microsoft Internet Mail and News is a common client (now being replaced in the market by Outlook Express).

The default port for NNTP is 119, although this changes to 563 if SSL is used. When the client connects to the service, it requests a list of available newsgroups. The NNTP service authenticates the user, then sends the list of newsgroups.

The client picks a newsgroup to view and requests the list of articles. Authentication takes place again by the NNTP service, and then the list of articles is sent. The client then picks articles they want to see and the NNTP Service sends them.

Posting Articles

Posting of articles works in a similar fashion: NNTP verifies that the client is allowed to post to the newsgroup, and then takes the article, adds it to the newsgroup, and updates the index.

Every newsgroup has its own directory (with the same name as the newsgroup), and every article is stored as a separate file within that directory (with an .NWS extension). By default, %SystemRoot%\Inetpub\nntproot is the main directory.

Creating a New Newsgroup

When you create a new newsgroup (through the Groups property sheet of Internet Service Manager), NNTP automatically creates the new directory. Within the newsgroup directory, indexes are also stored. They have an extension of .XIX and one is created for every 128 articles.

The NNTP service starts automatically when the NT Server starts but can be paused, stopped, or started from the Services icon of the Control Panel (where it appears as Microsoft NNTP Service). It, like other IIS-related services, also can be paused, stopped, or started from the Microsoft Management Console.

Configuring Certificate Server

☑ Objective ▶   Microsoft Certificate Server enables you to generate, create and use keys for digital authentication. To use, you must first obtain a valid server certificate (generated with Key Manager) from a certificate authority. The following table lists the Web sites of several certificate authorities within the United States.

Note You can generate a certificate with certificate server without getting certified by an agency, but they aren't considered valid.

BankGate	`http://www.bankgate.com`
GTE CyberTrust	`http://www.cybertrust.gte.com`
Thawte Consulting	`http://www.thawte.com`
Verisign	`http://www.verisign.com`

Once you've created a certificate or a certificate authority has issued you a valid certificate, use Key Manager to activate the certificate.

Configuring Index Server

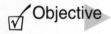**Objective** Index Server is configured based upon the size of the site and the number of documents it contains. Four items should be taken into consideration when configuring Index Server:

- ▶ Number of documents in the corpus
- ▶ Size of the corpus
- ▶ Rate of search requests arriving at the server
- ▶ Complexity of queries

Increasing the amount of memory and going with the fastest CPU available increases Index Server performance. The disk space needed for the data is always roughly 40 percent the size of the corpus.

Index Server can be used to index multiple servers by sharing a folder on the remote volume and creating a virtual directory on the indexing server. The biggest difficulty in doing this is maintaining link integrity.

Managing MIME Types

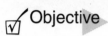 **Objective**

MIME is an acronym for Multipurpose Internet Mail Extension, and is used to define the type of file sent to the browser, based upon the extension. If your server is supplying files in multiple formats, it must have a MIME mapping for each file type or browsers will most likely be unable to retrieve the file.

MIME mappings for IIS 4.0 are different than they were in previous versions. The mappings are kept in the Registry under KEY_LOCAL_MACHINE\SOFTWARE\Classes\MIME\Databases\ Content Type, and can be viewed, edited, or have new ones added by using Regedit, or Regedt32. Figure 3.12 shows an example of the MIME mapping for text files in Regedt32.exe.

Figure 3.12

The MIME mapping for text files.

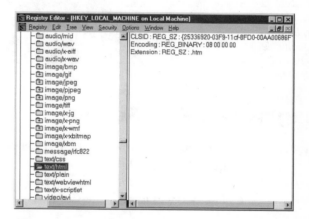

 Note

These mappings occur whether or not IIS is installed. It appears to be a Windows common registry of Mime types.

If you aren't comfortable with editing the Registry directly (and you probably should not be), you also can add entries to the Registry through the HTTP Headers tab of any directory or virtual directory. The File Types button at the bottom of the properties page enables you to enter MIME maps in a much simpler way than editing the Registry. The button is shown in Figure 3.13.

Selecting this button enables you to specify new MIME types by giving the associated extension and the content type, as shown in Figure 3.14.

Figure 3.13

The MIME Map option appears on the HTTP Headers tab.

MIME Map option ——

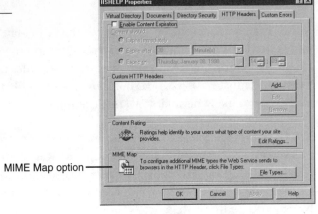

Figure 3.14

The MIME Map option enables you to specify file type extensions and content type.

Managing the FTP Service

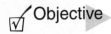 **Objective**

Once installed and running, the FTP service can be managed through two main utilities:

▶ The Services icon of the Control Panel

▶ Internet Service Manager

Using the Control Panel Method

The first utility of note is the Services icon in the Control Panel. From here you can start, pause, or stop the FTP Publishing Service, as well as configure it for startup in three ways:

▶ Automatic (the default)—The service is started when all of IIS starts.

▶ Manual—Requiring interaction from the administrator to actively start it.

▶ Disabled—It does not start at all.

Once started, the service can be stopped or paused (as well as started again after either of the other two). When the service is stopped, it is unloaded, whereas when it is paused, it remains loaded with the intention of it being restarted again.

FTP Site Options with Internet Service Manager

From the Internet Service Manager, you can select your FTP site and choose to stop, pause, or start the site by right-clicking it. You also can manage all properties of the site from here, as shown in Figure 3.15.

Figure 3.15

The Properties sheets for an FTP site.

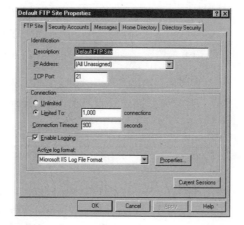

There are five tabs to the properties, each containing specific information on the Web site. Each tab is discussed in the paragraphs that follow in the order, which are arranged in the order that they appear by default.

FTP Site Tab

The FTP Site tab enables you to change the description (name) of the FTP site, the IP address, and the TCP port. As has been pointed out before, port 21 is the default TCP port, but changing it to another value enables the site to become hidden. Additional settings on this tab enable you to specify a number of seconds for a connection timeout, limit the number of connections allowed (if bandwidth is an issue; the default is limited to 1,000 connections) and enable logging. By default, the logs are written to %SystemRoot%\System32\Logfiles.

You can choose for the log files to be created in a number of different time periods. The way in which you choose for them to be created governs the name of the log files created (which always consist of some combination of variables.) The table that follows summarizes the log files.

Log Time Period	Log File Name
Daily	inyymmdd.log
Weekly	inyymmww.log
Monthly	inyymm.log
Unlimited File Size	inetsv#.log
When file size reaches (19MB is the default, but another MB can be specified)	inetsv#.log

Security Accounts Tab

The Security Accounts tab enables you to allow or disallow anonymous access, and define which Windows NT user accounts have operator privileges. You also can choose to allow only anonymous connections and enable automatic password synchronization.

 Tip

An important point when studying for the exam—it is a two-stepped approach—you cannot configure only anonymous access until you have first enabled anonymous access.

Messages Tab

The Messages tab enables you to specify a message to be displayed when users access the site. This can be done in three ways:

▶ Upon welcome

▶ Upon exit

▶ Upon there being too many users (maximum connections reached)

Home Directory Tab

The Home Directory tab enables you to specify a home directory in either of two ways:

▶ On this computer (the default)

▶ As a share on another computer

If you are specifying a directory on this computer, you must give the path. If you are specifying a share on another computer, you must give the UNC path (\\server\share). In either scenario, you then assign permissions for that directory of Read and/or Write, and choose if you want to log access. You also must specify whether directory listings should appear in UNIX style or MS-DOS style. UNIX is the default and should be left as such in most implementations for maximum compatibility.

Directory Security Tab

The Directory Security tab enables you to configure IP address and Domain Name restrictions. When configuring, you have two choices:

▶ Specify all addresses that are prohibited

▶ Specify all addresses that are allowed access

Recall that the three ways to enter addresses are as a single computer (by IP address), a group of computers (by IP address), or by domain name. Refer to Chapter 1, "Planning," for more information about entering addresses.

Managing the WWW Service

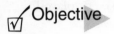 Once installed and running, the WWW service can be managed through two main utilities:

> ▶ The Services icon of the Control Panel

> ▶ Internet Service Manager

Using the Control Panel Method

The first utility of note is the Services icon in the Control Panel. From here, you can start, pause, or stop the World Wide Web Publishing Service, or configure it for startup in three ways:

> ▶ Automatic (the default)—The service is started when all of IIS starts.

> ▶ Manual—Start it.

> ▶ Disabled—It does not start at all.

WWW Site Options with Internet Service Manager

From the Internet Service Manager, you can select your Web site (or any Web site if you have multiples) and choose to stop, pause, or start the site by right-clicking it.

You also can manage all properties of the site from here, as shown in Figure 3.16.

There are nine tabs to the properties, each containing specific information about the Web site. In the order that they appear by default, each tab is discussed in the paragraphs that follow.

Figure 3.16

The Properties sheets for a Web site.

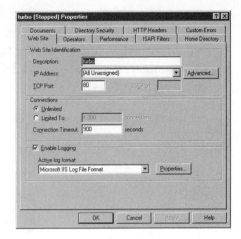

Web Site Tab

The Web Site tab enables you to change the description (name) of the Web site, the IP address, and the TCP port. As has been pointed out before, port 80 is the default TCP port, but changing it to another value allows the site to become hidden. This is useful in a situation where you want to create an intranet and avoid traffic from the Internet. The Advanced tab enables you to assign multiple identities for the Web site. Additional settings on this tab enable you to configure the SSL port, limit the number of connections allowed (if bandwidth is an issue; the default is unlimited) and enable logging. By default, the logs are written to the following directory:

%SystemRoot%\System32\Logfiles

Note

What is presented here is an example. There's no good reason for changing a port number, unless you want to use blind security. The best way to handle filtering Internet traffic would be to change the host security settings for the site, rather than changing the port.

You can choose for the log files to be created in a number of different time periods. The way in which you choose for them to be created governs the name of the log files created (which always consist of some combination of variables). The table that follows summarizes this process.

Log Time Period	Log File Name
Daily	inyymmdd.log
Weekly	inyymmww.log
Monthly	inyymm.log
Unlimited File Size	inetsv#.log
When file size reaches 19MB (19MB is the default, but another MB can be specified)	inetsv#.log

Operators Tab

The Operators tab simply enables you to define which Windows NT user accounts have operator privileges.

Performance Tab

The Performance tab enables you to tune the Web site according to the number of hits you expect each day. There are three settings:

▶ Fewer than 10,000

▶ Fewer than 100,000 (the default)

▶ More than 100,000

You also can enable bandwidth throttling from the Performance tab to prevent the entire network from being slow to service the Web site. By default, bandwidth throttling is not enabled. Finally, on the Performance tab you can configure HTTP Keep-Alives to be enabled. This maintains the open connection and uses it for the next account so that a new connection doesn't have to be created each time a user accesses the site.

ISAPI Filters Tab

The ISAPI Filters tab enables you to add or remove filters for the site. ISAPI filters are discussed in great detail in Chapter 5.

Home Directory Tab

The Home Directory tab enables you to specify a home directory in three ways:

▶ On this computer (the default)

▶ As a share on another computer

▶ As an URL to be redirected to

If you are specifying a directory on this computer, you must give the path. If you are specifying a share on another computer, you must give the UNC path (\\server\share). In either scenario, you then assign permissions for that directory. If you go with the third option and redirect the home directory to an URL, you must specify the URL and choose how the client will be sent. You can send the client as one of the following:

▶ The exact URL you enter

▶ A directory below the URL you enter

▶ A permanent redirection for the resource

Documents Tab

The Documents tab enables you to define the default documents to display if a specific document is not specified in the URL request. Multiple files can be listed, and the first one in the list is always used unless it is unavailable. If it is unavailable (or unable to be found), then the next one in the list is used.

Directory Security Tab

The Directory Security tab enables you to configure anonymous access and authentication, as well as secure communications and IP address and domain name restrictions. When configuring the latter, you have two choices:

▶ Specify all addresses that are prohibited

▶ Specify all addresses that are allowed access

The three ways to enter addresses are as a single computer (by IP address), a group of computers (by IP address), or by domain name.

HTTP Headers Tab

The HTTP Headers tab enables you to specify an expiration time for your content (the default is none), set custom headers, assign a rating to your content (to alert parents to pornography, and so on) and configure MIME maps (see the section "Managing MIME Types," earlier in this chapter).

Custom Errors Tab

The last tab, Custom Errors, enables you to configure the error message returned to the user when an event occurs. For example, error 400 is, by default, a Bad Request, and the file 400.htm is used to return the message 404 is Not Found, and so on.

Exercises

Exercise 3.1: Changing Permissions for a File

The following exercise illustrates how to add Write permissions to a file:

1. Start Internet Service Manager.

2. Select a file, right-click it, and choose Properties.

3. Beneath Access Permissions, check the Write check box.

4. Click OK.

Exercise 3.2: Creating a Virtual Directory

The following exercise walks you through the steps of creating a virtual directory named Scott:

1. Start Internet Service Manager.

2. Double-click the Internet Information Server until servers are displayed.

3. Double-click a server.

4. Highlight Default Web Site and right-click.

5. Choose New, Virtual Directory.

6. For a directory alias, enter **Scott**. Press Next.

7. Click the Browse button for a physical path, and find My Briefcase. Select it and then click Next.

8. Change the permissions for the virtual directory so that only Read access is allowed.

9. Select Finish.

10. Double-click the Default Web Site. Scott should now appear as a directory.

Exercise 3.3: Preventing a Host from Accessing Your Site

The following exercise walks you through the steps of denying access to a host based upon its IP address:

1. Start Internet Service Manager.

2. Double-click the Internet Information Server until servers are displayed.

3. Double-click a server.

4. Highlight Default Web Site and right-click.

5. Choose Properties and select the Directory Security tab.

6. Beneath the IP Address and Domain Name Restrictions frame, click the Edit button.

7. Make certain the active radio button on the IP Address and Domain Name Restrictions screen is Granted Access, and click Add.

8. With the active option button on the Deny Access On screen being on Single Computer, enter the IP address 195.200.200.001 and click OK.

9. The word Deny should appear on the IP Address and Domain Name Restrictions screen beside the IP address entered. Click OK.

10. Back at the Directory Security tab, click either OK or Apply and you have now restricted host 195.200.200.001 from accessing your site.

Exercise 3.4: Allow only a Set of Hosts to Access Your Site

The following exercise walks you through the steps of restricting access to your site to only 128 hosts based upon their IP address:

1. Start Internet Service Manager.

2. Double-click the Internet Information Server until servers are displayed.

3. Double-click a server.

4. Highlight Default Web Site and right-click.

5. Choose Properties and select the Directory Security tab.

6. Beneath the IP Address and Domain Name Restrictions frame, click the Edit button.

7. Make certain the active radio button on the IP Address and Domain Name Restrictions screen is Denied Access, and click Add.

8. With the active option button on the Grant Access On screen being on Group of Computers, enter the IP address 195.200.200.001 and the subnet value 255.255.255.128.

9. Click OK.

10. The word Grant should now appear on the IP Address and Domain Name Restrictions screen beside the IP address entered, with the subnet value in parentheses beside it.

11. Click OK.

12. Back at the Directory Security tab, click either OK or Apply and you have now restricted access to your site to 128 hosts only, beginning with 195.200.200.001 and progressing incrementally.

Exercise 3.5: Set a Default Document

The following exercise walks you through the steps of enabling a default document to be displayed when someone accesses your site without specifying a file name:

1. Start Internet Service Manager.

2. Double-click the Internet Information Server until servers are displayed.

3. Double-click a server.

continues

Exercise 3.5: Continued

   4. Highlight Default Web Site and right-click.

   5. Choose Properties and select the Documents tab.

   6. Click the Enable Default Document check box.

   7. Click the Add button.

   8. Enter the name of your default document (such as DEAULT.HTM or DEFAULT.ASP) in the Default Document Name field and click OK.

   9. The document now appears in the text field. Following steps 7 and 8, you can enter multiple documents to be displayed in successive order if the first document is unavailable (the first one in the list will always be displayed if it is available).

Exercise 3.6: Disable HTTP Keep-Alives

The following exercise walks you through the steps of disabling HTTP Keep-Alives:

   1. Start Internet Service Manager.

   2. Double-click the Internet Information Server until servers are displayed.

   3. Double-click a server.

   4. Highlight Default Web Site and right-click.

   5. Choose Properties and select the Performance tab.

   6. Beneath the Connection Configuration frame, click the HTTP Keep-Alives Enabled check box to remove the default checkmark.

   7. Click the OK or Apply buttons.

Exercise 3.7:   Change the Web Service TCP Port

This exercise walks you through the steps of changing the TCP port of the Web service to hide it from browsers not specifically pointed to it:

1. Start Internet Service Manager.

2. Double-click the Internet Information Server until servers are displayed.

3. Double-click a server.

4. Highlight the Web site you want to hide and right-click.

5. Choose Properties and select the Web Site tab.

6. At the TCP Port field, change the default value of 80 to the new port number (such as 7500).

7. Click the OK or Apply buttons.

Review Questions

1. TCP port 80 is the default for which service?

   A. NNTP

   B. SMTP

   C. WWW

   D. FTP

2. By default, anonymous access is enabled for which of the following services following installation?

   A. WWW

   B. FTP

   C. SMTP

   D. NNTP

3. What permissions are assigned to a WWW directory by default during the site creation by the wizard?

   A. Allow Read Access

   B. Allow Write Access

   C. Allow Directory Browsing

   D. Allow Script Access

4. Rob is having difficulty with users properly accessing resources on an intranet Web site that he created. For the directory in question, NTFS permissions allow Read for everyone, but he has removed the Read permission for IIS. What is the effect of this action?

   A. no one can read the files in the directory.

   B. only those users recognized by NT are allowed to read the files in the directory.

   C. all users can read the files because NTFS overrides IIS permissions.

   D. only users coming from NT Workstation or NT Server can read the files in the directory.

5. The default user name for the anonymous account on a computer named SPENCER for the WWW service is which of the following?

    A. SPENCER

    B. IUSR

    C. IUSR_SPENCER

    D. SPENCER_IUSR

6. When creating virtual directories, they should reside where?

    A. on the server

    B. in the domain

    C. on the WAN

    D. anywhere

7. Karen has created a number of virtual directories at her site, but cannot get them to appear in directory listings. This is most likely caused by which of the following?

    A. inappropriate permissions

    B. a port other than 80 being used

    C. virtual directories beyond the server

    D. a failure to use links in HTML files

8. Multi-homing is also known as creating which of the following?

    A. virtual files

    B. virtual directories

    C. virtual servers

    D. virtual private networks

9. In the DNS name www.microsoft.com, what does microsoft represent?

   A. the last name of the host

   B. the domain in which the host is located

   C. the IP address of the building in which the host is located

   D. the directory in which the host name file is located

10. The wc utility included in the Windows NT Resource Kit can be used to count which of the following items in a log file?

    A. words

    B. characters

    C. lines

    D. paragraphs

11. TCP port 25 is the default for which service?

    A. NNTP

    B. SMTP

    C. WWW

    D. FTP

12. How many SMTP sites are allowed for the SMTP service?

    A. 0

    B. 1

    C. 2

    D. unlimited

13. By default in SMTP, how many users can receive a single message?

    A. 1

    B. 100

    C. 256

    D. 512

14. Allan, a new administrator, notices traffic on TCP port 563. SSL is in use. What service is using port 563, by default?

    A. NNTP

    B. SMTP

    C. WWW

    D. FTP

15. By default, into what directory are FTP log files written to?

    A. %SystemRoot%

    B. %SystemRoot%\Inetpub

    C. %SystemRoot%\Inetpub\Logfiles

    D. %SystemRoot%\System32\Logfiles

Review Answers

1. **C**. The default TCP port for the WWW Service is 80.

2. **A, B**. By default, anonymous access is enabled for WWW and FTP during installation.

3. **A, D**. Allow Read Access and Allow Script access are selected by default.

4. **A.** Taking away the Allow Read Access permission in IIS prevents users from viewing files in the directory.

5. **C**. The default anonymous account user name is always `IUSR_computername`.

6. **B**. Virtual directories should always be stored on servers within the same NT domain as the IIS server resides.

7. **D**. Virtual directories do not appear in directory listings, and must be accessed through explicit links within HTML files.

8. **C**. Multi-homing is another word for using virtual servers.

9. **B**. The path specifies a host named www in a domain microsoft. The domain microsoft is located in the top-level domain com.

10. **A, B, C**. The wc utility can be used to count characters, words, or lines in a log file.

11. **B**. The default TCP port for the SMTP Service is 25.

12. **B**. Regardless of the size of the site, only one SMTP service is allowed.

13. **B**. By default, in SMTP 100 users can receive a single message.

14. **A**. By default, NNTP operates at TCP port 563 with SSL.

15. **D**. By default, FTP log files are written to the %SystemRoot%\System32\Logfiles directory.

Answers to Test Yourself Questions at Beginning of Chapter

1. The default TCP port used for the WWW service is 80. See "Creating and Sharing Directories."

2. Virtual directories should always be stored on servers within the same NT domain as the IIS server resides. See "Creating and Sharing Virtual Directories."

3. Virtual servers allow one server to alias multiple domain names. See "Creating and Sharing Virtual Servers."

4. The wc utility can be used to count the number of lines in a log file, as well as the number of words or characters. See "Writing Scripts for Service Management."

5. WebMaps enable you to view your site with a tree view, or Cyberbolic view (or both). See "Using Content Analyzer."

6. The default TCP port for the SMTP service is port 25. See "Configuring SMTP."

7. By default, and in the absence of SSL, NNTP uses TCP port 119. See "Configuring NNTP."

8. After generating the digital certificate, it must be registered with a certificate authority. See "Configuring Certificate Server."

9. The Index Server data, in all cases, is approximately 40 percent of the size of the corpus. See "Configuring Index Server."

10. MIME is an acronym for Multipurpose Internet Mail Extension. See "Managing MIME Types."

11. FTP logs can be created on a Daily, Weekly, or Monthly basis. See "Managing the FTP Service."

12. A WWW site can be made hidden by changing the default TCP port. See "Managing the WWW Service."

Chapter 4

Integration and Interoperability

This chapter helps you prepare for the exam by covering the following objectives:

> ▶ Configure IIS to connect to a database. There is only one task. Configuring ODBC.
>
> ▶ Configure IIS to integrate with Index Server. The tasks include the following:
>
> > ▶ Specifying query parameters by creating the .IDQ file
> >
> > ▶ Specifying how the query results are formatted and displayed to the user by creating the .HTX file

Test Yourself! Before reading this chapter, test yourself to determine how much study time you will need to devote to this section.

1. What are the two file extensions used by ODBC to determine how the database is accessed and how the output Web page is constructed?

2. What is the conditional expression that can be used in an .IDQ file to see if one entry is a subset of a second entry?

Answers are located at the end of the chapter....

This chapter examines integration between the WWW service of IIS and other servers and services. The other servers and services discussed fall into one of two categories: databases or Index Server. Connecting IIS to a database enables you to pull or update information from a server dedicated to such a task—such as SQL. Integrating with Index Server enables you to make the available data visible and searchable by those accessing your site. The chapter is organized as follows:

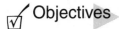 **Objectives**

▶ Configuring IIS to Connect to a Database

▶ Configuring Integration with Index Server

Configuring IIS to Connect to a Database

With the expansion of the World Wide Web into homes around the United States came the expectation that Web browsers would allow users to retrieve data specific to a need. Users grew frustrated at looking at static screen pages and wanted to be able to pull up data and forms based on their requests. From an HTML coding standpoint, creating a Web page for every conceivable request is impractical. The sheer volume of pages would be incomprehensible, and the action of updating the pages each time a piece of data changed would be more than any one person could handle.

To solve the problem, such databases as Oracle or Microsoft SQL (Structured Query Language) Server can be used with Microsoft Internet Information Server (IIS) 4. The databases can supply the information to fulfill a query, update information, and add new data through the Web almost as easily as if a user were sitting at a PC on a Local Area Network.

Databases have been around since the early days of computing, and Web servers have been around for a number of years. What is new is the integration of the two to create the dynamic Web sites expected today.

Because Windows NT Server is growing in popularity exponentially, and it is the platform on which Internet Information Server runs, it is not uncommon to expect the database to which you connect to be Microsoft SQL Server. This is the expectation for the exam and the thrust of the discussion that follows.

Understanding ODBC

Open Database Connectivity (ODBC) is an API (Application Programming Interface) that provides a simple way to connect to an existing database (whether that database be SQL or any ODBC-compliant database). It was designed by Microsoft to address the issue of any number of applications needing to interface with SQL server.

The greatest advantage that ODBC offers is that it defines a clear distinction between the application and the database, and thus does not require any specific programming. To use it, you create a query and template for how the output will look.

There are four major components to IIS's implementation of ODBC:

▶ **.HTM**—The file containing the hyperlink for a query. The request comes from the browser and merely specifies the URL for the .IDC (Internet Database Connector) file on IIS.

▶ **.IDC**—The file containing the data source file information and SQL statement.

▶ **.HTX**—A file of HTML extensions containing the template document with placeholders for the result.

Figure 4.1 illustrates the processes involved in answering a query request.

Figure 4.1

The process of resolving a data-base query in IIS.

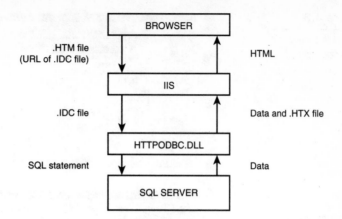

Implementing ODBC

Implementing ODBC is extremely easy and can be broken into the following steps:

1. Double-click the ODBC icon in the Control Panel.

2. Select the System DSN tab from the ODBC Data Source Administrator dialog box (shown in Figure 4.2).

Figure 4.2

The System DSN tab enables you to configure data sources.

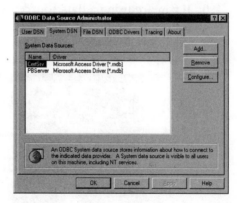

3. Choose Add and select the driver (SQL, Access, and Oracle appear as choices). This is illustrated by Figure 4.3.

4. Specify the name and description of the data source on the Create a New Data Source dialog box shown in Figure 4.4.

Figure 4.3

Select the new data sources.

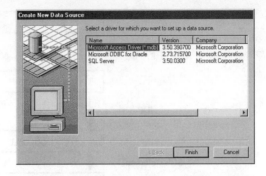

Figure 4.4

You must specify a name, description, and server for the data source.

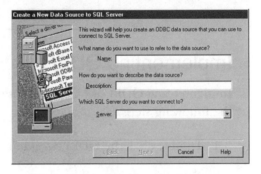

5. Specify the server to connect to and click Next.

6. If you are using a data source that can perform authentication, such as SQL Server, then specify how authentication is to be done (shown in Figure 4.5).

Figure 4.5

Specify how authentication will be handled.

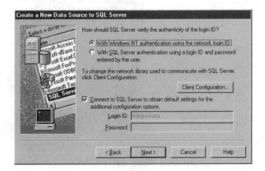

Authentication can be done by Windows NT or SQL Server. If SQL Server is chosen, it uses standard logon security and a SQL Server user ID and password must be given for all connections. If you choose to use Windows NT authentication, the Windows NT user account is associated with a SQL Server user account, and integrated security is used to establish the connection.

Note

In reality, to get Windows NT logins to work, three things must be done:

▶ SQL Server security must be set to Integrated (NT only) or Mixed (NT & SQL).

▶ Named Pipes or Multiprotocol must be set up as the connection type—this is because NT refuses to send your password as clear text.

▶ You must use SQL Security Manager to assign NT users to SQL users.

The security mode on the server is critical.

Figure 4.5 also shows a Client Configuration button. This can be used to customize the configuration if you are using nonstandard pipes.

The Login ID and Password boxes at the bottom of Figure 4.5 are used only if you have selected SQL Server authentication, and become grayed out if you are using Windows NT authentication.

Other ODBC Tabs

Other tabs in the ODBC Data Source Administrator dialog box include the following:

▶ User DSN

▶ File DSN

▶ ODBC Drivers

▶ Tracing

▶ About

The User DSN tab, shown in Figure 4.6, is used to add, delete, or change the setup of data source names (DSNs). The data sources specified here are local to a computer and can only be used by the current user.

Figure 4.6

The User DSN tab enables you to configure data sources specific to a user.

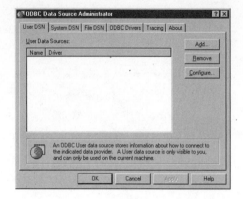

The File DSN tab is used to add, delete, or change the setup of data sources with file data source names. File-based data sources can be shared between all users that are using the same drivers and are not dedicated to individual users or local machines.

The ODBC Drivers tab shows information about the ODBC drivers that are currently installed. The information given includes the name, version, filename, and created date of every ODBC driver (and the name of the company responsible for it.)

The Tracing tab, shown in Figure 4.7, enables you to configure how the ODBC Driver Manager will trace ODBC calls to functions. Choices include all of the time, dynamically, by a custom DLL, or for one connection only (as well as not at all.)

Figure 4.7

The Tracing tab of the ODBC Data Source Administrator.

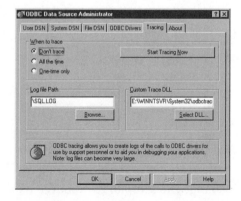

The About tab lists the ODBC core components, as well as the actual files they consist of, and the versions. An example of the information it provides is shown in Figure 4.8.

Figure 4.8

The About tab of the ODBC Data Source Administrator.

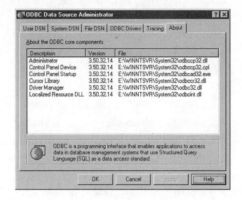

Creating and Developing Files

Once the registration has been completed and ODBC has been configured, the remaining steps involve creating and developing the files to be used.

The .IDC File

The .IDC file contains the SQL command used to interface between IIS and the Httpodbc.dll library. There are four required parameters to the file:

- ▶ Datasource

- ▶ Username

- ▶ Template

- ▶ SQLStatement

The Datasource is simply the name of the ODBC data source that has been defined in the ODBC Data Source Administrator dialog box available from the Control Panel.

The Username is the username required to access the data source, and can be any valid logon name for the SQL Server database. This (as well as the Password field, if used) is ignored if you use integrated security or if the database doesn't have security installed.

The Template specified the name of the file (.HTX) that will be used as a template to display (and do any necessary interpretation) of the SQL results.

The SQLStatement is the list of commands you want to execute. Parameter values can be used if they are enclosed in percent signs (%). If multiple lines are required, a plus sign (+) must be the first character on each line.

An example of an .IDC file follows:

```
Datasource: Synergy
Username:   sa
Template:   syn_temp.htx
SQLStatement:
+SELECT employeeno, dob, doh
+FROM pubs.dbo.synergy
+WHERE salary>50000
```

The preceding code pulls the employee number, date of birth, and date of hire information from the pubs.dbo.synergy database for every employee exceeding $50,000 in salary. Once the data has been extracted, it is combined with an .HTX file (in this case syn_temp.htx) for formatting.

Optional fields that can be used in the .IDC file include the following:

▶ DefaultParameters—To specify default values in the event nothing is specified by the client

▶ Expires—The number of seconds to wait before refreshing

▶ MaxFieldSize—The maximum buffer space per field (beyond this, truncation takes place)

▶ MaxRecords—The maximum number of records to return per query

- ▶ ODBCConnection—Can either be set to POOL to add the connection to the connection pool (keeping open for future requests) or NONPOOL to not do so

- ▶ Password—The password for the username given

- ▶ RequiredParameters—Parameters that have to be filled in by the client before you can do the query. Parameters are separated by a comma, and if the user does not provide them all, then Httpodbc.dll returns an error message to them.

- ▶ Translationfile—The path for non-English characters to be found before being returned to the browser

- ▶ Content-type—A valid MIME type describing what goes back to the client. If the .HTX file has HTML, then this usually is text/html.

The .HTX File

The .HTX file is an HTML template that fills in its blanks with information returned from a query. It accepts SQL information in, and returns HTML information out. A quick look at an .HTX file shows that it looks very much like an HTML file, and contains many of the same fields.

Database fields that it receives are known as containers and are identified by field names surrounded by percent signs (%) and angle brackets (<>). Thus the employeeno field that comes from the SQL database is known as <%employeeno%> in an .HTX file.

All processing is done in loops that start with <%begindetail%> and end with <%enddetail%>. Logic can be included with <%if…%> and <%endif%>, as well as <%else%> statements. You also can use the four standard programming operators:

- ▶ EQ—Equal to

- ▶ GT—Greater than

- ▶ LT—Less than

- ▶ CONTAINS

An example of an .HTX file would be

```
<HTML>
<HEAD>
<TITLE>Welcome to Synergy</TITLE>
</HEAD>
<H2>Employees with Salaries greater than $50,000</H2>
<%begindetail%>
<b>Employee number:</b><%employeeno%> <b>Date of birth and hire:
➥</b><%dob%>, <%doh%><P>
<%enddetail%>
</HTML>
```

Some useful samples of .HTX files can be found on your system, and located by using the NT Find utility from the Start menu to look for files ending in that extension. Three useful ones for working with Index Server are located in the %systemroot%\system32\inetsrv\iisadmin\isadmin directory of your system, and an example of one is given at the end of this chapter.

Configuring Integration with Index Server

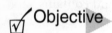 Objective

Index Server has already been examined several times in this book, including the explanation of it in Chapter 1, "Planning," and details about how to configure it in Chapter 3, "Configuring and Managing Resource Access." This section covers how it handles queries and returns results. For most intents and purposes, this discussion is very much like the earlier discussion of .HTX files (used to format and return the query results to the user).

The difference exists in the files used to hold the queries. Rather than using the .IDC file previously discussed, Index Server uses an .IDQ (Internet Data Query) file. The .IDQ file should always be placed in the Scripts directory, and it requires Execute or Script permission to function properly.

There are two sections to the file and it begins with a tag of <Query> (the first section) and is followed by the [Names] section. The Names section is purely optional and not used most of the time.

If it is used, it defines nonstandard column names that are referred to in a query. The Query section of the file is all that is required, and it can contain parameters, variables, and conditional expressions.

Restrictions are that lines must start with the variable you are trying to set, and only one variable can be set per line. Additionally, percent signs (%) are used to identify the variables and references.

Using Variables in .IDQ Files

The variables that can be used in .IDQ files are as follows:

- ▶ CiCatalog—Sets the location for the catalog. If the value is already set, the value here overrides that one.

- ▶ CiCodepage—Sets the server's code page. Again, if the value is already set, the entry here overrides the previous one.

- ▶ CiColumns—Defines a list of columns that will be used in the .HTX file.

- ▶ CiDeferNonIndexedTrimming—By default is not used, but can be set if the scope of the query must be limited.

- ▶ CiFlags—Query flags can be set to DEEP or SHALLOW to determine if only the directory listed in CiScope is searched.

- ▶ CiForceUseCi—By setting to TRUE, you can force the query to use the content index even if it is out of date.

- ▶ CiLocale—Specifies the locale used to issue the query.

- ▶ CiMaxRecordsInResultSet—Specifies the maximum number of results that can be returned from the query.

- ▶ CiMaxRecordsPerPage—Specifies the maximum number of records that can appear on a display page.

- ▶ CiRestriction—A restriction that you are placing on the query.

- ▶ CiScope—Specifies the starting directory for the search.

- ▶ CiSort—Specifies whether the results should be sorted in an order of ascending, or descending.

- ▶ CiTemplate—Specifies the full path of the .HTX file from the root. Index Server is bound by the Windows NT shell limit of 260 characters per path.

As with most script files, a pound sign (#) can be used to specify a comment. At whatever point the # sign is in the line, from there on the line will be ignored.

Using Conditional Expressions in .IDQ Files

The following conditional expressions can be used in .IDQ files:

- ▶ CONTAINS—Is true if any part of the first value is found in the second value

- ▶ EQ—Equal to

- ▶ GE—Greater than or equal to

- ▶ GT—Greater than

- ▶ ISEMPTY—Is true if the value is null

- ▶ LE—Less than or equal to

- ▶ LT—Less than

- ▶ NE—Not equal to

An Example of the .IDQ File

The following is an example of an .IDQ file:

```
[Query]
CiColumns=employeeno,dob,doh
CiMaxRecordsInResultSet=50
CiMaxRecordsPerPage=20
#20 used for compatibility with most browsers
```

```
CiScope=/
CiFlags=DEEP
CiTemplate=/scripts/synergy.htx
```

In the example, three columns are queried in the database: employeeno, dob, and doh. The maximum number of records that will be returned is 50, with up to 20 on each page of display. The fifth line is a comment line added by the person who created the file. It has no effect on operation whatsoever. The CiScope is set to the root directory with the search (CiFlags) set to go through all subdirectories. The template to use is then specified by the CiTemplate variable.

The Scan .IDQ File

One of the best examples of an efficient .IDQ file is SCAN.IDQ, located in the %systemroot%/system32\inetsrv\iisadmin\isadmin folder of your system. It is used with QUERY.HTM as a query file, and printed in its entirety here (line numbers have been added to help explain how it works):

```
1.   [Names]
2.   #
3.   # Query Metadata propset
4.   MetaVRootUsed(DBTYPE_BOOL)      = 624c9360-93d0-11cf-a787-
➥00004c752752 2
5.   MetaVRootAuto(DBTYPE_BOOL)      = 624c9360-93d0-11cf-a787-
➥00004c752752 3
6.   MetaVRootManual(DBTYPE_BOOL)    = 624c9360-93d0-11cf-a787-
➥00004c752752 4
7.   MetaPropertyGuid(DBTYPE_GUID)   = 624c9360-93d0-11cf-a787-
➥00004c752752 5
8.   MetaPropertyDispId(DBTYPE_I4)   = 624c9360-93d0-11cf-a787-
➥00004c752752 6
9.   MetaPropertyName(DBTYPE_WSTR)   = 624c9360-93d0-11cf-a787-
➥00004c752752 7
10. StorageType(DBTYPE_UI4)         = b725f130-47ef-101a-a5f1-
➥02608c9eebac 4

11. # This is the query file for the query.htm query form.
12. #

13. [Query]
```

```
14. # The CiCatalog variable must point to where the catalog
➥(index) files
15. # are stored on your system.  You will probably have to
➥change this
16. # value.  If this value is not specified, a default value is
➥read from
17. # the registry from:
18. # HKEY_LOCAL_MACHINE\System\CurrentControlSet\Control\
➥ContentIndex\IsapiDefaultCatalogDirectory

19. # CiCatalog=d:\

20. # These are the columns that are referenced in the .htx files
21. # when formatting output for each hit.

22. CiColumns=vpath, path, metavrootused, metavrootauto,
➥metavrootmanual, storagetype

23. # The CiRestriction is the query.  Here, it's just pass in
➥from the
24. # form in the .htm file.

25. CiRestriction=#vpath *

26. # Don't allow more than 300 total hits in the result set. It
➥can be
27. # expensive for the server to allow this value to get too
➥large.

28. CiMaxRecordsInResultSet=300

29. # Display CiMaxRecordsPerPage hits on each page of output

30. CiMaxRecordsPerPage=%CiMaxRecordsPerPage%

31. # CiScope is the directory (virtual or real) under which
➥results are
32. # returned.  If a file matches the query but is not in a
➥directory beneath
33. # CiScope, it is not returned in the result set.
34. # A scope of \ means all hits matching the query are
➥returned.
```

```
35. CiScope=VIRTUAL_ROOTS

36. # This is the .htx file to use for formatting the results of
➥the query.

37. CiTemplate=/iisadmin/isadmin/scan.htx

38. # This is the list of property names to use in sorting the
➥results.
39. # Append [a] or [d] to the property name to specify ascending
➥or
40. # descending.  Separate keys in multi-key sorts with commas.
41. # For example, to sort on file write date ascending, then
➥file size
42. # descending, use CiSort=write[a],filesize[d]

43. CiSort=%CiSort%

44. # Setting CiForceUseCi to true means that the index is
➥assumed to be
45. # up to date, so queries that might otherwise force a walk of
➥the
46. # directory structure (find files older than X), will instead
➥use
47. # the index and run more quickly.  Of course, that means that
➥the results
48. # might miss files that match the query.

49. CiForceUseCi=true
```

Lines 1 and 13 set up the two required sections of the file. Lines 2 and 12 are blank, used for aesthetic purposes when reading the file. All lines beginning with the pound character (#) are comment lines and are ignored during execution. Lines 4 through 10 define nonstandard column names that are referred to in the query.

Line 22 lists the columns referenced in the .HTX file, while line 25 really does not set a restriction, as the restriction itself is preceded by the pound sign (#), commenting it out. The maximum number of records returned is limited to 300 by line 28, and the number of records per page is set by line 30.

The search begins at the virtual roots—per line 35—and the template used for formatting the results is scan.htx, per line 37 (listed in the following section). Line 43 defines the sort, while line 49 forces the index to be assumed to be up to date.

After the data has been returned, SCAN.HTX comes into play, so that file is examined next.

The Scan .HTX File

After SCAN.IDQ has performed its function, results are returned to SCAN.HTX, also located in the %systemroot%/system32\inetsrv\iisadmin\isadmin folder of your system. It is printed in its entirety here (line numbers have been added to help explain how it works):

```
1.  <HTML>

2.  <!--
3.  <%CiTemplate%>

4.  This is the formatting page for query results. This file
➡defines
5.  how the result page header, rows, and footer will appear.
6.  -->

7.  <HEAD>
8.  <!-- The title lists the # of documents -->

9.  <%if CiMatchedRecordCount eq 0%>
10. <TITLE><%escapeHTML CiRestriction%> - no documents matched.</
➡TITLE>
11. <%else%>
12. <TITLE><%escapeHTML CiRestriction%> - documents
➡<%CiFirstRecordNumber%> to <%CiLastRecordNumber%></TITLE>
13. <%endif%>
14. </HEAD>

15. <BODY BGCOLOR="#FFFFFF" TEXT="#000000" LINK="#000066"
➡VLINK="#808080" ALINK="#FF0000" TOPMARGIN=0>

16. <TABLE>
```

```
17. <TR>
18. <TD><IMG SRC ="/iisadmin/isadmin/64x_book.jpg"
➥ALIGN=Middle></TD>
19. <TD VALIGN=MIDDLE><H1>Index Server</H1><br><center><h2>Search
➥Results</h2></center></TD>
20. </TR>
21. </TABLE>

22. <!-- Print a header that lists the query and the number of
➥hits -->

23. <H5>
24. <%if CiMatchedRecordCount eq 0%>
25. No virtual roots matched the query "<%EscapeHTML
➥CiRestriction%>".
26. <%else%>
27. Virtual roots <%CiFirstRecordNumber%> to
➥<%CiLastRecordNumber%> of
28. <%CiMatchedRecordCount%> matching the query
29. "<%EscapeHTML CiRestriction%>" for catalog <%CiCatalog%>
30. <%endif%>
31. </H5>

32. <!--
33. This table has a link to a new query page, a previous button,
➥and
34. a next page button.  The buttons are only displayed when
➥appropriate.
35. -->

36. <TABLE WIDTH=80%>

37. <!--
38. Query.htm set HTMLQueryForm as the name of the page to return
➥to
39. for a new query.
40. -->

41. <!-- Define a "previous" button if this isn't the first page
➥ -->

42. <%if CiContainsFirstRecord eq 0%>
43. <TD ALIGN=LEFT>
44. <FORM ACTION="/iisadmin/isadmin/scan.idq" METHOD="GET">
45. <INPUT TYPE="HIDDEN"
```

```
46. NAME="CiBookMark" VALUE="<%CiBookMark%>" >
47. <INPUT TYPE="HIDDEN"
48. NAME="CiBookmarkSkipCount" VALUE="-<%EscapeRAW
➡CiMaxRecordsPerPage%>" >
49. <INPUT TYPE="HIDDEN"
50. NAME="CiRestriction" VALUE="<%CiRestriction%>" >
51. <INPUT TYPE="HIDDEN"
52. NAME="CiMaxRecordsPerPage" VALUE="<%EscapeRAW
➡CiMaxRecordsPerPage%>" >
53. <INPUT TYPE="SUBMIT"
54. VALUE="Previous <%CiMaxRecordsPerPage%> documents">
55. </FORM>
56. </TD>
57. <%endif%>

58. <!-- Define a "next" button if this isn't the last page -->

59. <%if CiContainsLastRecord eq 0%>
60. <TD ALIGN=RIGHT>
61. <FORM ACTION="/iisadmin/isadmin/scan.idq" METHOD="GET">
62. <INPUT TYPE="HIDDEN"
63. NAME="CiBookMark" VALUE="<%CiBookMark%>" >
64. <INPUT TYPE="HIDDEN"
65. NAME="CiBookmarkSkipCount" VALUE="<%EscapeRAW
➡CiMaxRecordsPerPage%>" >
66. <INPUT TYPE="HIDDEN"
67. NAME="CiRestriction" VALUE="<%CiRestriction%>" >
68. <INPUT TYPE="HIDDEN"
69. NAME="CiMaxRecordsPerPage" VALUE="<%EscapeRAW
➡CiMaxRecordsPerPage%>" >
70. <INPUT TYPE="SUBMIT"
71. VALUE="Next <%CiRecordsNextPage%> documents">
72. </FORM>
73. </TD>
74. <%endif%>
75. </TABLE>

76. <HR>

77. <!--
78. The begindetail/enddetail section describes how each row of
➡output
79. is be formatted.  The sample below prints:

80. record number
```

```
81. document title (if one exists) or virtual path of the file
82. the abstract for the file
83. the url for the file
84. the file's size and last write time
85. -->

86. <FORM ACTION="/iisadmin/isadmin/scan.ida" METHOD="GET">
87. <table>
88. <tr>
89. <th width=147 align="left">Virtual Root</th>
90. <th width=147 align="left">Physical Root</th>
91. <th width=147 align="left">Type</th>
92. <th colspan = 3 width=450 align="center">Type Of Scan</th>
93. </tr>

94. <!--
95. NAME: PROOT_<virtual root> VALUE: physical path to root
96. NAME: SCAN_<virtual root>  VALUE: "NoScan".
➥ Implies no scan will be performed
97. NAME: SCAN_<virtual root>  VALUE: "FullScan".
➥Implies full scan will be performed
98. NAME: SCAN_<virtual root>  VALUE: "IncrementalScan".
➥Implies incremental scan will be performed

99. -->

100. <%begindetail%>
101. <INPUT TYPE="HIDDEN" NAME="PROOT_<%if StorageType eq
➥1%>NNTP_<%endif%><%vpath%>" VALUE="<%path%>">
102. <%if metavrootused ne 0%>
103. <tr>
104. <td><%vpath%></td>
105. <td><%path%></td>
106. <td><%if StorageType eq 1%>News<%else%>Web<%endif%></td>
107. <td><input type=radio checked name="SCAN_<%if StorageType eq
➥1%>NNTP_<%endif%><%vpath%>" value="NoScan"> No Scan </td>
108. <td><input type=radio name="SCAN_<%if StorageType eq
➥1%>NNTP_<%endif%><%vpath%>" value="IncrementalScan">
➥Incremental Scan </td>
109. <td><input type=radio name="SCAN_<%if StorageType eq
➥1%>NNTP_<%endif%><%vpath%>" value="FullScan"> Full Scan </td>
110. </tr>
```

```
111.  <%endif%>
112.  <%enddetail%>
113.  </table>

114.  <INPUT TYPE="SUBMIT"
115.  VALUE="Submit changes">
116.  </FORM>
117.  <P>

118.  <!-- Only display a line if there were any hits that
➥matched the query -->

119.  <%if CiMatchedRecordCount ne 0%>
110.  <HR>
111.  <%endif%>

112.  <TABLE WIDTH=80%>

113.  <!--
114.  Query.htm set HTMLQueryForm as the name of the page to
➥return to
115.  for a new query.
116.  -->

117.  <TD> <A HREF="/iisadmin/isadmin/admin.htm">Administration
➥Main Menu</A> </TD>

118.  <!-- Define a "previous" button if this isn't the first page
➥-->

119.  <%if CiContainsFirstRecord eq 0%>
120.  <TD ALIGN=LEFT>
121.  <FORM ACTION="/iisadmin/isadmin/scan.idq" METHOD="GET">
122.  <INPUT TYPE="HIDDEN"
123.  NAME="CiBookMark" VALUE="<%CiBookMark%>" >
124.  <INPUT TYPE="HIDDEN"
125.  NAME="CiBookmarkSkipCount" VALUE="-<%EscapeRAW
➥CiMaxRecordsPerPage%>" >
126.  <INPUT TYPE="HIDDEN"
127.  NAME="CiRestriction" VALUE="<%CiRestriction%>" >
128.  <INPUT TYPE="HIDDEN"
129.  NAME="CiMaxRecordsPerPage" VALUE="<%EscapeRAW
➥CiMaxRecordsPerPage%>" >
130.  <INPUT TYPE="SUBMIT"
```

```
131. VALUE="Previous <%CiMaxRecordsPerPage%> documents">
132. </FORM>
133. </TD>
134. <%endif%>

135. <!-- Define a "next" button if this isn't the last page -->

136. <%if CiContainsLastRecord eq 0%>
137. <TD ALIGN=RIGHT>
138. <FORM ACTION="/iisadmin/isadmin/scan.idq" METHOD="GET">
139. <INPUT TYPE="HIDDEN"
140. NAME="CiBookMark" VALUE="<%CiBookMark%>" >
141. <INPUT TYPE="HIDDEN"
142. NAME="CiBookmarkSkipCount" VALUE="<%EscapeRAW
➥CiMaxRecordsPerPage%>" >
143. <INPUT TYPE="HIDDEN"
144. NAME="CiRestriction" VALUE="<%CiRestriction%>" >
145. <INPUT TYPE="HIDDEN"
146. NAME="CiMaxRecordsPerPage" VALUE="<%EscapeRAW
➥CiMaxRecordsPerPage%>" >
147. <INPUT TYPE="SUBMIT"
148. VALUE="Next <%CiRecordsNextPage%> documents">
149. </FORM>
150. </TD>
151. <%endif%>
152. </TABLE>

153. <P><BR>

154. <!--
155. If the index is out of date (for example, if it's still
➥being created
156. or updated after changes to files in an indexed directory)
➥let the
157. user know.
158. -->
159. <%if CiOutOfDate ne 0%>
160. <P><BR>
161. <I><B>The index is out of date.</B></I>
162. <%endif%>

163. <!--
164. If the query was not executed because it needed to enumerate
➥to
165. resolve the query instead of using the index, but
➥CiForceUseCi
```

```
166. was TRUE, let the user know
167. -->

168. <%if CiQueryIncomplete eq 1%>
169. <P><BR>
170. <I><B>The query is too expensive to complete.</B></I>
171. <%endif%>

172. <!-- Output a page number and count of pages -->

173. <%if CiTotalNumberPages gt 0%>
174. <P>
175. Page <%CiCurrentPageNumber%> of <%CiTotalNumberPages%>
176. <P>
177. <%endif%>
178. </HTML>
```

The preceding file is too long for a discussion of every line. Fortunately, it's necessary only to look at the lines of greatest interest to this discussion.

Lines 9 through 13 look for the number of total matches found, and return a title corresponding to zero or more than zero. Lines 24 to 30 fashion the results based on the number of virtual servers found.

Other lines continue to format the display based on the results found (should there be a Next button, and so on). Notice the constant checks for results (finds, pages, and so on) greater than zero: lines 119, 146, 183, and so on. An example of how this screen looks is shown in Figure 4.9.

Figure 4.9

An example of the SCAN.HTX page.

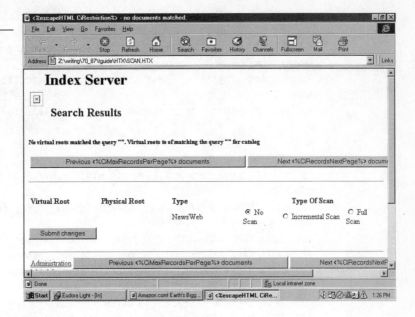

The Query .HTM File

The two preceding sections discussed the .IDQ file that gathers results and the .HTX file that formats those results. Missing from the equation is the .HTM file, which first queries for the results. One of the best examples of this file is QUERY.HTM, located in %systemroot$\InetPub\iissamples\ISSamples. It is this file which sends the query to the IDQ file. The following is the complete list of the Query .HTM code lines:

```
1.  <!DOCTYPE HTML PUBLIC "-//IETF//DTD HTML 3.0//EN" "html.dtd">
2.  <HTML>

3.  <HEAD>

4.  <!--
```

```
5.  *****        INSTRUCTIONS FOR CUSTOMIZING THIS FORM        *****

6.  To customize this form, look for remarks in the file
➥beginning with
7.  5 stars ("*****"). These lines contain instructions for
➥easily
8.  customizing the most common query form elements.

9.  -->

10. <TITLE>Index Server 2.0 Sample HTM/IDQ/HTX Search Form</
➥TITLE>
11. <META NAME="DESCRIPTION" CONTENT="Sample query form for
➥Microsoft Index Server">
12. <META NAME="AUTHOR"       CONTENT="Index Server Team">
13. <META NAME="KEYWORDS"     CONTENT="query, content, hit">
14. <META NAME="SUBJECT"      CONTENT="sample form">
15. <META NAME="MS.CATEGORY" CONTENT="Internet">
16. <META NAME="MS.LOCALE"    CONTENT="EN-US">
17. <META HTTP-EQUIV="Content-Type" CONTENT="text/html;
➥charset=Windows-1252">
18. </HEAD>

19. <!-- ***** To change the form's background pattern, simply
save your background pattern
20. using the name IS2BKGND.GIF in the same directory as this
➥form. ***** -->
21. <BODY background="is2bkgnd.gif">

22. <TABLE>

23. <TR><TD><A href="http://www.microsoft.com/ntserver/search"
➥target="_top" style="text-decoration: none">

24. <!-- ***** To change the form's logo, simply save your logo
➥ using the name IS2LOGO.GIF
25. in the same directory as this form. -->
26. <IMG SRC ="is2logo.gif" VALIGN=MIDDLE ALIGN=LEFT>

27. </A></TD></TR>
28. <TR><TD ALIGN="RIGHT"><H3>
```

```
29. <!-- ***** The following line of text is displayed next to
➥the form logo. -->
30. Sample HTM/IDQ/HTX Search Form

31. </H3></TD></TD></TR>
32. </TR>
33. </TABLE>

34. <FORM ACTION="query.idq" METHOD="GET">
35. <TABLE WIDTH=500>
36. <TR>
37. <TD>Enter your query below:</TD>
38. </TR>
39. <TR>
40. <TD><INPUT TYPE="TEXT" NAME="CiRestriction" SIZE="80"
➥ MAXLENGTH="100" VALUE=""></TD>
41. <TD><INPUT TYPE="SUBMIT" VALUE="Go"></TD>
42. </TR>
43. <TR>
44. <TD ALIGN="RIGHT"><A HREF="ixqlang.htm">Tips for searching</
➥A></TD>
45. </TR>
46. <TR>
47. <TD>
48. <P><INPUT NAME="FreeText" TYPE=CHECKBOX>Search for any
➥combination of words entered above.
49. </TD>
50. </TR>
51. </TABLE>

52. <!-- The CiScope parameter allows you to control which
➥documents are searched. To search
53. the entire document set, use a value of "/", which
➥corresponds to the root of your web
54. virtual namespace. To search a subset of your documents,
➥set the value equal to the
55. virtual directory you want to search.  -->
56. <INPUT TYPE="HIDDEN" NAME="CiScope" VALUE="/">

57. <INPUT TYPE="HIDDEN" NAME="CiMaxRecordsPerPage" VALUE="10">
58. <INPUT TYPE="HIDDEN" NAME="TemplateName" VALUE="query">
```

```
59. <INPUT TYPE="HIDDEN" NAME="CiSort" VALUE="rank[d]">
60. <INPUT TYPE="HIDDEN" NAME="HTMLQueryForm" VALUE="query.htm">
61. </FORM>


62. <!-- BEGIN STANDARD MICROSOFT FOOTER FOR QUERY PAGES -->

63. <hr width=500 align=left>
64. <p>
65. <table border="0" cellpadding="0" cellspacing="0"
➥width="500">
66. <tr>
67. <!-- IIS GIF -->
68. <td>
69. <a href="http://www.microsoft.com/iis"><img src="/IISSamples/
➥Default/nts_iis.GIF" alt="Learn more about Internet Information
➥Server!" width="88" height="31" border="0"></font></a>
70. </td>

71. <!-- Microsoft Legal Info -->
72. <td align=center>
73. <font size="1" face="Verdana, Arial, Helvetica"> (c)1997
➥Microsoft Corporation. All rights reserved.<br></font><a
➥href="http://www.microsoft.com/misc/cpyright.htm"><font size="1"
➥face="Verdana, Arial, Helvetica">Legal Notices.</font></a>
74. </td>

75. <!-- Best with IE GIF -->
76. <td align=right>
77. <a href="http://www.microsoft.com/ie"><img src="/IISSamples/
➥Default/IE.GIF" alt="Download Internet Explorer!" width="88"
➥height="31" border="0"></a>
78. </td>
79. </tr>
80. </table>

81. <!-- END STANDARD MICROSOFT FOOTER FOR QUERY PAGES -->

82. </BODY>
83. </HTML>
```

The results of running the file are shown in Figure 4.10. They are self-explanatory in nature.

Figure 4.10

An example of the QUERY.HTM page.

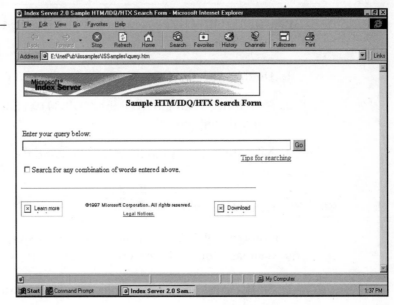

Exercises

Exercise 4.1:   Examine the ODBC Core Components

To see which ODBC core components are installed on your system, follow these steps:

1. Double-click the ODBC icon in the Control Panel.

2. Select the About tab from the ODBC Data Source Administrator dialog box.

3. Note the core components installed and the version number of each.

Exercise 4.2:   Edit the QUERY.HTM File

To modify the QUERY.HTM file to perform a query based upon your database, follow these steps:

1. Start a word processing application such as Microsoft Word 97.

2. Select the File, Open menu, switch to All Files, and find the existing copy of QUERY.HTM (by default, in InetPub\iissamples\ISSamples.

3. What appears is the HTML result. Select View, HTML Source and the code is displayed.

4. Make the changes to reflect your system and database.

5. Choose File, Save, and then Exit. Lastly, confirm that it is saved as an .HTM file.

Exercise 4.3:   Examine the Sample Files on Your System

To examine the sample .HTM, .IDQ, and .HTX files on your system, follow these steps:

1. Start a word processing application such as Microsoft Word 97.

2. Select the File, Open menu and go to InetPub\iissamples\ISSamples. You may need to change the file type to All Files in order to see the listings.

3. What appears is a number of sample files to use in creating your own scripts. Bring each one up and you will see the HTML result. Select View, HTML Source and the code is displayed.

Review Questions

1. When specifying a template path, how many characters can be used in the path specification?

   A. 8

   B. 255

   C. 256

   D. 260

2. Of the following file extensions, which can be used to contain queries?

   A. HTM

   B. IDC

   C. IDQ

   D. HTX

3. Which of the following files can be used to contain templates?

   A. HTM

   B. IDC

   C. IDQ

   D. HTX

4. Where can Login Authentication to a SQL Server accessed through IIS be done?

   A. On the NT Server

   B. On the SQL Server

   C. On the IIS Server

   D. On the Index Server

5. In which file would the <Query> tag be found

    A. Sample.htm

    B. Sample.idc

    C. Sample.idq

    D. Sample.htx

6. In which file would the SQL Statement parameter be found?

    A. Sample.htm

    B. Sample.idc

    C. Sample.idq

    D. Sample.htx

7. What is the comment character used as the first character in script files to prevent the line from being processed?

    A. %

    B. <

    C. [

    D. #

8. Joe calls Steve, the new administrator, and says that he is doing some deletion of unnecessary files and has come across one called HTTPODBC.DLL. How could this file be explained?

    A. It is the dynamic link library providing ODBC support on the server

    B. It is the file used to install ODBC support on the server

    C. It is needed for HTTP operations

    D. It should be deleted after installation

9. In which file would the MaxRecords parameter be found?

   A. Sample.htm

   B. Sample.idc

   C. Sample.idq

   D. Sample.htx

10. In which file would the CiCodePage variable be found?

   A. Sample.htm

   B. Sample.idc

   C. Sample.idq

   D. Sample.htx

Review Answers

1. **D**. The limit is 260 characters on any NT-based pathname.

2. **B, C**. Queries can be in either .IDC or .IDQ files.

3. **D**. .HTX files signify templates.

4. **A, B**. SQL Server Login Authentication can be done by SQL Server or NT Server.

5. **C**. The <Query> tag is used in .IDQ files.

6. **B**. SQLStatement is one of required parameters of the .IDC file.

7. **D**. The pound sign (#) is used to signify comments.

8. **A**. HTTPODBC.DLL is the dynamic link library providing ODBC support on the server.

9. **D**. MaxRecords is a parameter that can be used in .HTX files.

10. **C**. CiCodePage is one variable that can be used in .IDQ files.

Answers to Test Yourself Questions at Beginning of Chapter

1. Files with .IDC extensions stipulate how the data is accessed, while those with .HTX extensions stipulate how the data is presented. See "Configuring IIS to Connect to a Database."

2. The CONTAINS expression in an .IDQ file checks to see if one entry is a subset of another entry. See "Configuring Integration with Index Server."

C h a p t e r

Running Applications

5

This chapter helps you prepare for the exam by covering the following objectives:

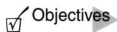 Objectives

▶ Configure IIS to support server-side scripting

▶ Configure IIS to run ISAPI applications

▶ Configure IIS to support ADO associated with the WWW service

Test Yourself! Before reading this chapter, test yourself to determine how much study time you will need to devote to this section.

1. What are the three items that can be contained within Active Server Pages?

2. What are the two ways that ISAPI can be implemented?

3. What three types of files can ADO be used to access?

Answers are located at the end of the chapter...

This chapter addresses the scripting side of IIS and other servers and services. The topics discussed are ways that scripts can be created and implemented to automate tasks on the IIS server—primarily in conjunction with the WWW service. It is imperative that you understand the material in Chapter 3, "Configuring and Managing Resource Access," and Chapter 4, "Integration and Interoperability," before attempting to understand scripting.

The sample Web site included with IIS 4.0, "Exploration Air," includes some examples of scripting and Active Server Pages. This material is highly recommended. The files are very useful and can provide you with a lot of insights into IIS 4.0 capabilities.

The specific topics covered in this chapter include the following:

▶ Configuring IIS to support server-side scripting

▶ Configuring IIS to run ISAPI applications

▶ Configuring ADO support

Configuring IIS to Support Server-Side Scripting

 Objective ▶

Microsoft Internet Information Server (IIS) 4.0 enables an administrator or Webmaster to use Active Server Pages (ASP) to do Web application programming. ASP simplifies server-side programming and offers support for ActiveX objects (also known as server-side objects), as well as HTML tags and all Active scripting commands.

The .ASP extension is assigned to all ASP scripts, and the files include text, HTML tags, and ASP script commands. While HTML tags begin with < and end with >, ASP tags begin with <% and end with %>. The tags also are known as *delimiters*, and it is the delimiters that signal the server that processing is required at that point. Look at the following example:

```
It is now <%= Time %>
```

Once the server processes the script command, the following is displayed:

It is now 14:52:10

The easiest way to create ASP files is to start with standard HTML files and add the script commands to them (as well as rename the file from .htm to .asp).

 Tip

> For purposes of passing the exam, also know that *primary script commands* are those within <%%>.

Active Server Pages can be used with VBScript, Jscript, PerlScript, or any other recognized scripting language. Not only can you use a variety of languages, but you also can use multiple languages within the same script. The syntax for doing so follows:

```
<SCRIPT LANGUAGE="VBScript" RUNAT=SERVER>
routine
</SCRIPT>
<SCRIPT LANGUAGE="PerlScript" RUNAT=SERVER>
routine
</SCRIPT>
```

In addition to defining variables by an operation (such as DATE, TIME, and so on), you also can set variables and reference them within the scripts. This is done through the use of the SET command, and the variable is then referenced in a manner similar to how the Time variable was referenced. You can also create an array of data to reference through use of the Session variable if you wanted the value to persist between scripts, which is unique for the life of the session. Look at the following example:

```
Session ("City") = "Anderson"
Set Session ("State") = "IN"
How is the weather in <%= Session("City") %>?
```

This is displayed as the following:

How is the weather in Anderson?

As mentioned, the Session variables are kept for the entire duration of the session, and abandoned afterward. To force the purging of the variables, you can use the Session.Abandon call. This loses the variables (and ends the session).

The Use of Cookies

Clients using ASP first establish unique session keys, a process carried by the use of HTTP cookies. No buffering is used, by default, so all operations that take place are immediately sent to the browser. This causes a session cookie to be sent for every browser interaction, but you can elect to turn on buffering and prevent the sending of some unnecessary cookies.

Note

Cookies are components of a session or information stored on the client's machine.

A Walkthrough of the Steps Involved in Active Server Pages

The following is a simplified example of how ASPs work:

1. The browser sends an HTTP request for an Active Server Page. The server knows it to be an Active Server Page due to the .ASP extension.

2. The server sends the file to ASP.DLL for execution of all code.

3. Processing is done and the server sends back an HTML page.

4. If there is any client-side code, it is executed on the client, and the page is displayed in the browser.

Note that during this process, no server-side scripting is sent to the client, so the clients can't view the script.

Scripting Hosts

Scripting hosts are designed to improve Operating System operations, and there are two scripting hosts available with IIS:

▶ A command-based scripting host

▶ A Windows-based scripting host

The hosts are very similar in nature. The command-based one is called by Cscript.exe, and the Windows-based host is called by Wscript.exe.

Parameters that can be used with Cscript.exe are as follows:

▶ //?—Shows the command line parameters.

▶ //B—Places the engine in batch mode.

▶ //C—Causes Cscript to be the default engine used by running scripts.

▶ //I—The opposite of //B, it places the engine in interactive mode.

▶ //logo—Shows a logo at execution time.

▶ //nologo—Does not display a logo at execution time.

▶ //R—Registers known script extensions with the engine. Known script extensions include .js, .vbs, and .tcl. This operation is done by default and you need not use the parameter.

▶ //S—Saves the current command line options for the user

▶ //T:nn—The timeout specified in number of seconds. The default is no limit, but you can specify a value to prevent excessive script execution.

Figure 5.1 shows the Wscript configuration screen (available from the Run command or any command line).

Figure 5.1

*The Wscript con-
figuration box.*

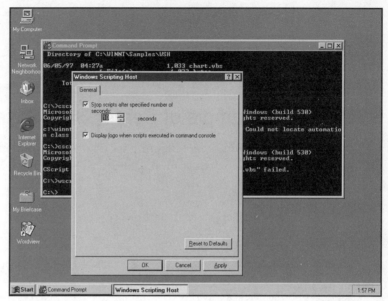

The options for Wscript configuration enable you to specify a
number of seconds after which to stop script execution (equivalent to //T:nn in Cscript), and enable you to toggle the banner on
and off (//logo and //nologo in Cscript). Wscript does not have the
capability for interactive or batch modes.

Adding Conditions

You can add conditional processing to your scripts by using
IF..Then..Else logic. The syntax is as follows:

```
If {condition exists} Then
{action to perform}
Else
{another action to perform
End If
```

You also can run an operation a number of times by using
For..Next loops:

```
For Each {variable} in {set}
{action to perform}
Next
```

As with most scripting languages, indentation is not required, but it is used to make it easier to read and debug the script. Additionally, ASP itself is not case sensitive, but the language used to execute the commands may be.

An Example of Server-Side Scripting

The following is an example based on a script file included with IIS. The Shortcut.vbs file uses Wscript to create a NotePad shortcut on the desktop:

```
' Windows Script Host Sample Script
'
' ------------------------------------------------------------
'               Copyright (C) 1996 Microsoft Corporation
'
' You have a royalty-free right to use, modify, reproduce and
distribute
' the Sample Application Files (and/or any modified version) in
any way
' you find useful, provided that you agree that Microsoft has no
warranty,
' obligations, or liability for any Sample Application Files.
' ------------------------------------------------------------
'
' This sample demonstrates how to use the WshShell object.
' to create a shortcut on the desktop


Dim WshShell, MyShortcut, MyDesktop, DesktopPath

' Initialize WshShell object
  Set WshShell = WScript.CreateObject("WScript.Shell")

' Read desktop path using WshSpecialFolders object
  DesktopPath = WshShell.SpecialFolders("Desktop")

' Create a shortcut object on the desktop
  Set MyShortcut = WshShell.CreateShortcut(DesktopPath &
➡"\Shortcut to notepad.lnk")
```

```
' Set shortcut object properties and save it
  MyShortcut.TargetPath =
➥WshShell.ExpandEnvironmentStrings("%windir%\notepad.exe")
  MyShortcut.WorkingDirectory =
➥WshShell.ExpandEnvironmentStrings("%windir%")
  MyShortcut.WindowStyle = 4
  MyShortcut.IconLocation = WshShell.ExpandEnvironmentStrings
➥("%windir%\notepad.exe, 0")
  MyShortcut.Save
```

Configuring IIS to Run ISAPI Applications

 Objective ▶

ISAPI—Internet Server API (Application Programming Inter-face)—applications are an alternative to Active Server Pages. In fact, the ASP scripting engine is an ISAPI filter. Like ASP, ISAPI can be used to write applications that Web users can activate by filling out an HTML form or clicking a link in an HTML page on your Web server. The user-supplied information can then be re-sponded to and the results returned in an HTML page or posted to a database.

ISAPI was a Microsoft improvement over popular CGI (Common Gateway Interface) scripting, and offers much better performance than CGI because applications are loaded into memory at server run-time. This means that they require less overhead and each request does not start a separate process. Additionally, ISAPI ap-plications are created as DLLs on the server, and allow pre-pro-cessing of requests and post-processing of responses, permitting site-specific handling of HTTP requests and responses.

ISAPI filters can be used for applications such as customized au-thentication, access, or logging. You can create complex sites by combining ISAPI filters and applications.

ISAPI works with OLE connectivity and the Internet Database Connector. This allows ISAPI to be implemented as a DLL (in essence, an executable) or as a filter (translating another execut-able's output). If ISAPI is used as a filter, then it is not called when the browser accesses an URL, but is summoned by the server in response to an event (which could easily be an URL request). Common uses of ISAPI filters include the following:

▶ Tracking URL usage statistics

▶ Performing authentication

▶ Adding entries to log files

▶ Compression

For the Exam

If you want to become an ISAPI programmer, then you'll need a book three times the length of this one to learn the language. If you want to pass the exam, (the purpose of this book), then there are several things you need to know:

▶ ISAPI applications effectively extend server applications to the desktop.

▶ ISAPI is similar to CGI but offers better performance.

▶ Although created by Microsoft, ISAPI is an open specification that third parties can write to.

▶ ISAPI filters can do pre- or post-processing.

Configuring ADO Support

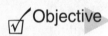 Objective ▶ The newest enhancement to Microsoft's Web service offering is ADO—ActiveX Data Objects. ADO combines a set of core functions and unique functions for each implementation. ADO was designed to replace the need for all other data access methods, and Microsoft recommends migration of all applications to ADO when it is feasible.

ADO can access the following:

▶ Text

▶ Relational databases

▶ Any ODBC-compliant data source

ADO grew out of ASP (Active Server Pages) and offers the following benefits:

- ▶ Low memory overhead

- ▶ Small disk footprint

- ▶ Ease of use

- ▶ De-emphasis on object hierarchy

- ▶ Ability to use ODBC 3.0 connection pooling

Connection pooling enables you to open database connections and manage sharing across different user requests while reducing the number of idle connections. In order to use it, you must set a timeout property in the Registry. When a user times out, rather than the connection being totally lost, it is saved into a pool. When the next request comes in, that connection is used, rather than a whole new connection being created each and every time.

While ADO has a number of benefits, its greatest downside is that it is mostly read-only on the browser. All filtering and processing must be done on the server, and when it reaches the browser, it is in its final state. Although there are ways around this, they are more cumbersome and difficult than other options.

For the Exam

As with ISAPI, if you want to become an ADO programmer, you'll need to purchase a book specific to that end. If you want to pass the exam then there are only a few things you need to know:

- ▶ ADO objects are small, compact, and easy to write to.

- ▶ ADO knows what data to access through DSN (Data Source Name) files.

- ▶ It is the DSN that contains the user security, database configuration, and location information.

▶ The DSN can be an actual file (text) or merely an entry in the Registry. ODBC enables you to create three types of DSNs—User (in Registry), System (in Registry) or File (text file).

▶ A system DSN applies to all users logged into the server.

▶ A user DSN applies to a specific user (or set of).

▶ A file DSN gives access to multiple users and can be transferred between servers by copying the file.

▶ DSN files are created through the ODBC icon of the Control Panel.

▶ ADO connections are written in the files with variable names such as *cn*. Look at the following example:

```
Set cn = Server.CreateObject("ADODB.Connection")
Cn.Open "FILEDSN=Example.dsn"
```

▶ A RecordSet is a table or query from a subset of the object that you wish to retrieve. Rather than retrieving the entire Access or SQL database, you retrieve a component of it, known as a RecordSet object.

▶ ADO commands are written in the files as variables, such as *cm*. Look at the following example:

```
Set cm = Server.CreateObject("ADODB.Command")
Cm.CommandText = "APPEND INTO Array (X, Y) VALUES"
```

Exercises

Exercise 5.1:   Run the Chart.VBS program

This exercise illustrates how to run a script program in Cscript and Wscript.

1. Open a command line

2. Enter:

   Cscript {*root path*}\Samples\Wsh\Chart.VBS

3. Enter:

   Cscript //logo {*root path*}\Samples\Wsh\Chart.VBS

4. Enter:

   Cscript //nologo {*root path*}\Samples\Wsh\Chart.VBS

5. From the Run command, enter:

   Wscript {*root path*}\Samples\Wsh\Chart.VBS

Review Questions

1. What file extension is used to signify, and required for, Active Server Pages?

   A. ASP

   B. EXE

   C. COM

   D. HTM

2. Which of the following would not be a component of Active Server Pages?

   A. HTML

   B. text

   C. access data

   D. script commands

3. The line of code "<*BODY*>" would be considered:

   A. an Active Server tag

   B. an HTML tag

   C. an ADO tag

   D. an ISAPI tag

4. Which variable in Active Server Pages is erased from existence when a connection is no longer there?

   A. BROWSER

   B. USER

   C. USERSESSION

   D. SESSION

5. What are the scripting hosts included with IIS?

    A. Cscript

    B. Wscript

    C. Uscript

    D. Pscript

6 Which of the following commands would make PerlScript active to process the .ASP file?

    A. `</SCRIPT="PerlScript">`

    B. `<SCRIPT="PerlScript">`

    C. `</SCRIPT LANGUAGE="PerlScript">`

    D. `<SCRIPT LANGUAGE="PerlScript">`

7. What command can be used to force the purging of variables?

    A. `Session.purge`

    B. `Session.abandon`

    C. `Abandon.session`

    D. `Purge.session`

8. Which Cscript parameter is the opposite of the `//B` parameter?

    A. `//T`

    B. `//R`

    C. `//S`

    D. `//I`

    E. `//C`

9. Conditional script commands in .ASP files that begin with IF must end with:

    A. FI

    B. END IF

    C. ENDIF

    D. IF END

10. Which type of processing can ISAPI filters do?

    A. pre-processing only

    B. post-processing only

    C. both pre- and post-processing

    D. neither pre- nor post-processing

11. ISAPI is implemented as

    A. a TSR

    B. a DLL

    C. an EXE

    D. as ASP

12. It would be Microsoft's recommendation that all sites with the time and resources to do so convert Web\data interaction to what type?

    A. ISAPI

    B. CGI

    C. ADO

    D. ASP

13. Which of the following are benefits of ADO?

    A. small disk footprint

    B. high memory overhead

C. improved authentication

D. emphasis on object hierarchy

14. What are the two types of DSNs?

A. HTML files

B. text files

C. registry entries

D. executables

15. To what group does a System DSN apply?

A. specific users

B. specific groups

C. all users logged on the server

D. multiple users

16. Which of the following variable names is recommended by Microsoft to use when specifying a connection in an ADO file?

A. cm

B. cn

C. co

D. recordset

Review Answers

1. **A**. Active Server Pages must have the .asp file extension.

2. **C**. Access data would not be Active Server Pages.

3. **B**. <BODY> is an HTML tag.

4. **D**. The *SESSION* variable goes away when the session (or connection) is no longer there.

5. **A, B**. Both Cscript and Wscript are included with IIS.

6. **D**. `<SCRIPT LANGUAGE="PerlScript">` would make PerlScript active for that portion of the .asp file.

7. **B**. `Session.abandon` can be used to force the purging of variables.

8. **D**. `//I` places the engine in interactive mode—the opposite of `//B`, which places it in batch mode.

9. **B**. Conditional script commands in .asp files that begin with `IF` must end with `END IF`.

10. **C**. ISAPI filters can do both pre- and post-processing.

11. **B**. ISAPI is implemented as a DLL.

12. **C**. It would be Microsoft's recommendation that all sites with the time and resources to do so convert Web\data interaction to ADO.

13. **A**. A benefit of ADO is its use of a small disk footprint.

14. **B, C**. DSNs can be text files or Registry entries.

15. **C**. A System DSN applies to all users logged on to the server.

16. **B**. `Cn` is used to specify a connection in an ADO file.

Answers to Test Yourself Questions at Beginning of Chapter

1. Active Server Pages can contain text, HTML code, and script commands. See "Configuring IIS to Support Server-Side Scripting."

2. ISAPI can be implemented as a DLL or a filter. See "Configuring IIS to Run ISAPI Applications."

3. ADO can be used to access text files, relational databases, or ODBC-compliant data sources. See "Configuring ADO Support."

Chapter 6

Monitoring and Optimization

This chapter will help you prepare for the exam by covering the following objectives:

 Objectives

▶ Maintain a log for fine-tuning and auditing purposes. Tasks include

  ▶ Importing log files into a Usage Import and Report Writer Database

  ▶ Configuring the logging features of the WWW service

  ▶ Configuring the logging features of the FTP service

  ▶ Configuring Usage Import and Report Writer to analyze logs created by the WWW service or the FTP service

▶ Monitor performance of various functions by using Performance Monitor. Functions include HHTP and FTP sessions.

▶ Analyze performance. Performance issues include

  ▶ Identifying bottlenecks

  ▶ Identifying network-related performance issues

  ▶ Identifying disk-related performance issues

  ▶ Identifying CPU-related performance issues

continues

▶ Optimize performance of IIS

▶ Optimize performance of Index Server

▶ Optimize performance of Microsoft SMTP Service

▶ Optimize performance of Microsoft NNTP Service

▶ Interpret performance data

▶ Optimize a Web site by using Content Analyzer

Test Yourself! Before reading this chapter, test yourself to determine how much study time you will need to devote to this section.

1. As the administrator for your IIS 4 Web site, you're asked to produce a report showing the daily Web traffic to your site. Which tool do you use and can you automate this task?

2. You are a consultant for a company that uses IIS 4. IIS 4 runs a Web site and FTP site under IIS 4. You are asked to track the number of anonymous users currently attached to the site. What do you do?

3. When administering IIS 4, you want to keep an eye out for hardware bottlenecks that may occur. What are some of the tools you can use to watch for these?

4. You're the administrator of your IIS 4 Web site. The Web site is responding sluggishly, and you notice some inactive clients are staying connected to your server. How can you change this?

5. On your company's Web site, you run Microsoft Index Server. You have between 100,000 and 150,000 documents stored on it. How much RAM is recommended for this number of documents?

6. You are an IIS 4 consultant working with a large company that has asked you to set up a smart host. What is this?

7. The Microsoft NNTP news server you administer allows too many clients to connect to it simultaneously, resulting in a poorly performing server. How can you change it so only a specific number of clients can connect at the same time?

8. What are the statistical measurements called that are used in Performance Monitor?

9. To help you manage your company's Web site, you use the Content Analyzer. Name three ways you can use this tool to optimize your site.

Answers are located at the end of the chapter...

Microsoft makes it very easy to monitor and optimize your IIS 4 Web site. Each time a user interacts with your Web site and requests resources from it, such as a Web page, image file, or similar item, a hit is recorded in a log file. You can log each IIS 4 service to help you fine-tune and optimize your site, plan for future expansion, and review the security of your site. IIS 4 enables you to send log data to a text file or to an Open Database Connectivity (ODBC)–compliant database, such as Microsoft SQL Server or Microsoft Access.

In this chapter you learn how to monitor and optimize your site, including the WWW and FTP services, the Index Service, and the Microsoft SMTP and NNTP services. Specific topics covered include

- ▶ Maintaining IIS 4 logs

- ▶ Monitoring performance of various functions using Performance Monitor

- ▶ Analyzing performance

- ▶ Optimizing the performance of IIS

- ▶ Optimizing the performance of Index Server

- ▶ Optimizing the performance of Microsoft SMTP Service

- ▶ Optimizing the performance of Microsoft NNTP Service

- ▶ Interpreting performance data

- ▶ Optimizing a Web site using Content Analyzer

Maintaining IIS 4 Logs

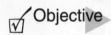 **Objective**

Maintaining IIS 4 logs is one of the most important tasks in fine-tuning and auditing an IIS site. In the following sections, you learn how to configure WWW and FTP services logging, configure Report Writer and Usage Import to analyze logs created by these services, and automate the Report Writer and Usage Import.

Importing Log Files into a Report Writer and Usage Import Database

The Report Writer and Usage Import Database help you analyze and create reports based on logs created by IIS. Report Writer creates analysis reports based on the log file data. Usage Import, on the other hand, reads the log files and places the data into a relational database.

To begin using these tools, you import the log file or files you want to analyze into a Report Writer and Usage Import database. The database is essentially a container that holds imported data from a log file.

Both Report Writer and Usage Import connect to this database when they start. You can see the name of the database each tool connects to by looking at the bottom of its screen on the status bar (see Figure 6.1). If Report Writer or Usage Import cannot find the database it is configured to connect to, you are prompted to enter the name of a valid database.

Figure 6.1

You can view the database that Report Writer connects to by looking at the status bar.

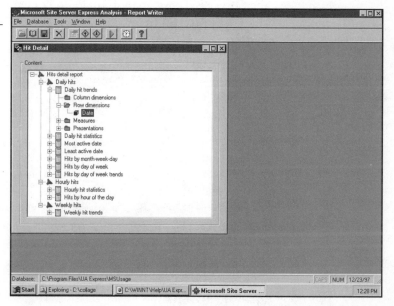

Relational databases are used because of their efficient use of data storage. Relational databases do not require redundant information from your log file to be stored. This results in smaller databases and less required disk space. In some cases, the database may be 10–20 percent smaller than the original log file.

Relational databases are also used because they enable you to analyze your data in a more flexible way. You can cross-reference over 200 different Internet server usage data properties.

To import log files into Usage Import so that you can analyze your site's data in Report Writer, perform the following steps:

1. Make sure you can access the Internet server log file on the local computer.

2. Select Start | Programs | Windows NT 4.0 Option Pack | Microsoft Site Server Express 2.0 | Usage Import. Usage Import starts. The first time you start Usage Import, you need to configure an Internet site in a database, because no sites are configured yet. Usage Import displays the Microsoft Site Server Express Analysis dialog box (see Figure 6.2), which informs you that you must use the Server Manager to configure your Internet site.

Figure 6.2

The Microsoft Site Server Express Analysis dialog box.

 Tip

If the Microsoft Site Server Express Analysis dialog box does not display, you've already configured a site under Usage Import. You can start Server Manager again by selecting File | Server Manager after Usage Import starts. Right-click on the Log Data Source item in the Server Manager and click on New Server. The Server Properties dialog box displays, which is explained in step 5.

3. Click OK. The Log data source Properties dialog box displays (see Figure 6.3).

Figure 6.3

The Log data source Properties dialog box.

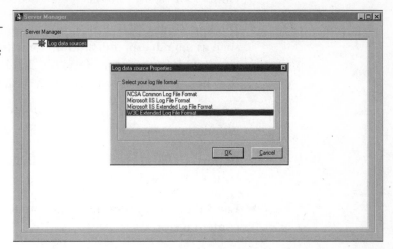

4. From the Log data source Properties dialog box, click the log file format for your log data source. Some of the file formats include NCSA Common Log File Format, Microsoft IIS Log File Format, Microsoft IIS Extended Log File Format, W3C Extended Log File Format, and others. The options available here correspond to the type of server you are analyzing. You can read more about the log file types supported in the "Configuring the Logging Features of the WWW Service" and "Configuring the Logging Features of the FTP Service" sections, later in this chapter.

 Tip

To create customizable log files, use the W3C Extended Log File Format. Compared to other log file formats, such as NCSA Common Log File Format and Microsoft IIS Log Format, the W3C Extended Log File Format also records the greatest amount of information about your Web site, including referring URL and cookie information.

5. Click OK. The Server Properties dialog box displays (see Figure 6.4). Set the following items on this dialog box:

▶ **Server type.** Sets the type of server for which your log file is configured. You can select World Wide Web, FTP, Gopher, or RealAudio servers.

▶ **Directory index files.** Enter your server's index file, such as default.asp, index.html, home.htm, or other name. This is the name of the file that is displayed in the client when the URL ends in a slash (/).

▶ **IP address.** Enter the IP address of the server. This field is optional.

▶ **IP port.** Enter the server's IP port number. The default is 80.

▶ **Local timezone.** Enter the local time zone where your content is stored.

▶ **Local domain.** Enter the domain name for the local network that is hosting your content. This setting is used to distinguish hits from internal and external clients. If you use a hosting service (such as IQuest), enter the domain of that service, such as **iquest.net**.

Figure 6.4

*The Server Prop-
erties dialog box.*

6. Click OK. The Site Properties dialog box displays (see Figure 6.5).

7. Enter the URL of the home page in the Home page URLs field on the Basic tab. This information is required. As an

optional entry, fill in the Server filesystem paths for this Site field. If you have multiple URLs, list them all in this field.

Figure 6.5

*The Site Proper-
ties dialog box.*

8. Click the Excludes tab (see Figure 6.6). Here you can set log file information that should be excluded from the database. These settings are optional. You can enter the name of hosts you want to exclude in the Hosts to exclude from import field. To exclude log file information based on inline image requests, enter the image file types in the Inline images to exclude from import field. Some common file types you might enter here include gif, jpg, jpeg, and png. You might opt to exclude these entries to decrease the time it takes to import the log file and make the database smaller.

 Tip

Although you have excluded inline images, you will still get accurate bandwidth calculations.

9. Click OK. The Usage Import window displays with the Log File Manager and Server Manager windows (see Figure 6.7). The Log File Manager organizes, filters, and imports log files for analysis. The Server Manager, on the other hand, sets up the site structure for which the logs are imported. Before any data can be imported into a database, the servers and sites that created the log data must be configured in the Service Manager.

Figure 6.6

The Excludes tab on the Site Properties dialog box.

Figure 6.7

The Usage Import window.

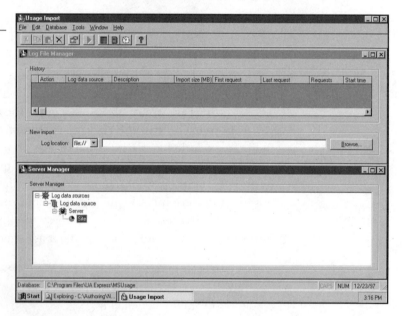

10. In the Log File Manager window, enter the complete path for your log file in the Log location field. Click Browse to locate the file graphically.

11. Click the Start Import button on the Usage Import window toolbar (this tool is a green right-facing arrow). After Usage Import finishes importing the log file, the Microsoft Site Server Express Analysis dialog box displays, telling you the import is completed and how long the import process took (see Figure 6.8).

Figure 6.8

The Microsoft Site Server Express Analysis dialog box.

12. Click OK. The Usage Import Statistics dialog box displays (see Figure 6.9).

Figure 6.9

The Usage Import Statistics dialog box.

13. Click Close.

When you are ready to create a report of a log file in Report Writer, perform the following steps:

1. Select Start | Programs | Windows NT 4.0 Option Pack | Microsoft Site Server Express 2.0 | Report Writer. Report Writer starts and displays the Report Writer opening dialog box (see Figure 6.10).

Figure 6.10

The Report Writer dialog box.

2. Select the From the Report Writer catalog option on the Report Writer dialog box. You can create your own report using the From scratch option. However, you should use the Report Writer catalog option the first few times you run Report Writer to see how the tool works.

3. Click OK. The Report Writer dialog box with the Report Writer catalog field displays (see Figure 6.11).

Figure 6.11

The Report Writer catalog field displaying in the Report Writer dialog box.

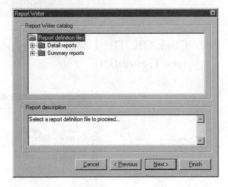

4. Select the plus sign next to the Detail reports or Summary reports folders, depending on the type of summary you want to create.

5. Click a report type, such as Hits detail report. To read about each type of report, click on it and view a description in the Report Description area at the bottom of the Report Writer dialog box.

6. Click Next. The Report Writer dialog box shown in Figure 6.12 displays. You set the date range of the data to analyze from this dialog box. The default is Every request you've imported. You also can narrow the date ranges, such as This week, This year, or a specific range (Before 12/25/98, for example).

Figure 6.12

Set the date range of the log file data to analyze from this Report Writer dialog box.

7. Click Next. The Report Writer dialog box shown in Figure 6.13 displays. From this dialog box, you can filter log file data using Boolean expressions and items included in the Filter name reference drop-down list. To use an item in the drop-down list, select the down arrow, click on the item, and drag the item to the Filter field. This enables you to create expressions and drag and drop Filter name reference items into your expressions.

Figure 6.13

You can filter log file data using this Report Writer dialog box.

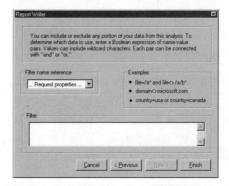

8. Click Finish. The Detail window for the report you want to generate displays (see Figure 6.14). From this window you can see the types of information that will be included in your new report. You can delete items from this window by selecting the item and pressing Delete.

Figure 6.14

The Hit Detail window.

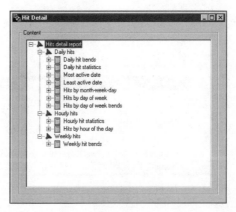

9. Click the Create Report Document toolbar button on the Report Writer toolbar. The Report Document dialog box displays (see Figure 6.15).

Figure 6.15

The Report document dialog box.

10. Enter a filename and select the format of the report. The default report format is HTML, which automatically displays in your Web browser. You also can select Microsoft Word and Microsoft Excel, which you can display in those applications. Click the Template button if you want to specify a report template that you have created.

11. Click OK. The report document is created. The Report Writer Statistics dialog box displays as well. Click Close to close this dialog box. If you specified the HTML format in step 10, your registered Web browser will launch with the report displayed (see Figure 6.16).

Figure 6.16

A Report Writer document displaying in Internet Explorer 4.0.

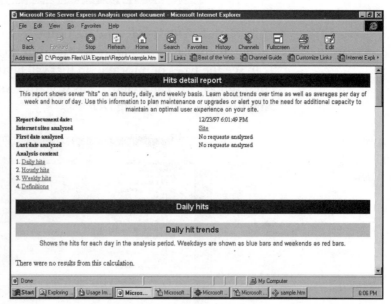

Configuring the Logging Features of the WWW Service

Probably one of the first actions you want to do when administering your IIS 4 site is to configure the logging features of the WWW and FTP services. When looking at log file information, you should keep in mind that this information does not show definitive information about users and visitors to your sites. Because Internet protocols are stateless, there cannot be sustained connections between clients and servers.

Log file data can give you a historical record of who has visited your site (based on visiting IP addresses), content exchanges (client downloads and uploads), which pages are the most popular ones on your site, and other information. A log file can be studied, for example, to see what traffic patterns develop on your site for maintenance issues (when you can perform daily, weekly, and monthly maintenance).

 Tip

Your log file can be accessed only after you stop your site. You can do this by starting Internet Service Manager, selecting the site, and clicking the Stop button on the Internet Service Manager toolbar. Click the Start button to start the site again.

 Note

See the next section, "Configuring the Logging Features of the FTP Service," for information on configuring logging features for the FTP service.

To configure logging features for your WWW service, perform the following steps:

1. Select Start | Programs | Windows NT 4.0 Option Pack | Microsoft Internet Information Server | Internet Service Manager. Internet Service Manager opens in the Microsoft Management Console (MMC) (see Figure 6.17).

Figure 6.17

Internet Service Manager displayed in MMC.

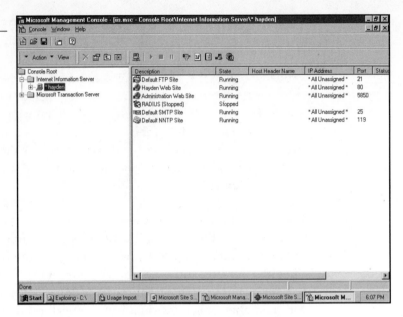

2. Right-click the Web site you want to configure.

3. Click Properties. The Web Site Properties dialog box displays (see Figure 6.18).

Figure 6.18

The Web Site Properties dialog box.

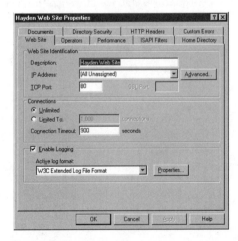

4. Click the Enable Logging option.

5. Click the Active log format drop-down list and select the type of log format you want to create. The following are the supported log file formats:

▶ **Microsoft IIS Log Format.** This is a fixed ASCII format that records basic logging items, including username, request date, request time, client IP address, number of bytes received, HTTP status code, and other items. This is a comma-delimited log file, making it easier to parse than other ASCII formats.

▶ **NCSA Common Log File Format.** This is a fixed ASCII format endorsed by the National Center for Supercomputing Applications (NCSA). The data it logs includes remote hostname, username, HTTP status code, request type, and the number of bytes received by the server. Spaces separate different items logged.

▶ **ODBC Logging.** This is a fixed format that is logged to a database. This log includes client IP address, username, request date, request time, HTTP status code, bytes received, bytes sent, action carried out, and the target. When you choose this option, you must specify the database for the file to be logged to. In addition, you must set up the database to receive that log data.

▶ **W3C Extended Log File Format.** This is a customizable ASCII format endorsed by the World Wide Web Consortium (W3C). This is the default setting. You can set this log format to record a number of different settings, such as request date, request time, client IP address, server IP address, server port, HTTP status code, and more. Data is separated by spaces in this format.

The following steps show how to configure the W3C Extended Log File Format.

6. Click the Properties button. The Extended Logging Properties dialog box displays (see Figure 6.19). If you selected a log format other than W3C Extended Log File Format from the Active log format drop-down list, the properties dialog box for that format displays.

7. In the New Log Time Period section, set the period when you want IIS to create a new log file for the selected Web site.

The default is Daily, but you can select Weekly, Monthly, Unlimited file size, or When file size reaches. If you select the last option, you need to set a maximum file size the log file can reach before a new file is created. The default here is 19MB. For active Web sites, the log file can reach sizes of over 100MB very quickly.

Figure 6.19

The Extended Logging Properties dialog box for the W3C Extended Log File Format.

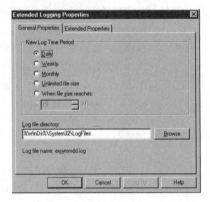

8. Enter the directory in which you want to store the log file. The default is %WinDir\System32\LogFiles. Click the Browse button to locate a new directory graphically.

Note

The log filename syntax is shown next to the Log file name label; an example of the syntax is exyymmdd.log. The first two characters in the name, *ex*, denote the type of log file format you selected in step 5. These characters include *in* for Microsoft IIS Log File Format, *nc* for NCSA Common Log File Format, and *ex* for W3C Extended Log File Format.

The remaining characters in the log filename syntax correspond to the date the file is created: *yy* is the year, *mm* is the month, and *dd* is the day.

If you select the ODBC Logging format, you must specify a Data Source Name (DSN), which does not follow these naming schemes.

9. Click the Extended Properties tab to display the logging options (see Figure 6.20) you can set (this tab is available

only when you select the W3C Extended Log File Format option). On this tab, you can set the options described in Table 6.1.

Figure 6.20

The Extended Properties tab.

Table 6.1

W3C Extended Log File Format logging options.

Option	Description
Date	Date the activity occurred
Time	Time the activity occurred
Client IP Address	IP address of the client attaching to your server
User Name	Name of user who accessed your server
Service Name	Client computer's Internet service
Server Name	Server name where the log entry was created
Server IP	Server IP address where the log entry was created
Server Port	Shows the port number to which the client is connected
Method	Shows the action the client was performing
URI Stem	Logs the resource the client was accessing on your server, such as an HTML page, CGI program, and so on

continues

Table 6.1   Continued

Option	Description
URI Query	Logs the search string the client was trying to match
HTTP Status	Shows the status (in HTTP terms) of the client action
Win32 Status	Shows the status (in Windows NT terms) of the client action
Bytes Sent	Shows the number of bytes sent by the server
Bytes Received	Shows the number of bytes received by the server
Time Taken	Shows the amount of time to execute the action requested by the client
User Agent	Reports the browser used by the client
Cookie	Shows the content of any cookies sent or received by the server
Protocol Version	Shows the protocol used by the client to access the server (HTTP or FTP)
Referrer	Shows the URL of the site from where the user clicked on to get to your site

Note   The default Extended Logging Options for the W3C Extended Log File Format include Time, Client IP Address, Method, URI Stem, and HTTP Status.

10. Click OK to close the Extended Logging Properties dialog box.

11. Click OK to close the Web Site Properties dialog box.

Log files can grow very large, so be sure your server on which the log file resides has plenty of free disk space. Logging shuts down if your server runs out of disk space when trying to add a new log entry to a file. When this happens, you'll see an event logged in the Windows NT Event Viewer. Another event will be logged when IIS is able to continue logging IIS activities (when disk space is freed up, for example).

Configuring the Logging Features of the FTP Service

As with the WWW service, you can configure the logging features of the FTP service in IIS 4. To do this, perform the following steps:

1. Select Start | Programs | Windows NT 4.0 Option Pack | Microsoft Internet Information Server | Internet Service Manager. Internet Service Manager opens in the Microsoft Management Console (MMC) (refer to Figure 6.17).

2. Right-click on the FTP site you want to configure.

3. Click Properties. The Default FTP Site Properties dialog box displays (see Figure 6.21).

Figure 6.21

The Default FTP Site Properties dialog box.

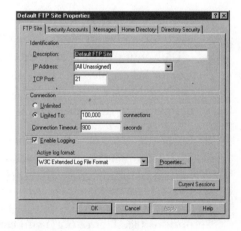

4. Click the Enable Logging option.

5. Click the Active log format drop-down list and select the type of log format you want to create. You can choose from Microsoft IIS Log File Format, ODBC Logging, and W3C Extended Log File Format. NCSA Common Log File Format is not supported on FTP sites. See step 5 in the preceding section for an explanation of these formats.

The following steps show how to configure the W3C Extended Log File Format.

6. Click the Properties button. The Extended Logging Properties dialog box displays (see Figure 6.22). If you selected a log format other than W3C Extended Log File Format from the Active log format drop-down list, the properties dialog box for that format displays.

Figure 6.22

The Extended Logging Properties dialog box for the W3C Extended Log File Format.

7. In the New Log Time Period section, set when you want IIS to create a new log file for the selected FTP site. The default is Daily, but you can select Weekly, Monthly, Unlimited file size, or When file size reaches. If you select the last option, you need to set a maximum file size the log file can reach before a new file is created. The default here is 19MB.

8. Enter the directory in which you want to store the log file. The default is %WinDir\System32\LogFiles. Click the Browse button to locate a new directory graphically.

9. Click the Extended Properties tab to display the logging options (see Figure 6.23) you can set (this tab is available only when you select the W3C Extended Log File Format option). On this tab, you can set the options described in Table 6.1.

10. Click OK to close the Extended Logging Properties dialog box.

11. Click OK to close the FTP Site Properties dialog box.

Figure 6.23

The Extended Logging Properties tab.

Configuring Report Writer and Usage Import to Analyze Logs Created by the WWW Service or the FTP Service

You learned earlier how to import a log file into Usage Import and how to create a report in Report Writer. You learn here how to configure Report Writer and Usage Import to analyze logs that are created by your WWW or FTP service.

The Usage Import Options

In Usage Import, you can access the Usage Import Options dialog box by selecting Tools | Options. This dialog box (see Figure 6.24) enables you to configure several settings and save them as your default settings or use them only during the current Usage Import session. If you opt not to save them as default settings, the next time you start Usage Import the previous settings are used.

Figure 6.24

The Usage Import Options dialog box.

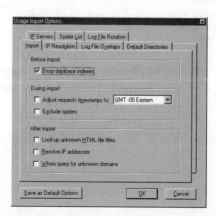

On the Import tab, you can set the following options:

▶ **Drop database indexes.** For analysis purposes, database indexes must be created. After you have a large amount of data in a database, however, you can enable this option and drop indexes during the import process.

▶ **Adjust requests timestamps to.** Turn on this option if you want all time stamps in log files to adjust to the time zone shown in the drop-down list. This is handy if you have Web sites in servers in multiple time zones.

▶ **Exclude spiders.** By selecting this option, you tell IIS to disregard hits from Internet search engines (which use spiders to search the Internet) and other agents shown on the Spider List tab.

▶ **Lookup unknown HTML file titles.** Performs HTML title lookups on HTML files added to the database during the log file import.

▶ **Resolve IP Addresses.** Resolves unresolved IP addresses found in log files during the import process.

▶ **Whois query for unknown domains.** Tells Usage Import to perform a Whois query for unknown organization names.

 Tip

On any of the Usage Import Options tabs, click the Save As Default Options button if you want your changes to be saved.

The IP Resolution tab (see Figure 6.25) includes the following options:

▶ **Cache IP resolutions for *n* days.** Enables you to set the number of days between IP lookups.

▶ **Timeout a resolution attempt after *n* seconds.** Enables you to set the number of seconds for Usage Import to attempt to resolve an IP address. After this time, Usage Import will stop attempting to resolve the IP address. Higher values mean better results, but will slow down the import process.

Figure 6.25

The IP Resolution tab.

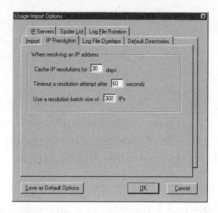

▶ **Use a resolution batch size of *n* IPs.** Specifies the batch size Usage Import uses for IP resolution.

 Tip

A large number setting in the Use a Resolution Batch Size of *n* IPs option may cause your DNS server to crash. Report Writer may also show a large number of unresolved addresses, which may not be correct.

The Log File Overlaps tab (see Figure 6.26) includes the following two options:

Figure 6.26

The Log File Overlaps tab.

▶ **To be considered an overlap, records must overlap by at least *n* minutes.** Sets the overlap period by the import module. Overlap periods are redundancies introduced in your log file database because of log files being accidentally reimported, resuming interrupted logging actions, concatenating two log files, and running logs on separate servers. If you specify shorter periods, overlaps may be reduced, but later analysis may be adversely affected.

▶ **If an overlap is detected.** Enables you to choose an action Usage Import should do when an overlap is detected. You can choose from these options: Import All Records, Stop the Import, Stop All Imports, and Discard Records and Proceed.

The Default Directories tab (see Figure 6.27) includes one option, the Log Files field. Use this field to specify the default directory for log files and import files.

Figure 6.27

The Default Directories tab.

The IP Servers tab (see Figure 6.28) includes these two options:

Figure 6.28

The IP Servers tab.

▶ **HTTP Proxy**. Import uses the proxy server host name (if specified) and port number for all HTML title lookups.

 Tip

For proxy servers that require usernames and passwords, use the syntax *username:password@hostname*.

▶ **Local domain of DNS server.** Clarifies hosts returned from IP resolutions. Enter your DNS server here, or, if an ISP maintains your DNS server, enter your ISP's setting here.

The Spider List tab (see Figure 6.29) includes common spider agents you want to exclude if the Exclude spiders option is selected on the Import tab. You can delete any agent here by selecting it and pressing Delete. Or you can add to the list by placing an asterisk (*) after the Freeloader item and then entering the word **and**, followed by the name of the agent. No spaces are allowed between words.

Figure 6.29

The Spider List tab.

Finally, the Log File Rotation tab (see Figure 6.30) includes the item At the end of an import. This option enables you to control the treatment of data that is cut off due to file rotation. This is data that is divided at the end of one file and begins again at the start of a new log. You can select from these options: commit open visits to database, discard open visits, and store open visits for next import.

Figure 6.30

The Log File Rotation tab.

Click OK on the Usage Import Options dialog box to close it and to use the settings you've configured.

The Report Writer Options

You can configure Report Writer options by opening Report Writer and selecting Tools | Options. The Report Writer Options dialog box displays (see Figure 6.31).

Figure 6.31

The Report Writer Options dialog box.

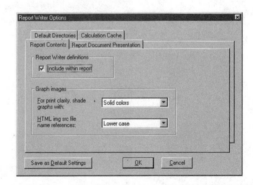

 Tip

On any of the Report Writer Options tabs, click the Save As Default Options button if you want your changes to be permanently saved.

On the Report Contents tab (refer to Figure 6.31), you can set the following options:

▶ **Include within report.** Use this option to have Report Writer include usage definitions at the bottom of every report. You may, after you become more familiar with Report Writer documents, want to disable this option so your reports don't have these definitions.

▶ **For print clarity, shade graphs with.** Use this option to specify Solid colors and Pattern lines for graph shading. For printed reports on noncolor printers, select the Pattern lines option.

▶ **HTML img src file name references.** Select which case to use when naming image and source files. For UNIX systems, use the correct case option for your system. In most situations, lowercase is the best choice.

On the Report Document Presentation tab (see Figure 6.32), you can set the following options on how the report is styled:

Figure 6.32

The Report Document Presentation tab.

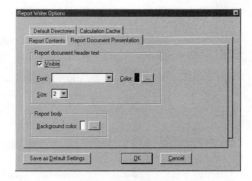

▶ **Visible.** Specify this option so Report Writer displays header information, including analysis time period, site analyzed, and report sections.

▶ **Font, Color, and Size options.** Use these options to specify the font, color, and size of the header information text.

▶ **Background color.** Click the ... button to display the Color dialog box in which to specify a background color for your report.

The Default Directories tab (see Figure 6.33) includes these two options:

Figure 6.33

*The Default
Directories tab.*

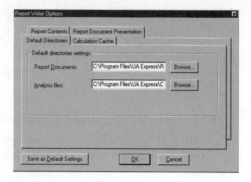

▶ **Report Documents.** Set the path for your completed reports in this field.

▶ **Analysis files.** Set the path for your completed analysis files in this field.

Finally, the Calculation Cache tab (see Figure 6.34) includes these options:

Figure 6.34

*The Calculations
Cache tab.*

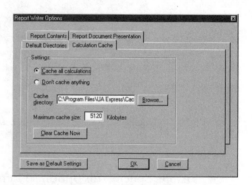

▶ **Cache all calculations.** Enables you to cache report calculations in the Cache folder for future use. By using cache calculations, you can speed up report generations.

▶ **Don't cache anything.** Turns off the calculation cache feature.

▶ **Cache directory.** Sets the directory in which calculations are cached.

> ▶ **Maximum cache size.** Sets the maximum amount of cached material the Cache directory can hold. This setting is in kilobytes.

> ▶ **Clear Cache Now.** Click this button when you want to clear the calculations cache.

Click OK in the Report Writer Options dialog box to close it and to use the settings you've configured.

Automating the Use of Report Writer and Usage Import

A handy feature of the Report Writer and Usage Import is the automation capability. Automating Report Writer and Usage Import is done by using the Scheduler tool. You can set up Scheduler so that a report is generated every day when you arrive at work or a report is created at the end of the week to be dispersed to your Internet site administration team.

When you use Scheduler, you create jobs that have tasks scheduled to begin at specific times and days. Tasks are simply activities, such as importing a log or creating a report. After you set up a job, Scheduler creates a batch file that will run to execute the specific tasks.

To create a new job in Usage Import, perform the following steps:

1. Open Usage Import and click on the Scheduler toolbar button (or select Tools|Scheduler). The Scheduler window displays (see Figure 6.35).

Figure 6.35

The Scheduler window.

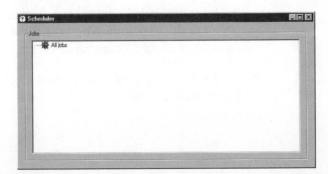

2. Double-click the All jobs item. The Job Properties dialog box displays (see Figure 6.36).

Figure 6.36

*The Job Proper-
ties dialog box.*

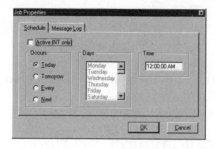

3. Click the Active (NT only) check box. If this is cleared, the Scheduler does not run the specified job. This is handy if you want to disable a specific job without deleting it entirely. This way you have the option of enabling it again without going through the process of setting up the job again.

4. In the Occurs area, select when you want the job to start.

5. If you chose Every or Next in the preceding step, select the day(s) you want the job to run in the Days area. Press Ctrl to select multiple days.

6. Enter the time you want the job to run in the Time field.

 Tip   Times are entered in 24-hour format, so 3:00 p.m. is denoted as 15:00 hours.

7. Click the Message Log tab (see Figure 6.37). You can save messages about the results of each task in a log file by entering the path and filename for the log file in the Message Log field. From the drop-down list, you can select variables to be added to the filename. When the file is created, the variables, such as *$d(23)*, are replaced by actual values.

8. Click OK to save your new job to the Scheduler window (see Figure 6.38).

Figure 6.37

The Message Log tab.

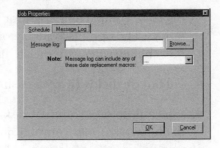

Figure 6.38

Your new job added to the Scheduler window.

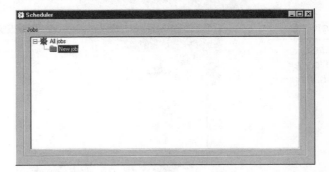

 Tip

You can click on the New job name twice (do not double-click it) to rename the job.

You now need to add tasks to your new job. Perform the following steps:

1. Right-click your new job and select New Task. The Task Properties dialog box displays (see Figure 6.39).

Figure 6.39

The Task Properties dialog box.

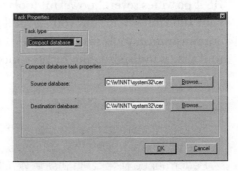

2. Select the type of task you want to add to your job by clicking on the Task type drop-down list. If you want to automate the

database compacting tasks, for instance, select Compact database. The options available on the Task Properties dialog box change when you pick a different task.

3. Fill out the fields (if any are shown) for the task you select.

4. Click OK to save your new task. The Scheduler window shows the new task under your new job (see Figure 6.40). Again, you can rename the new task by clicking on it twice.

Figure 6.40

A new task added to your new job.

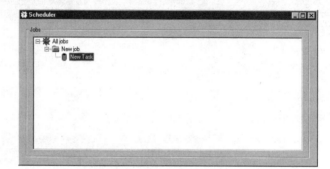

5. Continue adding tasks to your job by repeating steps 1–4.

6. When finished, close the Scheduler window and click Yes when prompted to start the job.

Monitoring Performance of Various Functions Using Performance Monitor

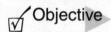 Objective ▶

IIS 4 provides several powerful tools to monitor and administer your Internet server, but you can still use common Windows NT administration tools to monitor IIS 4's performance. One such tool that is indispensable for IIS 4 monitoring is Performance Monitor.

 Note ▶

You should already be familiar with Performance Monitor before proceeding with this objective. You can learn more about Performance Monitor in *Inside Windows NT 4.0 Server*, New Riders Publishing.

With Performance Monitor you can monitor functions relating to HTTP and FTP sessions. Performance Monitor is used when you want to see trends and patterns in your site's usage. When you install IIS 4, new objects relating to Web and FTP services are added to Performance Monitor along with specific counters for those services. Objects are individual occurrences of a system resource, such as Web Service, FTP Service, Active Server Pages, Browser, and other items. Counters, on the other hand, are statistics relating to the objects, such as Debugging Requests, Memory Allocated, and Request Wait Time (all of which relate to the Active Server Pages object).

Performance Monitor can be started from the Administrative Tools (Common) folder. To specify the object and counter(s) you want to track, select Edit | Add to Chart. The Add to Chart dialog box displays (see Figure 6.41).

Figure 6.41

Add objects and counters to Performance Monitor from the Add to Chart dialog box.

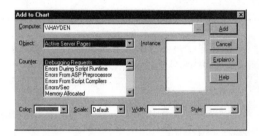

The Performance Monitor screen shown in Figure 6.42 is monitoring functions relating to Web and FTP service. The following objects and counters are used:

▶ Web Services object with Anonymous User/sec, Bytes Sent/sec, and Maximum NonAnonymous Users counters selected

▶ FTP Server object with Bytes Total/sec, Current Anonymous Users, and Maximum Connections counters selected

Table 6.2 lists the objects and counters available in Performance Monitor to help you monitor IIS 4.

Figure 6.42

An example of monitoring Web and FTP services in Performance Monitor.

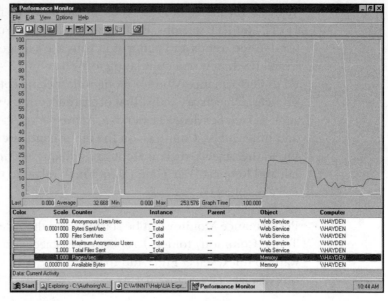

Table 6.2

IIS 4-related objects and counters in Performance Monitor.

Object	Counter
Active Server Pages	Debugging Requests
	Errors During Script Runtime
	Errors From ASP Preprocessor
	Errors From Script Compilers
	Errors/Sec
	Memory Allocated
	Request Bytes In Total
	Request Bytes Out Total
	Request Execution Time
	Request Wait Time
	Requests Disconnected
	Requests Executing
	Requests Failed Total

Object	Counter
	Requests Not Authorized
	Requests Not Found
	Requests Queued
	Requests Rejected
	Requests Succeeded
	Requests Timed Out
	Requests Total
	Requests/Sec
	Script Engines Cached
	Session Duration
	Sessions Current
	Sessions Timed Out
	Sessions Total
	Template Cache Hit Rate
	Template Notifications
	Templates Cached
	Transactions Aborted
	Transactions Committed
	Transactions Pending
	Transactions Total
	Transactions/Sec
FTP Service	Bytes Received/Sec
	Bytes Sent/Sec
	Bytes Total/Sec
	Current Anonymous Users
	Current Connections
	Current NonAnonymous Users
	Maximum Anonymous Users

continues

Table 6.2 Continued

Object	Counter
	Total Anonymous Users
	Total Connection Attempts
	Total Files Received
	Total Files Sent
	Total Files Transferred
	Total Logon Attempts
	Total NonAnonymous Users
Internet Information Services Global	Cache Flushes
	Cache Hits
	Cache Hits %
	Cache Misses
	Cached File Handles
	Current Blocked Async I/O Requests
	Directory Listings
	Measured Async I/O Bandwidth Usage
	Objects
	Total Allowed Async I/O Requests
	Total Blocked Async I/O Requests
	Total Rejected Async I/O Requests
NNTP Server	Article Map Entries
	Article Map Entries/Sec
	Articles Deleted
	Articles Deleted/Sec
	Articles Posted
	Articles Posted/Sec
	Articles Received
	Articles Received/Sec

Object	Counter
	Articles Sent
	Articles Sent/Sec
	Articles Total
	Bytes Received/Sec
	Bytes Sent/Sec
	Bytes Total/Sec
	Control Messages Failed
	Control Messages Received
	Current Anonymous Users
	Current Connections
	Current NonAnonymous Users
	Current Outbound Connections
	Failed Outbound Logons
	History Map Entries
	History Map Entries/Sec
	Maximum Anonymous Users
	Maximum Connections
	Maximum NonAnonymous Users
	Moderated Postings Failed
	Moderated Postings Sent
	Sessions Flow Controlled
	Total Anonymous Users
	Total Connections
	Total NonAnonymous Users
	Total Outbound Connections
	Total Outbound Connections Failed
	Total Passive Feeds
	Total Pull Feeds

continues

Table 6.2 Continued

Object	Counter
	Total Push Feeds
	Total SSL Connections
	Xover Entries
	Xover Entries/Sec
SMTP Server	% Recipients Local
	% Recipients Remote
	Avg Recipients/Msg Received
	Avg Recipients/Msg Sent
	Avg Retries/Msg Delivered
	Avg Retries/Msg Sent
	Bytes Received Total
	Bytes Received/Sec
	Bytes Sent Total
	Bytes Sent/Sec
	Bytes Total
	Bytes Total/Sec
	Connection Errors/Sec
	Directory Drops Total
	Directory Drops/Sec
	Directory Pickup Queue Length
	DNS Queries Total
	DNS Queries/Sec
	ETRN Messages Total
	ETRN Messages/Sec
	Inbound Connections Current
	Inbound Connections Total
	Local Queue Length
	Local Retry Queue Length

Object	Counter
	Message Bytes Received Total
	Message Bytes Received/Sec
	Message Bytes Sent Total
	Message Bytes Sent/Sec
Message Bytes Total	Message Bytes Total/Sec
	Message Delivery Retries
	Message Received/Sec
	Message Send Retries
	Messages Delivered Total
	Messages Delivered/Sec
	Messages Received Total
	Messages Refused for Address Objects
	Messages Refused for Mail Objects
	Messages Refused For Size
	Messages Retrieved Total
	Messages Retrieved/Sec
	Messages Sent Total
	Messages Sent/Sec
	NDRs Generated
	Number of MailFiles Open
	Number of QueueFiles Open
	Outbound Connections Current
	Outbound Connections Refused
	Outbound Connections Total
	Remote Queue Length
	Remote Retry Queue Length
	Routing Table Lookups Total
	Routing Table Lookups/Sec
	Total Connection Errors

continues

Table 6.2   Continued

Object	Counter
Web Service	Anonymous Users/Sec
	Bytes Received/Sec
	Bytes Sent/Sec
	Bytes Total/Sec
	CGI Requests/Sec
	Connection Attempts/Sec
	Current Anonymous Users
	Current Blocked Asyn I/O Requests
	Current CGI Requests
	Current Connections
	Current ISAPI Extension Requests
	Current NonAnonymous Users
	Delete Requests/Sec
	Files Received/Sec
	Files Sent/Sec
	Files/Sec
	Get Requests/Sec
	Head Requests/Sec
	ISAPI Extension Requests/Sec
	Logon Attempts/Sec
	Maximum Anonymous Users
	Maximum CGI Requests
	Maximum Connections
	Maximum ISAPI Extension Requests
	Maximum NonAnonymous Users
	Measured Async I/O Bandwidth Usage
	NonAnonymous Users/Sec

Object	Counter
	Not Found Errors/Sec
	Other Request Methods/Sec
	Post Requests/Sec
	Put Requests/Sec
	System Code Resident Bytes
	Total Allowed Async I/O Requests
	Total Anonymous Users
	Total Blocked Async I/O Requests
	Total CGI Requests
	Total Connection Attempts
	Total Delete Requests
	Total Files Received
	Total Files Sent
	Total Files Transferred
	Total Get Requests
	Total Head Requests
	Total ISAPI Extension Requests
	Total Logon Attempts
	Total Method Requests
	Total Method Requests/Sec
	Total NonAnonymous Users
	Total Not Found Errors
	Total Other Request Methods
	Total Post Requests
	Total Put Requests
	Total Rejected Async I/O Requests
	Total Trace Requests

Analyzing Performance

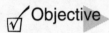 As the IIS 4 administrator, you are responsible for analyzing the performance of the Internet site. But you also need to pay close attention to other server performance issues. These performance issues include the following:

▶ Identifying Bottlenecks

▶ Identifying Network-Related Performance Issues

▶ Identifying Disk-Related Performance Issues

▶ Identifying CPU-Related Performance Issues

Identifying Bottlenecks

Bottlenecks occur when one (or several) hardware resources is being used too much, sometimes resulting in the draining of another hardware resource. The result is a performance reduction over the entire network. A bottleneck may occur as a result of insufficient server memory or because of too little bandwidth available to the connected users. A bottleneck is the largest source of delay that can be reduced. You need to know how to recognize bottlenecks on your system before you can even attempt to remedy them.

Finding a bottleneck can be a slow and arduous task at times. You must don your "detective" hat when looking for the combination of hardware and software that is creating the bottleneck. Start looking for bottlenecks by running Performance Monitor to create a baseline of activities for your site.

You also can use Event Viewer to record events and audit situations on your computer that may require your attention. Another useful tool to use to locate bottlenecks is the Task Manager. Task Manager shows you all the ongoing tasks and threads on your computer.

One performance bottleneck you should be aware of is logging to a database. As IIS 4 logs activities to a database, an ODBC connection must be established. This connection process may take a relatively long time, causing a performance bottleneck to occur. If you cannot speed up the ODBC connection time, consider switching to file-based logging. File-based logging is faster than database logging.

The following sections explore some common bottlenecks that you should become familiar with when administering IIS 4.

Identifying Network-Related Performance Issues

Because IIS 4 may reside on your local area network server, you should become aware of some of the network-related performance issues that can affect the performance of your Internet site.

According to Microsoft, for medium-to-very-busy sites, you can expect IIS to saturate a 10Mbps ethernet network adapter. If this happens, it will certainly cause bottlenecks to occur that are network-related. However, it is almost impossible for a Web server to saturate a 10Mbps ethernet adapter. It *could* saturate a 56KB link or a T1. Remember that a T1 line provides 15 percent of the speed of an ethernet connection. To check for network saturation, check for CPU % Utilization on both the client and server. To prevent the server from becoming network-bound, increase network bandwidth to the server by using one of the following solutions:

▶ Use multiple 10MB Ethernet cards

▶ Install a 100MB Ethernet or FDDI network card

Identifying Disk-Related Performance Issues

You may encounter hard disk bottlenecks if you have a very large file set, such as an application in the range of 5MB or larger, that is being accessed by clients in a random pattern. To identify a bottleneck of this sort, perform the following steps:

1. Start Performance Monitor.

2. Select Edit | Add To Chart.

3. From the Add to Chart dialog box (see Figure 6.43), select the PhysicalDisk item from the Object drop-down list object.

Figure 6.43

Select the PhysicalDisk object and % Disk Time counter from the Add to Chart dialog box.

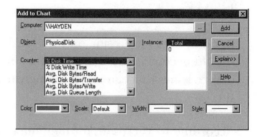

4. From the Counter list, select % Disk Time.

5. Click Add.

6. Click Done.

The % Disk Time counter shows the percentage of elapsed time the disk is busy servicing read or write requests. If there is a bottleneck involving disk access, the PhysicalDisk % Disk Time counter will be high, because the percentage of the CPU utilization will remain low and the network card will not be saturated.

When you notice a disk-related bottleneck, you can improve performance in a few ways. The best answer to a disk bottleneck is striping or mirroring. You also can use a redundant array of inexpensive drives (RAID).

Identifying CPU-Related Performance Issues

You can identify CPU bottlenecks by measuring the amount of the server CPU that is being utilized. Perform the following steps to measure this value:

1. Start Performance Monitor.

2. Select Edit | Add To Chart.

3. From the Add To Chart dialog box, select the Processor item from the Object drop-down list object.

4. From the Counter list, select % Processor Time.

5. From the Instance list, select the number of instances you want to view.

6. Click Add.

7. Click Done.

You'll notice CPU bottlenecks if you notice very high CPU % Processor Time numbers while the network card remains well below capacity. If the CPU % Processor Time value is high, try the following remedies:

▶ Upgrade the CPU to a faster one.

▶ Add additional CPUs to your server.

▶ Move other applications (such as database applications) you run on the Web server to another computer.

▶ Add more computers on which you replicate your site and then distribute traffic across them.

Optimizing the Performance of IIS

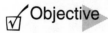

One of the greatest improvements to IIS 4 is the inclusion of the Microsoft Management Console (MMC) to help you manage and administer IIS. With MMC, you can make global performance changes (such as limiting bandwidth usage), set service master properties, and configure other IIS properties to help optimize its performance.

To change global performance properties under IIS, perform the following steps:

1. Open Internet Service Manager in MMC.

2. Right-click the server you want to modify.

3. Select Properties to display the Server Properties dialog box for that server (see Figure 6.44).

Figure 6.44

The Server Properties dialog box.

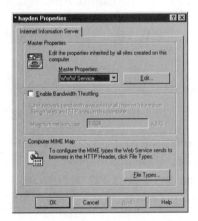

4. Click the Performance tab, then the Enable Bandwidth Throttling option to control the amount of bandwidth consumption by all IIS services. You may want to do this if your network card is set up to handle multiple services, such as email and Web services. In the Maximum network use field, enter a bandwidth value in KB/S (kilobytes/second).

 Tip

To get a bandwidth value for your server, begin with a value that is 50 percent of your connection bandwidth. You can then increase or decrease this value to tweak your system requirements.

5. Click the Master Properties drop-down list. This displays the services (WWW and/or FTP) you have installed and those for which you can customize default master properties. Master properties are standard settings for all the Web sites or FTP sites hosted on your server. After you set master properties for all your sites, you can still modify settings for individual sites. Master Properties provides you with an easy and quick way to set common parameters for all your sites.

6. Select the service you want to modify.

7. Click Edit. The Service Master Properties dialog box for your site displays (see Figure 6.45).

Figure 6.45

The Service Master Properties dialog box.

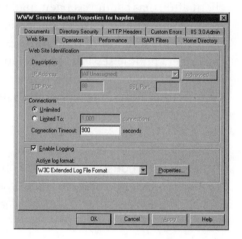

From this dialog box you can set the following performance parameters:

▶ Connections

▶ Performance Tuning

▶ Enable Bandwidth Throttling

▶ HTTP Keep-Alives

These parameters are discussed in more detail in the following sections.

Connections

You find the Connections area on the Web Site tab of the Service Master Properties dialog box. This area includes the Unlimited and Limited To options that control the number of simultaneous connections your Web or FTP sites allow. Click the Limited To option to specify the number of simultaneous connections to your sites. Then enter a value in the connection field (the default is 1,000). If you do not want to limit the number of connections, select the Unlimited option (which is the default setting).

You also can set the timeout value for each inactive connection. This value is set in seconds and will automatically disconnect a client after that client has been inactive on your site for the set number of seconds. In the Connection Timeout field, enter a value for the amount of time your server should automatically disconnect an idle session. The default is 15 minutes (900 seconds), but an average setting is five minutes (300 seconds). For an infinite amount of time, enter all 9s in this field.

Note

Even if a connection is lost or a browser stops working, your site will continue to process data until the timeout value is reached. Setting an appropriate timeout value will limit the loss of resources due to these lost connections.

Performance Tuning

The Performance tab (see Figure 6.46) on the Service Master Properties dialog box includes the Performance Tuning option. This option is set to the estimated number of connections you anticipate for your site. Move the slider to the appropriate value. If you anticipate fewer than 10,000 visitors each day, move the slider to the far left; for a site with fewer than 100,000 visitors, keep the slider in the middle; and for a busy site that has over 100,000 visitors, move the slider to the far right.

Figure 6.46

The Performance tab on the Service Master Properties dialog box.

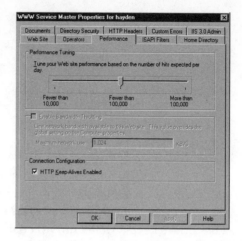

When you move the slider to a setting, IIS 4 alters the resources allocated to the service. Settings that are higher than the actual number of connections will result in faster connections and will improve Web server performance. This is because more resources are allocated to fewer connections. On the other hand, if you set the Performance Tuning slider to a number that is much higher than the actual number of connections, you will notice a decrease in overall server performance, because server memory is being wasted (basically it is not being utilized). This setting will devote more resources to your Web service and fewer resources to other server applications. You should compare your daily hit logs with the Performance Tuning setting to ensure this setting closely matches the actual connections to your site.

Enable Bandwidth Throttling

Another performance option you can set is also on thePerformance tab. The Enable Bandwidth Throttling option, which you were shown how to set at the server level in the "Optimizing the Performance of IIS" section, sets the global bandwidth used by your Web site.

Click the Enable Bandwidth Throttling option and set a bandwidth setting based on kilobytes per second (KB/S).

Note The value you set on the Performance tab overrides settings for bandwidth throttling set on the Computer Properties sheet. This is true even if the value on the Performance tab is set higher than that on the Computer Properties sheet.

HTTP Keep-Alives

The final performance optimization setting you can modify on the Performance tab is the Connection Configuration option. This includes the HTTP Keep-Alives Enable option. You can enable IIS 4's keep-alive feature to enable clients to maintain open connections. This way a client does not need to re-establish connections for each request, such as for each request for an image, document, or other resource. By enabling keep-alive, you not only decrease the amount of time a client waits to connect to another document or application on your site, but also increase the amount of resources devoted to this client.

Click the HTTP Keep-Alives Enabled option to turn on this feature to ensure that clients with slower connections are not prematurely closed. You should enable this feature for better server performance so that repeated requests from an individual client are not necessary when a page containing multiple elements is accessed.

Inheritance Overrides

If you make any changes to the Service Master Properties options, you also affect all individual sites under that service. When you click OK to save settings on the Service Master Properties dialog box (see Figure 6.47), the Inheritance Overrides dialog box will appear if a value you've changed will be overridden based on values of an individual site, or *child node*.

Select the child node(s) from the Descendants with overridden defaults for the current property that you want to change to match the new value you set on the Service Master Properties dialog box. Click OK.

Figure 6.47

*The Inheritance
Overrides dialog
box.*

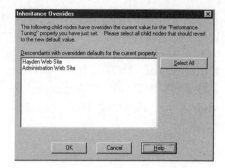

Optimizing the Performance of Index Server

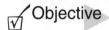 Objective ▶ Microsoft Index Server is used to index the contents and properties of Internet or intranet documents stored on an IIS server. You are shown how to install Index Server in earlier chapters, but one way to optimize its performance is to run it on a system with an optimum configuration. By and large, the basic Windows NT Server configuration provides adequate Index Server performance. This situation is probably best suited, however, for a small organization or an Internet site that does not expect a large amount of daily traffic.

To optimize the performance of Index Server, you should start by looking at the configuration of the computer on which it resides. The following are the factors that you need to measure to set this configuration:

▶ Number of documents in the corpus, which is the collection of documents and HTML pages indexed by Index Server

▶ Corpus size

▶ Rate of search requests

▶ Kind of queries

You'll find that the amount of memory you have installed will greatly affect the performance of Index Server. For sites that have fewer than 100,000 documents stored in the corpus, a minimum of 32MB is required and recommended. However, if you have

100,000 to 250,000 documents, the recommended amount of memory jumps to 64–128MB, whereas the minimum required still is 32MB. For sites with 250,000 to 500,000 documents, you need a minimum of 64MB of RAM, but it is recommended that you have 128–256MB. Finally, if you have over 500,000 documents, you must have 128MB of RAM installed, but at least 256MB is recommended.

Note

Keep in mind that complex search queries will run faster when Index Server is installed on a computer with a faster CPU. Also, a faster CPU and additional memory will improve indexing performance.

Another system configuration setting you should pay attention to is the amount of free hard disk space where the Index Server catalog is stored. If less than 3MB of free space is available on the index disk, indexing and filtering are temporarily paused until additional disk space is made available. The event log records a message that `Very low disk space was detected on drive` *drive*. `Please free up at least` *number*`MB of space for content index to continue.`

Tip

The minimum amount of disk space should be at least 30 percent of the corpus. However, during a master merge (which deletes redundant data and enables queries to run faster), you may need up to 45 percent of the corpus.

Optimizing the Performance of Microsoft SMTP Service

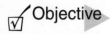

Objective

The Microsoft SMTP service enables IIS 4 to deliver messages over the Internet. Microsoft SMTP supports basic SMTP (Simple Mail Transfer Protocol) delivery functions and is compatible with SMTP mail clients.

When you install IIS 4, you also can install Microsoft SMTP. The default settings for Microsoft SMTP can be used, but you also can customize your SMTP Service to optimize it for your system. The following are some of the ways you can optimize Microsoft SMTP:

▶ Set connection limits

▶ Set message limits

▶ Specify a smart host

Setting Connection Limits

You can set the number of simultaneous connections for incoming and outgoing connections. To set this number, open Microsoft Manager Console (MMC), right-click on the SMTP site you want to modify, and select Properties. The SMTP Site Properties dialog box displays (see Figure 6.48).

Figure 6.48

The SMTP Site Properties dialog box.

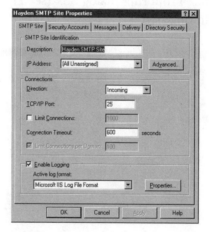

On the SMTP Site tab, perform the following steps to set the connection limit:

1. Click the Limit Connections option.

2. In the Limit Connections option field, enter the number of simultaneous connections for your SMTP Service. For incoming messages, the default is 1,000 and the minimum is 1. For outgoing messages, the default is 500 and the minimum is 1. *Outgoing messages* refers to the number of concurrent outbound connections to all remote domains.

3. In the Connection Timeout field, enter the period of time an inactive connection is disconnected. The default is 600 seconds for both incoming and outgoing messages.

4. In the Limit Connections per Domain field, enter the number of outgoing connections to a single remote domain. This option is available only with outgoing connections. The default is 100 connections and should be less than or equal to the value set in the Limit Connections field.

5. Click Apply.

Message Limits

You can set limits on the size and number of messages each connection can have. To do this, click the Messages tab of the SMTP Site Properties dialog box (see Figure 6.49) and perform the following steps:

Figure 6.49

The Messages tab of the SMTP Site Properties dialog box.

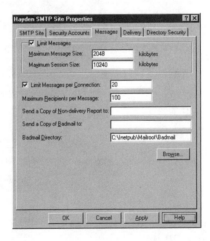

1. Click the Limit Messages option.

2. In the Maximum Message Size field, enter the value for the maximum size of a message (in kilobytes). The minimum size is 1KB; the default is 2048KB (2MB).

Note

If a single message exceeds the Maximum Message Size, it can still be processed by SMTP Server if it does not exceed the Maximum Session Size.

3. In the Maximum Session Size field, enter the value for the maximum size of a message before the connection will be closed. Set this value to the same or higher than the Maximum Message Size. The default is 10MB.

4. Click the Limit Messages per Connections option to specify the number of messages that can be sent in one connection. You can use this value to increase system performance by enabling SMTP Server to use multiple connections to deliver messages to a remote domain. When the limit is reached, a new connection is opened and the transmission continues until all messages are delivered.

Tip

To determine a value for the Limit Messages per Connections option limit, run Performance Monitor and select the SMTP Server object. In the Counter list, select Messages Sent/Sec. The Limit Messages per Connection value should be less than the value indicated by the performance counter.

5. Click Apply.

Specifying a Smart Host

Instead of sending all outgoing messages directly to a remote domain, you can route all messages through a smart host. A smart host enables you to route messages over a more direct or less costly connection than other routes.

Note

Smart hosts are similar to the route domain option for remote domains. With a remote domain, however, only messages for that remote domain are routed to a specific server. On the

continues

other hand, with smart hosts, all outgoing messages are routed to that server. If you set up a smart host, you can still designate a different route for a remote domain. The route domain setting overrides the smart host setting.

To set up a smart host, do the following:

1. Select the Delivery tab (see Figure 6.50) on the SMTP Site Properties dialog box.

Figure 6.50

The Delivery tab on the SMTP Site Properties dialog box.

2. In the Smart Host field, enter the name of the smart host server. You can enter a string or enter an IP address in this field. To increase system performance when using an IP address here, enclose the address in brackets. Microsoft SMTP will then look at the IP address as an actual IP address without looking at it as a string value first.

3. Select the Attempt Direct Delivery Before Sending to Smart Host option. This option is used if you want SMTP Service to attempt to deliver remote messages locally before forwarding them to the smart host server. The default is to send all remote messages to the smart host, not to attempt direct delivery.

4. Click OK.

Optimizing the Performance of Microsoft NNTP Service

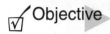
Objective ▶

The Microsoft NNTP Service is used to let users exchange communications via the Internet Network News Transport Protocol (NNTP). Users can post and view articles, much like they can when attached to the Usenet news service available on the Internet.

Similarly to the Microsoft SMTP Server, you can run Microsoft NNTP Service without modifying its default settings. However, you may want to tweak some of its properties to get better performance out of it. Two optimization tasks you can perform are changing connection settings and modifying client postings.

Changing Connection Settings

You can limit the number of simultaneous news client connections to a virtual server. You can set a value up to 2 billion, in other words, a relatively unlimited number of connections. To do this, open the Microsoft Management Console and right-click on the NNTP Site you want to modify. Select Properties to display the NNTP Site Properties dialog box (see Figure 6.51).

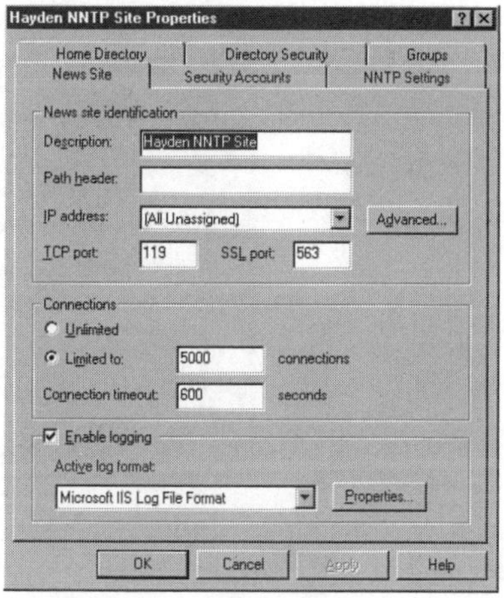

Figure 6.51

The NNTP Site Properties dialog box.

Hayden NNTP Site Properties	? X

| Home Directory | Directory Security | Groups |
| News Site | Security Accounts | NNTP Settings |

News site identification

Description: Hayden NNTP Site

Path header:

IP address: [All Unassigned] ▼ Advanced...

TCP port: 119   SSL port: 563

Connections

○ Unlimited

◉ Limited to: 5000   connections

Connection timeout: 600   seconds

☑ Enable logging

Active log format:

Microsoft IIS Log File Format ▼ Properties...

| OK | Cancel | Apply | Help |

On the News Site tab, perform the following steps:

1. Click the Unlimited option if you want to specify that there is no limit to the number of simultaneous connections.

2. Click the Limited to option and fill in the connections field with the number of simultaneous connections you want to limit NNTP to handling. The default is 5,000. Increase or decrease this value depending on your server size and needs.

3. In the Connection timeout field, enter a value for NNTP Server to automatically disconnect inactive clients. The default is 600 seconds.

4. Click Apply.

Modifying Client Postings

The NNTP Settings tab (see Figure 6.52) includes options for modifying client posting parameters. This tab enables you to set the maximum size of news articles posted to your NNTP Server.

Figure 6.52

The NNTP Settings tab.

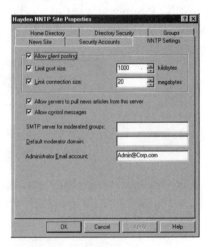

To modify client postings, perform the following steps:

1. Select the Limit post size option.

2. Enter a value to indicate the maximum size of a news article that a client can post to your NNTP Server. The default is 1,000KB. However, you may want to decrease this value if you want your news server to be set up to handle smaller articles. Increase this value, on the other hand, to allow larger articles to be posted. If an article exceeds this value, it still will be posted if the article does not surpass the Limit connection size value.

3. Click the Limit connection size option.

4. Enter a value to indicate the maximum size for articles that a news client can post to your news server. The default is 20MB.

5. Click OK.

Interpreting Performance Data

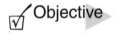 Objective   There are two tools primarily used for monitoring TCP/IP traffic, and these are the primary tools for gathering data for interpretation:

▶ Performance Monitor

▶ Network Monitor

Performance Monitor

The Performance Monitoris Windows NT's all-around tool for monitoring a network using statistical measurements called counters. It has the capability of collecting data on both hardware and software components, called objects, and its primary purpose is to establish a baseline from which everything can be judged. It offers the ability to check/monitor/identify the following:

▶ The demand for resources

▶ Bottlenecks in performance

▶ The behavior of individual processes

▶ The performance of remote systems

It also can

▶ Generate alerts to exception conditions

▶ Export data for analysis

Every object has a number of counters, and you should be familiar with those for the Paging File object - %Usage and %Usage Peak, which will tell whether a paging file is reaching its maximum size.

To get numerical statistics, use the Report (columnar) view. To see how counters change over a period of time, use the log feature. To spot abnormalities that occur in data over a period of time, use the Chart view.

To monitor a number of servers and be alerted if a counter exceeds a specified number, create one Performance Monitor alert for each server on your workstation. Enter your username in the Net Name on the Alert Options dialog box (below Send Network Message tab), and you will be alerted when the alert conditions arise. Only one name can be placed here, and the name can be that of a user or group, but not multiple users or groups.

If you are monitoring a number of performance counters and that monitoring is slowing down other operations on your workstation, the best remedy is to increase the monitoring interval.

To tune or optimize Windows NT, you need to be able to look at the performance of the server on many different levels.

Note

Two important pieces of information to remember: You *must* install the Network Monitor Agent to be able to see several of the network performance counters, and SNMP service *must* be installed in order to gather TCP/IP statistics.

Network Monitor

Network Monitor is a Windows tool that enables you to see network traffic that is sent or received by a Windows NT computer.
Network Monitor is included with Windows NT 4.0, but it must be
installed to be active.

To install Network Monitor, open Control Panel|Network and
then add the Network Monitor Tools and Agent from the Services
tab. The version of Network Monitor that comes with Windows
NT 4.0 is a simple version; it captures traffic only for the local
machines (incoming and outgoing traffic).

Microsoft's System Management Server, a network management
product, comes with a more complete version of Network Monitor
that enables you to capture packets on the local machine for the
entire local network segment. Both versions enable you to capture
the packets that are flowing in and out of your computer. The Full
version that comes with SMS also gives you extra functionality,
such as the ability to capture all packets on the local network or
on remote networks, edit those packets, and derive statistics about
protocols and users on the network.

There are two pieces to the Network Monitor. The Agent captures the data. The Monitor Tool can be used to view the data.
You also can filter out traffic that isn't important to the troubleshooting process.

The Network Monitor can be used to diagnose more complex
issues with connectivity by enabling you to see the actual packets
that are flowing on the network, verifying which steps are being
used to resolve names or which port numbers are being used to
connect.

Note

As with ISAPI, filters enable you to limit what you are viewing
and keep the data from being overwhelming. The most commonly used filters are INCLUDE and EXCLUDE, which capture, or
avoid capturing, specific data. The Network Monitor included

continues

with Windows NT Server can monitor only the specific system on which it is installed, unlike the Network Monitor in SMS, which can monitor other systems on the network.

Optimizing a Web Site Using Content Analyzer

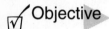 Objective ▶

The Site Server Express Analysis Content Analyzer (Content Analyzer for short) enables you to create WebMaps to give you a view of your Web site, helping you manage your Web site. WebMaps are graphical representations of resources on your site. These resources can include HTML documents, audio and video files, Java applets, FTP resources, and applications. Content Analyzer also enables you to manage your links. You can ensure that links are included in the resources and that they all work correctly.

You can use Content Analyzer to optimize your Web site. Here are some of the ways you can do this:

- ▶ Import usage data to review how users are using your site (see Figure 6.53). Important data you can view here includes how many hits a page receives, which pages are being hit the most, and from which URLs those hits are coming.

- ▶ Export the Tree view of your site's WebMap to be an HTML index or table of contents for your site. You also can use the index report from the Content Analyzer site report to serve as an HTML index of your site's contents.

- ▶ Assign helper applications to file types to edit source files. From Content Analyzer you can set helper applications to create and view site resources. This enables you quickly to check a broken link and fix it in an HTML editor, such as Microsoft FrontPage.

- ▶ View resource properties from within Content Analyzer. You can view name, size, load size, modification date, URL, MIME type, HTTP status, and other properties.

Figure 6.53

Content Analyzer provides a report of your site.

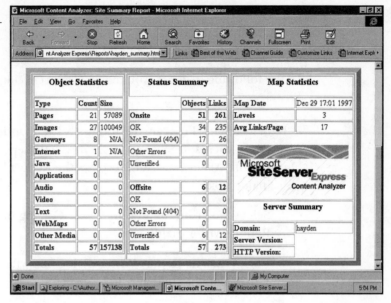

▶ View a resource's links in Content Analyzer. When viewing links within a resource, you can see the hyperlink text, MIME type, size, order, HTTP status, number of links, location of the linked document, hits, and other link information. Use this information to fine-tune or fix link-related problems in your documents.

▶ Verify onsite and offsite links. Links that are unavailable are shown in red. These links may be broken, or an offsite link may not have been available when you attempted to verify it.

 Note

This chapter does not teach you how to use Content Analyzer. For information on Content Analyzer, read the *Content Analyzer User's Guide*.

Exercises

In the following exercise, you make a report of a log file in Report Writer:

1. Select Start | Programs | Windows NT 4.0 Option Pack | Microsoft Site Server Express 2.0 | Report Writer. Report Writer starts and displays the Report Writer opening dialog box.

2. Select the From the Report Writer Catalog option on the Report Writer dialog box.

3. Click OK. The Report Writer dialog box with the Report Writer Catalog field appears.

4. Select the plus sign next to Detail Reports.

5. Click Hits detail report.

6. Click Next. The Report Writer dialog box displays. Set the date range of the data to analyze for a one-month time period.

7. Click Next. The Report Writer dialog box displays.

8. Click Finish. The Detail window for the report you want to generate displays.

9. Click the Create Report Document toolbar button on the Report Writer toolbar. The Report Document dialog box displays.

10. Enter a filename and keep the default report format of HTML.

11. Click OK. The report document is created.

The following exercise shows how to configure the logging features of the FTP service in IIS 4:

1. Select Start | Programs | Windows NT 4.0 Option Pack | Microsoft Internet Information Server | Internet Service Manager. Internet Service Manager opens in the MMC.

2. Right-click the FTP site you want to configure.

3. Click Properties. The FTP Site Properties dialog box displays.

4. Click the Enable Logging option.

5. Click the Active Log Format drop-down list and select the type of log format you want to create. The following steps show how to configure the W3C.

7. In the New Log Time Period section, set when you want IIS to create a new log file for the selected FTP site.

8. Enter the directory in which you want to store the log file. The default is %WinDir\System32\LogFiles.

9. Click the Extended Properties tab to display the logging options you can set (this tab is available only when you select the W3C Extended Log File Format option). On this tab, you can set the options described earlier in Table 6.1.

10. Click OK to close the Extended Logging Properties dialog box.

11. Click OK to close the FTP Site Properties dialog box.

Exercise 6.3: Creating Automatic Jobs in Usage Import

The following exercise shows how create a new job in Usage Import:

1. Open Usage Import and click on the Scheduler toolbar button. The Scheduler window displays.

2. Double-click on the All Jobs item. The Job Properties dialog box displays.

3. Click the Active (NT Only) check box. If this is cleared, the Scheduler does not run the specified job.

4. In the Occurs area, select when you want the job to start.

5. If you chose Every or Next in the preceding step, select the day(s) you want the job to run in the Days area. Press Ctrl to select multiple days.

6. Enter the time you want the job to run in the Time field.

7. Click the Message Log tab. You can save messages about the results of each task in a log file by entering the path and filename for the log file in the Message Log field. From the drop-down list, you can select variables to be added to the filename. When the file is created, the variables, such as *$d(23)*, are replaced by actual values.

8. Click OK to save your new job to the Scheduler window.

Review Questions

1. You administer an Internet site with IIS 4's Web and FTP service running. You have Microsoft Index Server installed and have a corpus with over 500,000 documents stored. What is the recommended amount of RAM your server should have?

   A. 32MB

   B. 64MB

   C. 128MB

   D. 256MB

2. On the same Index Server computer as discussed in Question 1, what is the minimum amount of RAM you need?

   A. 32MB

   B. 64MB

   C. 128MB

   D. 256MB

3. You are an IIS 4 consultant. Your client runs IIS 4 and needs a weekly report summarizing the number of users who access its site and the number of hits every hour. What tool should you use to generate this report?

   A. Microsoft Excel

   B. Microsoft Site Server Express Analysis—Report Writer

   C. Microsoft Site Server Express Analysis—Usage Import

   D. Crystal Reports

4. When setting up IIS 4 logging, you want to customize the type of data that is logged. Which logging option should you choose?

   A. NCSA Common Log File Format

   B. W3C Extended Log File Format

    C. ODBC Logging

    D. SQL Logging

5. IIS 4 is installed on a server with all IIS 4's default settings used. When you examine the Web Site tab on the Service Master Properties dialog box, what is the number of maximum connections listed in the Limited To field under the Connections area?

    A. 0

    B. 500

    C. 1000

    D. 100

6. The IIS 4 Web site you administer does not receive a large number of hits each day, but the server's performance is sluggish. Which one of the following statements is true?

    A. The Performance Tuning slider setting on the WWW Service Master Properties Performance tab is too high.

    B. The Performance Tuning slider setting on the WWW Service Master Properties Performance tab is too low.

    C. The site could be operating at a TCP port other than the default.

    D. You are probably using IDE drives rather than SCSI.

7. The IIS 4 server you manage performs slowly and has numerous hits reported for every client that connects to your site. Which one of the following may need to be enabled to alleviate this problem?

    A. Enable Bandwidth Throttling

    B. Enable Logging

    C. Connection Timeout

    D. HTTP Keep-Alives Enabled

8. To optimize the performance of your FTP site, you can set which of the following option(s) that you can also set for your Web site?

   A. Connection Timeout

   B. Enable Bandwidth Throttling

   C. Connection Limited To Value

   D. Home Directory Redirection to URL

9. Your company has IIS 4 installed with the Microsoft SMTP and Microsoft NNTP Services running. What is the default maximum size of news articles that can be posted to a Microsoft NNTP Service news server?

   A. Unlimited

   B. 2MB

   C. 1000KB

   D. 512KB

10. You run Performance Monitor periodically to check your IIS 4's performance. Which of the following counters is not a valid item under the Internet Information Services Global object?

   A. Current Blocked Async I/O Requests

   B. File Listings

   C. Measured Async I/O Bandwidth Usage

   D. Objects

11. You are an IIS 4 consultant. A client calls to report that Microsoft Index Server has stopped running, and a message says that there is not enough free disk space available. From the following choices, you know what about the amount of disk space at this point?

   A. The free disk space has dropped to 100MB.

   B. The free disk space has dropped to 3MB.

C. The free disk space is not 20 percent of the corpus.

D. The free disk space is not 50 percent of the corpus.

12. When installing Microsoft Index Server, you need to calculate the amount of free disk space to set aside for it. What is the amount you should set aside?

A. 20 percent of the corpus

B. 30 percent of the corpus

C. 45 percent of the corpus

D. 50 percent of the corpus

13. You administer your company's IIS 4's Internet site. You need to create a report based on your server's data logs using Report Writer. Before running Report Writer, what should you do?

A. Enable logging and install SQL Server or MS Access

B. Enable ODBC Logging file format

C. Run Usage Import and import the log file

D. Use Edit from the command line to convert the file to TXT

14. You use the Scheduler in Report Writer and Usage Import. What is the name of the items placed in a new job?

A. Job items

B. Categories

C. Subjobs

D. Tasks

15. You are a consultant for a company that uses IIS 4 to run its Web and FTP sites. You are asked to track the number of nonanonymous users currently attached to the site. Which Performance Monitor counter do you use to track this value?

    A. Current Anonymous Users

    B. Logged In Users

    C. Current NonAnonymous Users

    D. Users

16. You're the administrator of your IIS 4 Web site. The Web site is responding sluggishly, and you notice some inactive clients are staying connected to your server. What is an appropriate response?

    A. From the Web site's Service Master Properties dialog box, set the Connection Timeout field to a higher number.

    B. From the Web site's Service Master Properties dialog box, enable the Unlimited Connection option.

    C. From the Web site's Service Master Properties dialog box, set the Connection Timeout field to a lower amount.

    D. From the Web site's Service Monitor Properties dialog box, set the Connection Timeout field to a lower amount.

17. On your company's Web site, you run Microsoft Index Server. You have between 100,000 and 150,000 documents stored on it. How much RAM is recommended for this number of documents?

    A. 32MB

    B. 64MB

    C. 128MB

    D. 256MB

18. You are an IIS 4 consultant working with a large company that has asked you to set up a smart host. What should you do to increase performance if you enter an IP address for the smart host?

    A. Use brackets to surround the IP address.

    B. Use commas to separate octets.

    C. Use percent signs to surround the IP address.

    D. Use semicolons to separate octets.

Review Answers

1. **D.** If you have over 500,000 documents, you must have 256MB.

2. **C.** If you have over 500,000 documents, you must have 128MB of RAM installed.

3. **B.** Microsoft Site Server Express Analysis–Report Writer is the recommended tool for generating this report.

4. **B.** W3C Extended Log File Format enables you to customize the type of data that is logged.

5. **C.** 1000 is the default in the Limited To field.

6. **A.** The Performance Tuning slider on the WWW Service Master Properties Performance tab is set too high.

7. **D.** HHTP Keep-Alives Enabled can help alleviate the problem.

8. **A,C.** The Connection Timeout and Connection Limited To value pertain to both FTP and WWW sites.

9. **C.** The default maximum size of news articles that can be posted to a Microsoft NNTP Service news server is 1000KB.

10. **A,C,D.** Only File Listings is a valid IIS Global object.

11. **B.** When free space drops below 3MB, Index Server will stop running.

12. **B.** The amount of free space should be 30 percent of the corpus.

13. **C.** Run Usage Import and import the file in question.

14. **D.** Items placed in a new job are called Tasks.

15. **C.** Current NonAnonymous Users in Performance Monitor will track the number of nonanonymous users.

16. **C.** From the Web site's Service Master Properties dialog box, set the Connection Timeout field to a lower amount.

17. **B.** A minimum of 64MB is recommended for this many documents.

18. **A.** Use brackets to surround the IP address and increase performance.

Answers to Test Yourself Questions at Beginning of Chapter

1. To create a report of daily Web site activity, enable logging for your site, and use Report Writer to create a detailed report of the activity. You can use Scheduler in Report Writer or Usage Analyst to automate this task. See "Importing Log Files Into a Report Writer and Usage Import Database" for details.

2. Run Performance Monitor, select Edit I Add To Chart, and select the FTP Service from the Objects list. From the Counter list, select Current Anonymous Users and click Add. Click Done. See "Monitoring Performance of Various Functions by Using Performance Monitor."

3. You can use Performance Monitor, Event Viewer, and Network Monitor. See "Analyzing Performance" for more information.

4. From the Web site's Service Master Properties dialog box, set the Connection Timeout field to a lower amount. See "Optimizing the Performance of IIS."

5. If you have between 100,000 and 150,000 documents, you should have 64–128MB of RAM. The minimum required is only 32MB, but the higher number is recommended. See "Optimizing the Performance of Index Server."

6. Instead of sending all outgoing messages in Microsoft SMTP Service directly to a remote domain, you can route all messages through a smart host. A smart host enables you to route messages over a more direct or less costly connection than via other routes. See "Optimizing the Performance of Microsoft SMTP Service."

7. On the NNTP Site Properties dialog box, click the Limited To option and fill in the connections field with the number of simultaneous connections you want to limit NNTP to handle. The default is 5,000. See "Changing Connection Settings."

8. Performance Monitor uses statistical measurements called counters. See "Interpreting Performance Data."

9. You can import usage data to review how users are using your site, export the Tree view of your site's WebMap to be an HTML index or table of contents for your site, and assign helper applications to file types to edit source files. See "Optimizing a Web Site Using Content Analyzer."

Chapter 7

Troubleshooting

This chapter helps you prepare for the exam by covering the following objectives:

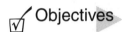

Objectives

- ▶ Resolve IIS configuration problems

- ▶ Resolve security problems

- ▶ Resolve resource access problems

- ▶ Resolve Index Server query problems

- ▶ Resolve setup issues when installing IIS on a Windows NT 4.0 computer

- ▶ Use a WebMap to find and repair broken links, hyperlink texts, headings, and titles

- ▶ Resolve WWW service problems

- ▶ Resolve FTP service problems

Test Yourself! Before reading this chapter, test yourself to determine how much study time you will need to devote to this section.

1. The three main values that must be entered to configure TCP/IP on a host with the ability to communicate beyond their network ID are what?

2. What NTFS permission enables a user to view any documents that are stored in a share, but does not enable them to make any changes to the documents?

3. Which command-line command should be given at a client to see the address of the DHCP server from which the client received its IP address?

4. By default, when does Index Server start?

5. To upgrade IIS 3.0 to IIS 4.0, what must you do?

6. What tool, new to IIS 4.0, can be used to administer Web site content to help you keep your Web site up-to-date and functioning correctly?

7. What is the default TCP control port for the WWW service?

8. What is the default TCP control port for the FTP service?

Answers are located at the end of the chapter...

This chapter covers the troubleshooting of IIS 4 problems in a number of areas, including the following:

▶ Resolving IIS configuration problems

▶ Resolving security problems

▶ Resolving resource access problems

▶ Resolving Index Server problems

▶ Resolving setup issues when installing IIS on a Windows NT Server 4.0 computer

▶ Using a WebMap to find and repair broken links, hyperlink texts, headings, and titles

▶ Resolving WWW Service problems

▶ Resolving FTP Service problems

Resolving IIS Configuration Problems

IIS configuration problems can usually be diagnosed rather quickly by the fact that nothing works. If the problem isn't with configuration (such as security, Index Server, and so on), then the problem is isolated to those services. If the problem is configuration, however, everything ceases to operate.

Configuration problems can be related to the installation of IIS or the configuration of TCP/IP. We will look at each of these in the following sections.

Installation Problems

Before you set up IIS 4, your system must meet or exceed the hardware requirements summarized in Tables 7.1 and 7.2. Table 7.1 shows requirements for a system running an Intel x86 processor; Table 7.2 lists requirements for a system running a DEC Alpha processor.

Table 7.1

IIS 4 hardware requirements for an Intel system	
Hardware Device	Requirements
CPU	Minimum of a 90 MHZ 486 DX processor. For better performance, you need a Pentium 133 or higher processor.
Hard disk space	Minimum of 50 MB, but it is recommended you have at least 120 MB. This does not include storage needed for files you plan to distribute via IIS.
Memory	Minimum of 32 MB. For a Web site on which you will store multimedia files or expect a great deal of traffic, 48 MB is the recommended minimum.
Monitor	Super VGA monitor with 800x600 resolution.

Table 7.2

IIS 4 hardware requirements for an Alpha system	
Hardware Device	Requirements
CPU	Minimum of 150 MHZ processor.
Hard disk space	Minimum of 120 MB, but you should allocate up to 200 MB for best performance.
Memory	Minimum of 48 MB. For better performance, have at least 64 MB.
Monitor	Super VGA monitor with 800x600 resolution.

Before you install IIS 4, remove any installations of a previous version of IIS. You'll also need to disable other versions of FTP, Gopher, or World Wide Web services you have installed under Windows NT Server 4.0. This includes the Windows Academic Center (EMWAC) service included with the Windows NT Resource Kit.

You also should have the following software installed:

▶ Windows NT Server 4.0

▶ Service Pack 3 for Windows NT Server 4.0

▶ Internet Explorer (4.01 or higher)

You also must be logged on to the Windows NT Server computer with Administrator privileges. Failing to have proper permissions or the required software installed almost always guarantees a failed installation.

TCP/IP Problems

Three main parameters specify how TCP/IP is configured on a host with the ability to communicate beyond its network ID: the IP address, the subnet mask, and the default gateway, which is the address of the router. These parameters are configured through the Protocols tab of the Network Properties dialog box. Although it's possible to receive an IP address from a DHCP server, for the moment this discussion focuses on parameters that are manually configured. DHCP related issues are discussed later, in the section "DHCP Client Configuration Problems."

These three TCP/IP parameters must be configured correctly or you cannot connect with TCP/IP. An incorrect configuration can result from typographical errors; if you type the wrong IP address, subnet mask, or default gateway, you may not connect properly or even be able to connect at all. To illustrate, if you dial the wrong number when making a telephone call, you can't reach the party you're calling. If you read the wrong phone number out of the phone book, you won't ever make a correct call, even if you dial the number you think is correct time and time again.

Whether the TCP/IP configuration parameters are wrong due to a typo or due to a mistaken number, the incorrect parameters affect communications. Different types of problems occur when each of these parameters has a configuration error.

IP Address Configuration Problems

While an incorrect TCP/IP address almost always causes problems, there are some instances when it does not. If you configure an IP address that's on the correct subnet but uses the wrong host ID and isn't a duplicate, the client may be able to communicate just fine. If, however, the correct IP address has been entered in a static file or database that resolves host names to IP addresses, such as an LMHOSTS file or a DNS database file, there can be some communication problems. Typically, therefore, an incorrect IP address does cause some problems.

Each TCP/IP parameter reacts differently if configured incorrectly. The following sections examine the effects that each TCP/IP parameter can have on IP communications.

IP Address

A TCP/IP address has two and sometimes three components that uniquely identify the computer the address is assigned to. At the very least, the IP address specifies the network address and host address of the computer. Also, if you are subnetting (using part of the host address to specify a subnet address), the third part of the address specifies the subnet address of the host.

▶ If the incorrect host (for example, 143.168.3.9) sends a message to a local client (for example, 133.168.3.20), the TCP/IP configuration of the sending host indicates that this is a remote address because it doesn't match the network address of the host initiating the communication. The packet won't ever reach the local client, because the address 133.168.3.20 is interpreted as a remote address.

▶ If a local client (133.168.3.6) sends a message to the incorrect host (143.168.3.9), the message never reaches its intended destination. The message is either routed (if the local client sends the message to the IP address as written) or it stays on the local subnet (if the local client sends it to what should have been the address, 133.168.3.9).

1. If the message is routed, the incorrect client does not receive the message because it is on the same segment of the network as the local client.

2. If the message is not routed, the message still doesn't reach the incorrect client because the IP address for the destination host (133.168.3.9) doesn't match the address as configured on the incorrect client (143.168.3.9).

Figure 7.1 gives an example of an incorrect IP address. In this case, a class A address is used, 33.x.x.x. The subnet mask (255.255.0.0) indicates the second octet is also being used to create subnets. In this case, even though the client has the same network address as the other clients on the same subnet, the client has a different subnet number because the address was typed incorrectly. The incorrect address specifies the wrong subnet ID. The client 33.5.8.4 is on subnet 5 while the other clients on the subnet have the address 33.4.x.x. If the client 33.5.8.4. tries to contact other clients on the same subnet, the message is routed because the subnet ID doesn't match the subnet number of the source host. If the client 33.5.8.4 tries to send a message to a remote host, the message is routed, but the message isn't returned to the client because the router doesn't handle subnet 5, only subnet 4.

Figure 7.1

An incorrect subnet address.

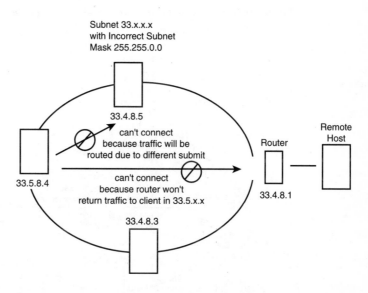

If a local client tries to send a message to 33.5.8.4, the message doesn't reach the client. If the local client uses the address as configured, the message is routed, which isn't the correct solution because the destination host is local. If the local client sends the message to what should have been the IP address, 33.5.8.4 doesn't receive the message because the IP address isn't configured correctly.

The last component of an IP address that can cause communication problems is the host address. An incorrect host address may not always cause a problem, however. In Figure 7.2, a local client has the wrong IP address, but only the host address portion of the address is wrong. The network address and subnet match the rest of the clients on the subnet. In this case, if a client sends a message to the client with the incorrect address, the message still reaches the client. However, if someone tries to contact the client with what should have been the address, he doesn't contact the client. In fact, he could contact another host that ended up with the address that was supposed to be given to the original host. If the original host ends up with the same IP address as another host through the configuration error, the first client to boot works, but the second client to boot may note the address conflict and not load the TCP/IP stack at all. In this case, the second client to boot isn't able to make any TCP/IP communications and this disrupts communications for both workstations (in a best-case scenario).

Figure 7.2

Incorrect host address.

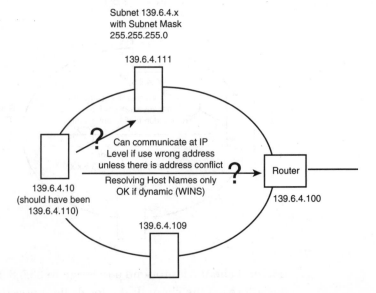

Subnet 139.6.4.x
with Subnet Mask
255.255.255.0

139.6.4.111

Can communicate at IP
Level if use wrong address
unless there is address conflict

Resolving Host Names only
OK if dynamic (WINS)

Router

139.6.4.10
(should have been
139.6.4.110)

139.6.4.100

139.6.4.109

Another problem comes in when the correct address was registered in static files, such as an LMHOSTS file or a DNS database, but an incorrect address is entered elsewhere. In this case, no one can communicate with this client by name because the name resolution for this host always returns the correct address, which can't be used to contact the host because the address has been typed incorrectly. Basically, the problems you encounter with an incorrect host address are intermittent. However, if the host was configured to be a WINS client, the host name is registered along with the incorrect address. Another WINS client trying to connect with this computer receives an accurate mapping for the host name.

Subnet Mask

The subnet mask specifies which portion of the IP address specifies the network address and which portion of the address specifies the host address. The subnet mask also can be used to take part of what would have been the host address and use it to further divide the network into subnets. If the subnet mask isn't configured correctly, your clients may not be able to communicate at all, or you may see partial communication problems.

Figure 7.3 shows a subnet on a TCP/IP network. The network uses a class B network address of 138.13.x.x. However, the third octet is used in this case for subnetting, so all the clients in the figure should be on subnet 4, as indicated by the common addresses 138.13.4.x. Unfortunately, the subnet mask entered for one client is 255.255.0.0. When this client tries to communicate with other hosts on the same subnet, it should be able to contact them because the subnet mask indicates they are on the same subnet, which is correct.

If the client tries to contact a host on another subnet, however, such as 138.13.3.x, the client fails. In this case, the subnet mask still interprets the destination host to be on the same subnet and the message is never routed. Because the destination host is on another subnet, the message never reaches the intended destination. The subnet mask is used to determine routing for outgoing communications, so the client with the incorrect subnet mask can receive incoming messages. However, when the client tries to re-turn communications, the message isn't routed if the source host is on the same network but on a different subnet. So in actuality, the client really can establish communications with only one side of the conversation. Contact with hosts outside the local network still works because those contacts are routed.

Figure 7.3

An incorrect subnet mask— missing the third octet.

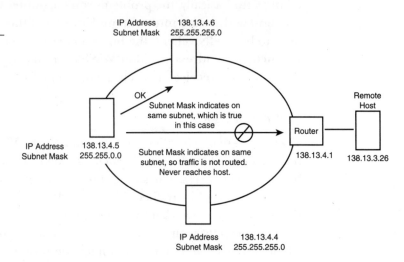

Figure 7.4 shows a subnet mask that masks too many bits. In this case, the subnet mask is 255.255.255.0. However, the network de-signers had intended the subnet mask to be 255.255.240.0, with four bits of the third octet used for the subnet and four bits as part of the host address. If the incorrect client tries to send a mes-sage to a local host and the third octet is the same, the message is not routed and thus reaches the local client. However, if the local client has an address that differs in the last four bits of the third octet, the message is routed and never reaches its destination. If the incorrect client tries to send a message to another client on another subnet, the message is routed because the third octet is different. The whole problem can be summed up by the incorrect subnet mask in the third octet.

Figure 7.4

Incorrect subnet mask—incorrect third octet.

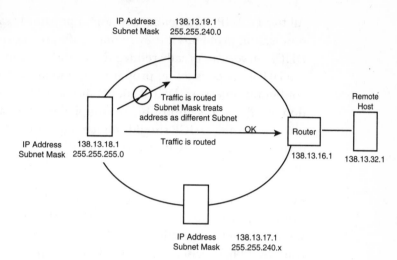

Subnet 138.13.16-31.x

IP Address   138.13.19.1
Subnet Mask   255.255.240.0

Traffic is routed
Subnet Mask treats
address as different Subnet

OK

Traffic is routed

Router

Remote
Host

IP Address   138.13.18.1
Subnet Mask   255.255.255.0

138.13.16.1   138.13.32.1

IP Address   138.13.17.1
Subnet Mask   255.255.240.x

Note

Problems with the subnet mask might appear as intermittent connections. Sometimes the connection works, sometimes it doesn't. The problems show up when the IP address of the destination host causes a packet to be routed when it shouldn't or to remain local when the packet should be routed.

Default Gateway

The default gateway address is the address of the router, the gateway to the world beyond the local subnet. If the default gateway address is wrong, the client with the wrong default gateway address can contact local hosts but isn't able to communicate at all beyond the local subnet. It's possible for the incorrect client to receive a message, because the default gateway is used only to send packets to other hosts. However, as soon as the incorrect client attempts to respond to the incoming message, the default gateway address doesn't work and the message doesn't reach the host that sent the original message. In many cases, the Default Gateway doesn't show up in an IPCONFIG/ALL (all variables of IP configuration) response if it hasn't been entered correctly.

DHCP Client Configuration Problems

All the TCP/IP parameters mentioned previously can cause communication problems if they're not configured correctly. Using a DHCP server can greatly reduce these configuration problems. If the DHCP scope is set up properly, without any typos or other configuration errors, DHCP clients shouldn't have any configuration problems. It's impossible to completely eliminate human error, but using DHCP should reduce the points of potential errors to just the DHCP servers rather than every client on the network.

Even when there are no configuration problems with DHCP addresses, DHCP clients can get a duplicate IP address from a DHCP server. If you have multiple DHCP servers in your environment, you should have scopes on each DCHP server for different subnets. Usually you have scopes with a larger number of addresses for the local subnet where the DHCP server is located and smaller scopes for other subnets. Creating multiple scopes on one server provides backup for giving clients IP addresses. If the server on the local scope is busy or down, the client can still receive an address from a remote DHCP server. When the router forwards this DHCP request to another subnet's server, it includes the address of the subnet it came from so that the remote DHCP server knows from which subnet scope of addresses to lease an address to the remote client. Using this type of redundancy, however, can cause problems if you don't configure the scopes on all the DHCP servers correctly.

The most important part of the configuration is to make sure you don't have duplicate addresses in the different scopes. On one server, for example, you could have a scope in the range 131.107.2.100 to 131.107.2.170. On the remote DHCP server, you could have a scope of 131.107.2.171 to 131.107.2.200. By setting up the scopes without overlap, you should not have any problems with clients receiving duplicate IP addresses. DHCP servers don't communicate with each other, so one server doesn't know anything about the addresses the other server has leased. Therefore, you must ensure that the servers never give out duplicate information by making sure the scopes for one subnet on all the different DHCP servers have unique IP addresses.

Another common problem with having multiple scopes on one server is entering the configuration parameters correctly. For example, if you enter the default gateway as 131.107.3.1 (instead of 131.107.2.1) for the scope 131.107.2.100 to 131.107.2.170, the clients receiving these addresses won't be able to communicate beyond the local subnet because they have the wrong router address. With one scope on a DHCP server, you're usually quite sure of what all the configuration parameters should be. With multiple scopes on one server, however, it's easy to get confused about which scope you're editing and what the parameters should be for that scope. To avoid this type of problem, check each scope's parameters very carefully to make sure the parameters match the address of the scope, not the subnet where the DHCP server is located.

Also, if the client doesn't receive an address because the server is down, or doesn't respond in a timely manner, the client isn't able to contact anyone. Without an IP address, the IP stack doesn't initialize and the client can't communicate at all with TCP/IP.

Resolving Security Problems

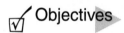

Security problems relate to a user or users being unable to utilize the resources you have made available to them—or to too many users being able to access what only one or two should be able to access. There are an unlimited number of reasons why these situations could occur, based upon what the resources are and how users access them.

Problem Areas

A number of different problem areas are examined in the following sections through the presentation of various issues involving server technologies.

In most Web server operations, you want to make the service available to the public, and to as many users as possible. Unfortunately, this can lead to the risk of allowing unwanted traffic in. Solutions to solving this problem are to use a firewall to restrict traffic, disable anonymous usage, or move the Web server service to a port other than its default 80—essentially hiding it from the outside world (discussed in more detail in this chapter's section on resolving WWW service problems).

▶ **Firewalls** can be used to restrict incoming traffic to only those services you are choosing to allow in. Additionally, a firewall can be used to prevent all traffic from coming in. If you're attempting to make data available on the Web, consider putting the Web server outside the firewall and allowing traffic to pass to it but to nothing else on your network.

▶ **Anonymous usage** is a staple of most public Web sites. If you don't wish to have a public Web site, however, consider disabling the logon. You can configure the Web server to use user authentication to verify that everyone accessing it has a valid Windows NT user account (they must give a username and password before being allowed to interact with the server).

▶ **Secure Sockets Layer (SSL) 3.0** is included with IIS and its use should be mandatory on any site holding sensitive data (such as medical information, credit card information, and so on). SSL enables a secure connection to be established between the browser and the server, and encryption to be used between them.

▶ **Server Certificates**, a part of SSL, can be created (unique digital identifications) to authenticate your Web site to browsers. This is used for public and private key (key pair) interactions of a secure nature.

▶ **NTFS permissions** can be used in conjunction with IIS to secure individual files and directories from those who should not access them. The five permission types follow:

 ▶ Change—Users can read and modify files, including deleting them and adding new ones to a directory.

 ▶ Full Control—The default for the Everyone group. Users can modify, move, delete, take ownership, and even change permissions.

▶ No Access—Overrides everything else and gives absolutely no access to the resource.

▶ Read—As the name implies, users can read the data.

▶ Special Access—User permissions have been set to something specific by the administrator.

Far and away, the No Access permission is the most powerful permission. When it is implemented, the user that has been assigned this permission has no access to that resource. It doesn't matter what other permissions have been assigned. The No Access permission overrides any other assigned permissions.

The Basic Steps in the Access Control Process

Solving most security problems involves using a great deal of common sense (if passwords are used, make them more than one character in length, and so on) and understanding what is taking place. The following steps illustrate the access control process:

1. The Web server receives a request from the browser to perform an operation.

2. The Web server checks to see if the IP address is permitted. If there are no restrictions on IP address ranges, or the request is coming from a valid range, processing continues.

3. The Web server checks to see if the user is permitted.

4. The Web server checks to see if its own permissions will enable access.

5. A check is made to see if the NTFS permissions will enable access.

If any of the preceding steps fail, then the access is denied. If they all succeed, then access is granted.

Resolving Resource Access Problems

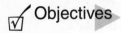 Objectives

Resource access problems are identified by a user or users being unable to access a resource. This problem can be caused by a lack of appropriate security or the TCP/IP configuration of the host or clients as discussed in the following section.

Using IPCONFIG to Resolve DHCP Address Problems

When a DHCP client gets an IP that isn't configured correctly, or if the client doesn't get an IP address at all, IPCONFIG can be used to resolve these problems. If the client gets incorrect IP parameters, it should be apparent from the results of IPCONFIG/all. You should be able to see that some of the parameters don't match the IP address or that some parameters are completely blank. For example, you could have the wrong default gateway (in which case the entry would not appear), or the client might not be configured to be a WINS client.

When a DHCP client fails to receive an address, the results of IPCONFIG /all are different. In this case, the client has an IP address of 0.0.0.0—an invalid address—and the DHCP server is 255.255.255.255—a broadcast address.

To fix this problem, you can release the incorrect address with IPCONFIG /release and then try to obtain a new IP address with IPCONFIG /renew. The IPCONFIG /renew command sends out a new request for a DHCP address. If a DHCP server is available, the server responds with the lease of an IP address. If there is no response, then it sends a request for a new one.

In many cases, the DHCP client acquires the same address after releasing and renewing. That the client receives the same address indicates the same DHCP server responded to the renewal request and gave out the address that had just been released back into the pool of available addresses. If you need to renew an address because the parameters of the scope are incorrect, you must fix the parameters in DHCP configuration before releasing and renewing the address. Otherwise, the client could receive the same address again with the same incorrect parameters.

 Note

Occasionally, a DHCP client won't acquire an address regardless of how many times you release and renew the address. One way to try to fix the problem is to manually assign the client a static IP address. Once the client is configured with this address, which you can verify by using IPCONFIG, switch back to DHCP.

Microsoft IP Configuration Troubleshooting Utilities

A number of tools come with TCP/IP when the protocol is installed on a Windows NT computer. After you have resolved any problems caused by the Windows NT network configuration, you can then focus on using the TCP/IP tools to solve IP problems. Some tools can be used to verify the configuration parameters. Other tools can be used to test the connectivity capabilities of TCP/IP as configured.

Using Ping to Test an IP Configuration

Ping is a command-line tool included with every Microsoft TCP/IP client (any DOS or Windows client with the TCP/IP protocol installed). You can use Ping to send a test packet to the specified address. If things are working properly, the packet is returned. Figure 7.5 shows the results of a successful Ping command. Note that four successful responses are returned. Unsuccessful pings can result in different messages, depending on the type of problem Ping encounters while trying to send and receive the test packet.

Although Ping is a simple tool to use (from the command prompt simply type Ping with the IP address or host name you want to ping), choosing what to ping is the key to using it for successful troubleshooting. The remainder of this section covers which IP addresses or hosts you should ping to troubleshoot TCP/IP connectivity problems.

Figure 7.5

The results of a successful Ping *command.*

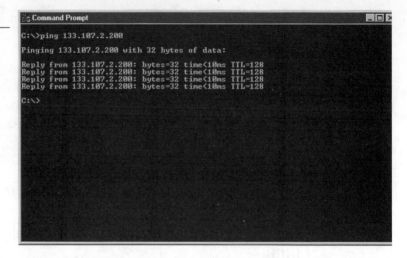

```
Command Prompt                                                  _ □ ×
C:\>ping 133.107.2.200

Pinging 133.107.2.200 with 32 bytes of data:

Reply from 133.107.2.200: bytes=32 time<10ms TTL=128
Reply from 133.107.2.200: bytes=32 time<10ms TTL=128
Reply from 133.107.2.200: bytes=32 time<10ms TTL=128
Reply from 133.107.2.200: bytes=32 time<10ms TTL=128

C:\>
```

Troubleshooting IP Protocol Installation by Pinging the Loopback Address

The first step in troubleshooting many problems is to verify that TCP/IP installed correctly on the client. You can look at the configuration through the Network Properties dialog box or with IPCONFIG, but to actually test the working status of the protocol stack you should try to ping the loopback address. The loopback address is 127.0.0.1. When you ping this address, a packet isn't sent on the network. Ping simply sends a packet down through the layers of the IP architecture and then up the layers again. If TCP/IP is installed correctly, you should receive an immediate successful response. If IP isn't installed correctly, the response fails.

To correct problems of this type, you should verify the NT network configuration and the protocol installation. You can check the following items:

▶ Make sure TCP/IP is listed on the installed protocols.

▶ Make sure the network adapter card is configured correctly.

▶ Make sure TCP/IP shows up in the bindings for the adapter card and that the bindings aren't disabled for TCP/IP.

▶ Check the system log for any errors indicating that the network services didn't start.

If you try the preceding steps, including rebooting the system, and have no success, you may have to remove TCP/IP and install it again. Sometimes Windows NT gets hung up somewhere and thinks things are really installed when they are not. Removing the protocol and then installing it again can often resolve this halfway state.

Troubleshooting Client Address Configuration by Pinging Local Addresses

Another step in verifying the TCP/IP configuration, after you have verified that TCP/IP is installed correctly, is to ping the address of the local host. Simply ping the IP address that you think is configured for the client. You should receive an immediate successful reply if the client address is configured as specified in the Ping command. You also can ping the name of the local host, but problems with name resolution are discussed later in this chapter's section "Name Resolution Problems." For the moment, you are concerned with raw TCP/IP connectivity—the capability to communicate with another IP host by using its IP address.

Correcting a failure at this level concerns checking the way the client address was configured. Was the address typed in correctly? Did the client receive the IP address from the DHCP server that you expected? Also, does the client have a connection on the network? Pinging the local host address doesn't cause a packet to be sent on the network, so if you have lost network connectivity, this ping won't indicate a network failure.

Troubleshooting Router Problems by Pinging the Default Gateway

If you can communicate with hosts on the same subnet but cannot establish communications with hosts beyond the subnet, the problem may be with the router or the way its address is configured. To communicate beyond the subnet, a router must be enabled with an address that matches the subnet address for the clients on the local subnet. The router also has other ports configured with different addresses, so it can send packets out to the network at large. Pinging the default gateway address tests the address you have configured for the router and also tests the router itself.

If the default gateway ping fails, there are several possible sources for the error:

▶ **The router has failed or is down.** In this case, you cannot make connections outside the subnet until the router is brought up again. However, you should be able to communicate with hosts on the same subnet.

▶ **The client has lost a physical connection with the router or with the network.** You can test a network connection at a hardware level and also through the software by trying to establish a session with a server with another protocol, such as NetBEUI, for example. If you only have TCP/IP on your network, you can temporarily install NetBEUI on the client and on another computer on the same subnet. Test connectivity by connecting to a file share on the other computer. Remember, the computer should be on the same subnet because NetBEUI packets don't route (but may be bridged).

▶ **The IP address on the router may be configured incorrectly.** The router address must match the client's default gateway address so that packets can move outside the subnet.

▶ **The client has the wrong router address.** Of course, if you ping the correct router address and it works, you also want to make sure the default gateway address configured on the client matches the address you successfully pinged.

▶ **The wrong subnet mask is configured.** If the subnet mask is wrong, packets destined for a remote subnet may not be routed.

You should also ping each of the IP addresses used by the different ports on your router. It's possible that the local interface for your subnet is working but other interfaces on the router, which actually connect the router to the other subnets on the network, have some type of problem.

Pinging a Remote Host

As a final test in using Ping, you can ping the IP address of a remote host, a computer on another subnet, or even the IP address of a Web server or FTP server on the Internet. If you can success-fully ping a remote host, your problem doesn't lie with the IP configuration; you're probably having trouble resolving host names.

If pinging the remote host fails, your problems may be with the router, the subnet mask, or the local IP configuration. However, if you have followed the earlier steps of pinging the loopback, local host address, and the default gateway address, you have already eliminated many of the problems that could cause this Ping to fail.

When a remote host Ping fails after you have tried the other Ping options, the failure may be due to other routers beyond the de-fault gateway used for your subnet. If you know the physical layout of your network, you can ping other router addresses along the path to the remote host to see where the trouble lies. Remember to ping the addresses on both sides of the router: the address that receives the packet and the address that forwards the packet on. You also can use the Route command, as described in the following section to find the path used to contact the remote host.

It is also possible that there is not a physical path to the remote host due to a router crash, a disruption in the physical network, or a crash on the remote host.

Many troubleshooters prefer to simply try this last step when using Ping to troubleshoot IP configuration and connectivity. If you can successfully ping a remote host, then the other layers of TCP/IP must be working correctly. In order for a packet to reach a remote host, IP must be installed correctly, the local client address must be configured properly, and the packet must be routed. If a Ping to the remote host works, then you can look to other sources (usu-ally name resolution) for your connection problems. If the Ping fails, you can try each preceding step until you find the layer where the problem is located. Then you can resolve the problem at that layer. You can either start by pinging the loopback address and working up through the architecture, or you can ping the remote host. Of course, if pinging the remote host works, you can stop. If not, you can work back through the architecture until you find a layer where Ping succeeds. The problem must therefore be at the next layer.

Diagnosing and Resolving Name Resolution Problems

Name resolution problems are easily identified as such with the PING utility. If you can ping a host using its IP address, but cannot ping it by its host name, then you have a resolution problem. If you cannot ping the host at all, then the problem lies elsewhere.

Problems that can occur with name resolution and their solutions fit into the following categories:

▶ **The entry is misspelled.** Examine the HOSTS or LMHOSTS file to verify that the host name is correctly spelled. If you're using the HOSTS file on a system prior to Windows NT 4.0, capitalization is important, as this file is case sensitive, because while LMHOSTS is not case sensitive (regardless of the Windows NT version number).

▶ **Comment characters prevent the entry from being read.** Verify that a pound sign is not at the beginning of the line (with the exception of entries such as #PRE and #DOM in LMHOSTS only), or anywhere on the line prior to the host name.

▶ **There are duplicate entries in the file.** Beacause the files are read in linear fashion, with any duplication, only the first entry is read and all others are ignored. Verify that all host names are unique.

▶ **A host other than the one you want is contacted.** Verify that the IP address entered in the file(s) is valid and corresponds to the host name.

▶ **The wrong file is used.** While similar in nature, HOSTS and LMHOSTS are really quite different, and not all that interchangeable. HOSTS is used to map IP addresses to host names, and LMHOSTS is used to map NetBIOS names to IP addresses.

In addition to PING, the all-purpose TCP/IP troubleshooting tool, useful name-resolution utilities include the following:

▶ NBTSTAT

▶ HOSTNAME

NBTSTAT

The NBTSTAT utility (NetBIOS over TCP/IP) displays protocol statistics and current TCP/IP connections. It is useful for trouble-shooting NetBIOS name resolution problems, and has a number of parameters and options that can be used with it:

▶ -a (adapter status)—lists the remote machine's name table given its name

▶ -A (Adapter status)—lists the remote machine's name table given its IP address

▶ -c (cache)—lists the remote name cache, including the IP addresses

▶ -n (names)—lists local NetBIOS names

▶ -r (resolved)—lists names resolved by broadcast and via WINS

▶ -R (Reload)—purges and reloads the remote cache name table

▶ -S (Sessions)—lists sessions table with the destination IP addresses

▶ -s (sessions)—lists sessions table converting destination IP addresses to host names via the LMHOSTS file

Hostname

The HOSTNAME.EXE utility, located in *systemroot*\System32 returns the name of the local host. This is used only to view the name and cannot be used to change the name. The host name is changed from the Network Control Panel applet.

If you have configured TCP/IP correctly and the protocol is installed and working, then the problem with connectivity is probably due to errors in resolving host names. When you test connectivity with TCP/IP addresses, you are testing a lower-level of connectivity than users generally use. When users want to connect to a network resource, such as mapping a drive to a server or connecting to a Web site, they usually refer to that server or Web site by its name rather than its TCP/IP address. In fact, users do not usually know the IP address of a particular server.

The name used to establish a connection must be resolved down to an IP address so that the networking software can make a connection. Once you've tested the IP connectivity, the next logical step is to check the resolution of a name down to its IP address. If a name cannot be resolved to its IP address or if it is resolved to the wrong address, users won't be able to connect to the network resource with that name, even if you can connect to it using an IP address.

Two types of computer names are used when communicating on the network. A NetBIOS name is assigned to a Microsoft computer, such as a Windows NT server or a Windows 95 client. A host name is assigned to a non-Microsoft computer, such as a UNIX server. (Host names also can be assigned to a Windows NT server running Internet Information Server. For example, the name www.microsoft.com refers to a Web server on the Microsoft Web site. This server is running on Windows NT.) In general, when using Microsoft networking, such as connecting to a server for file sharing, print sharing, or applications, you refer to that computer by its NetBIOS name. When executing a TCP/IP-specific command, such as FTP or using a Web browser, you refer to that computer by its host name.

A NetBIOS name can be resolved to a TCP/IP address in several ways. Figure 7.6 shows an example of how NetBIOS names are resolved. The TCP/IP client initiating a session first looks in its local name cache. If the client cannot find the name in a local cache, it then queries a WINS server if it is configured to be a WINS client. If the WINS server cannot resolve the name, the client tries a broadcast that only reaches the local subnet, because routers, by default, aren't configured to forward broadcasts. If the client cannot find the name through a broadcast, it looks for any LMHOSTS or HOSTS files, if it has been configured to do so. Finally, if the client cannot resolve a name in any other way, it queries a DNS server if it has been configured to be a DNS client. However, if the client specifies a name longer than 15 characters (the maximum length of a NetBIOS name), the client first queries DNS before trying a HOSTS file or WINS.

Figure 7.6

Resolving NetBIOS names.

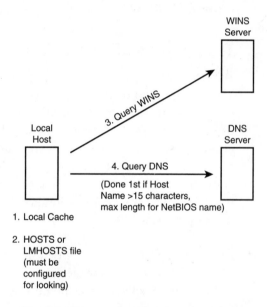

Host names are resolved in a similar manner. The client, however, checks sources that are used solely to resolve host names before trying sources that are used to resolve NetBIOS names. In resolving host names, the client first tries the local host name, then checks the HOSTS file next, followed by the DNS server (if it is configured to be a DNS client). These two sources only resolve host names. If the client cannot resolve the name, it checks the WINS server, if configured as a WINS client, tries a broadcast, then looks in the LMHOSTS file. The last three methods to resolve a name are used to resolve NetBIOS names, but it is possible for a host name to be listed in these sources.

Several tools are available to test name resolution. They are discussed in the following sections.

Testing Name Resolution with `Ping`

Just as you can use `Ping` to verify the TCP/IP configuration, you can also use `Ping` to verify host name resolution. If you can successfully ping a host name, then you have verified TCP/IP communication from the Network Interface layer of the TCP/IP architecture to the Transport layer. When you ping a host name, a successful reply shows the IP address of the host. This shows that the name has been successfully resolved to an IP address and that you can communicate with that host.

Testing NetBIOS Name Resolution by Establishing a Session

The ultimate test of connectivity is to establish a session with another host. If you can establish a session through mapping a drive or by executing a `Net Use` command (which is the command-line equivalent of mapping a drive), you have made a NetBIOS connection. If you can FTP, Telnet, or establish a Web session with another host, you have made a Sockets connection. NetBIOS connection and Sockets connection are the two main types of connections made by a TCP/IP client.

After the drive has been mapped with `Net Use`, you can switch to the new drive letter, view files and directories, and do any other things that are specified in the permissions of the share mapped to the drive letter. To get more information about the syntax of the `Net Use` command, type `net help use` in a command prompt.

A common problem in making NetBIOS connections is that the wrong NetBIOS name is used. Verify that the destination host has the same name that you are using to make the connection.

Another potential problem with the name configuration occurs when NetBIOS scope IDs are used. Only NetBIOS hosts with the same scope ID can communicate with each other. The scope ID is configured through the advanced TCP/IP parameters. Incorrect share permissions can prevent you from establishing a NetBIOS session. When you try to connect a drive to a share where you have No Access, you receive an Access Denied message. This message indicates that you can connect to the server, but your rights did not enable you to make a connection to this specific share. This type of failure has nothing to do with TCP/IP connectivity. Remember that if the administrator adds your account to a group that has access, and you want to try again, you must log out and log in again to receive a new access token with the updated permissions.

To resolve NetBIOS connectivity problems, you must know what sources are used to resolve NetBIOS names. The first place a client looks to resolve a NetBIOS name is the local cache. You can view the contents of the NetBIOS cache with the NBTSTAT command. You should verify that no incorrect entry is in the cache that maps the NetBIOS name to an incorrect IP address. If there is, however, you can remove the entry and then try to make another connection.

The next place to attempt NetBIOS name resolution is in a query to a WINS server. The client must be configured to be a WINS client. You can verify the address of the WINS server through the Advanced properties of TCP/IP or by using IPCONFIG/all. You can view the contents of the WINS database by using WINS Manager on the WINS server (or any computer where the management tools are installed). Verify that the host name is in the database and, if so, make sure it is mapped to the correct IP address.

If the WINS server is configured to do a DNS lookup, you have another way to get NetBIOS resolution. The WINS server queries DNS if the WINS server cannot resolve the name from its own database. You can view the contents of the DNS database files by using DNS Manager on the DNS server or by using the NSLOOKUP utility from any client.

The client next tries a broadcast to resolve NetBIOS names, although you cannot configure what the client finds through the broadcast. The next place the client looks for NetBIOS name resolution is the LMHOSTS file. You can configure the contents of this file. The client must be configured for LMHOSTS lookup in the advanced TCP/IP configuration. Also, the LMHOSTS file must be located in the correct directory path. On a Windows NT computer, the LMHOSTS file must be in the path <winnt root>\system32\drivers\etc.

Next, verify the entries in the LMHOSTS file. The correct host name and IP address must be entered in this file. If you have multiple entries in the file for a host name, only the first entry is used. If you added another entry for a host in the file, you must delete it so that it will not be used.

Domain names are another source of potential problems with LMHOSTS files in a non-WINS environment. The domain name must be registered with the IP address of the Primary Domain Controller (PDC) and #DOM (a switch that registers the server as a domain controller) on the same line. This entry is necessary to log on to the domain as well as to see the domain in a browse list.

Another problem with LMHOSTS files doesn't prevent connectivity, but it can greatly delay it. If you have #INCLUDE statements at the top of the LMHOSTS file, the files specified by #INCLUDE are included before any other entries lower in the LMHOSTS file are searched. You can speed connections to hosts entered in the LMHOSTS file by moving the #INCLUDE entries to the bottom of the LMHOSTS file.

Testing TCP Name Resolution by Establishing a Session

Typical TCP/IP connections from a Microsoft client, such as FTP or Telnet, use Windows Sockets. To test connectivity at this level, try establishing an FTP or Telnet session or try to connect to a Web server. When you successfully connect to a Web server, you see the site's Web page, and you can navigate through the page. When the connection fails, you receive a message on your Internet browser that the connection failed.

To resolve problems with a Windows Sockets connection, you must understand how a client resolves TCP host names. The first place a client looks to resolve a host name is the local host name. You can see what TCP/IP thinks the local host name is by executing the Hostname command. Verify the host name if the results of the Hostname command confirm that the local host is what you expect it to be. You can modify the host name in the DNS tab of the TCP/IP properties.

The next place the client looks is in a HOSTS file. This file must be located in the path <winnt root>\system32\drivers\etc. Verify that any entry in the file for the host is correct, with the correct host name and IP address. If multiple entries for the same host name are in the file, only the first name is used. The HOSTS file can also have links to HOSTS files on other servers. If links are specified in the local HOSTS file, you should make sure entries in the other HOSTS files also are correct.

The final place a client can use host name resolution is a DNS server. The client must be configured to use DNS on the DNS tab in the TCP/IP properties dialog box. The DNS server must have a zone file corresponding to the domain name specified in the host name, or it must be able to query another DNS server that can resolve the name.

Resolving Index Server Problems

 Objectives

Index Server works with IIS through queries that come in the form of .IDQ (Internet Data Query) files. It responds to those queries in the form of .IDQ files as well. In order to function properly, .IDQ files should always be placed in the Scripts directory, and they require Execute or Script permission.

As discussed in Chapter 4, there are two sections to .IDQ files with [Query] being required, and [Names] being optional (used only to define nonstandard column names that are referred to in a query). Refer to Chapter 4 for a listing of parameters, variables, and conditional expressions.

Most troubleshooting/trouble correction is implemented automatically with Index Server. For example, if the cache becomes corrupted, Index Server begins a recovery operation, and no administrator interaction is required. In all events, messages are written to the event log indicating the actions taking place, and administrators can monitor their Index Server installations from there.

Query Errors

Errors can, and often do, occur when improper syntax is used in queries, when files are corrupt, or when other problems occur. There is a series of standard messages returned to alert you that this is the cause of the problem, and this section examines those.

Syntax Errors

According to Microsoft's online documentation (file ixerrysn.htm), the error messages, as shown in Table 7.3, can be returned when executing a query.

Table 7.3

The ixerrysn.htm file.

Message	Explanation
Expecting closing parenthesis	Occurs when parentheses are mismatched.
Expecting closing square bracket	An opening square bracket was not followed by a closing square bracket. Usually the result of an ill-formed weight.
Expecting comma	Occurs when a reserved token or end-of-string occurs before the closing brace of a vector property. Example: @VectorString = {A1, B@}.
Expecting currency	A currency value was expected but not found. Occurs when a property of type DBTYPE_CY is fed incorrect input. Correct format for currency is #.#.
Expecting date	A date was expected but not found. Occurs when a property of type DBTYPE_DATE is fed incorrect input. Allowed formats for dates are yyyy/mm/dd, yyyy/mm/dd hh:mm:ss, and relative dates (-#y, -#m, -#w, -#d, -#h, -#n, -#s).

Message	Explanation
Expecting end of string	A complete restriction has been parsed, and there is still more input. Example: (@size = 100) sample.
Expecting GUID	A GUID (Globally Unique Identifier) was expected but not found. Occurs when a property of DBTYPE_GUID is fed incorrect input. Property format for a GUID is XXXXXXXX-XXXX-XXXX-XXXX-XXXXXXXXXXXX.
Expecting integer	An integer was expected but not found. Occurs when a property of an integer type (DBTYPE_I4, for example) is fed a nonnumeric value, or a nonnumeric vector weight is entered.
Expecting phrase	A textual phrase was expected and not found. This error occurs in a variety of situations where the query parser is expecting plain text and is given a special token instead.
Expecting property name	Occurs when a correctly formed property name is not found after an @ sign.
Expecting real number	A real number was expected but not found. Occurs when a property of a real type (DBTYPE_R4, for example) if fed a nonnumeric value.
Expecting regular expression	Similar to Expecting phrase error. Used when in regular-expression parsing mode.
The file <*file*> is on a remote UNC share. .IDQ, .IDA, and .HTX files cannot be placed on a remote UNC share	An .IDQ, .IDA, or .HTX file was found on a remote UNC share. None of these files can be on a remote UNC share.

continues

Table 7.3   Continued

Message	Explanation
Invalid literal	Occurs only when a query property is formatted poorly. Almost all conditions are covered by the Expecting Integer, Expecting Date, and other errors.
No such property	Property specified after @, #, or $ does not exist. It is not a default property and is not specified in the [Names] section of the .IDQ file.
Not yet implemented	An unimplemented feature of Index Server.
Out of memory	The server ran out of memory processing the `CiRestriction`.
Regular expressions require a property of type string	A property of a nontextual type (`DBTYPE_I4`, `DBTYPE_GUID`, and so on) was selected for regular-expression mode. For example, `#size 100*` would cause this error.
Unexpected end of string	There is a missing quotation mark in your query.
Unsupported property type	For future expansion. Will occur when a display-only property type is used in a query restriction.
Weight must be between 0 and 1000	Occurs when a query term weight is outside the legal range of 0 to 1000.

IDQ File Errors

According to Microsoft's online documentation in file ixerridg.htm, the messages in Table 7.4 are returned by use of the `CiErrorMessage` variable, accessible from .htx error pages.

Table 7.4

The ixerridq.htm file.	
Message	Explanation
The catalog directory cannot be found in the location specified by `'CiCatalog='` in file <*file*>.	The catalog location specified by the `CiCatalog` parameter did not contain a valid content index catalog.
`DBTYPE_BYREF` must be used with `DBTYPE_STR`, `DBTYPE_WSTR`, `DBTYPE_GUID`, or `DBTYPE_UI1` types.	`DBTYPE_BYREF` must always be used in conjunction with an indirect type in the [Names] section.
`DBTYPE_VECTOR` or `DBTYPE_BYREF` used alone.	The VECTOR and BYREF property modifiers must always be used with a type. Example: `DBTYPE_I4	DBTYPE_VECTOR`
Duplicate column, possibly by a column alias, found in the `'CiColumns='` specification in file <*file*>.	The same property was named more than once in the `CiColumns` line. It may have been mentioned with different friendly names that refer to the same property.
Duplicate property name.	The same property was defined twice in the [Names] section.
Expecting closing parenthesis.	Opening parenthesis in [Names] section is not followed by closing parenthesis in .IDQ file.
Expecting GUID.	Incorrectly formatted entry in the [Names] section of .IDQ file.
Expecting integer.	Incorrectly formatted entry in the [Names] section of .IDQ file.
Expecting property name.	Incorrectly formatted entry in the [Names] section of .IDQ file.
Expecting property specifier.	Invalid or missing property specifier in [Names] section. Property is named either by PROPID (integer) or string.

continues

Table 7.4 Continued

Message	Explanation
Expecting SHALLOW or DEEP in .IDQ file *<file>* on line 'CiFlags='.	The CiFlags parameter has a value other than SHALLOW or DEEP.
Expecting TRUE or FALSE in .IDQ file *<file>* on line 'CiForceUseCi='.	The CiForceUseCi parameter has a value other than TRUE or FALSE.
Expecting type specifier.	Incorrectly formatted entry in the [Names] section of .IDQ file.
Failed to set property name.	A resource failure. Usually out of memory.
The file *<file>* is on a network share. .IDQ, .IDA, and .HTX files cannot be placed on a network share.	You must put these files into a virtual root on the local computer.
The .HTX file specified could not be found in any virtual or physical path.	The file specified in the CiTemplate parameter could not be located.
The .IDQ file *<file>* contains a duplicate entry on line *<line>*.	A parameter in the [Query] section of the .IDQ file was given more than once.
The .IDQ file *<file>* could not be found.	Check the path to the .IDQ file and then make sure the .IDQ file is in that path.
An invalid 'CiScope=' or 'CiCatalog=' was specified in file *<file>*.	The .IDQ file cannot contain invalid parameters. Correct the condition and try again.
Invalid GUID.	A poorly formatted GUID was found in the [Names] section.
An invalid locale was specified on the 'CiLocale=' line in .IDQ file *<file>*.	The locale ID specified by the CiLocale parameter was not recognized as a valid locale ID.
Invalid property found in the 'CiColumns=' specification in file *<file>*.	A property specified in the CiColumns parameter is not a standard property and is not listed in the [Names] section of the .IDQ file.

Message	Explanation
Invalid property found in the 'CiSort=' specification in file *<file>*.	A property specified in the CiSort parameter is not a standard property and is not listed in the [Names] section of the .IDQ file.
An invalid sort order was specified on the 'CiSort=' line in file *<file>*. Only [a] and [d] are supported.	A sort-order specification following a property name in the CiSort parameter was unrecognized. Only [a] (for ascending) and [d] (for descending) are allowed.
One or more output columns must be specified in the .IDQ file *<file>*.	The CiColumns parameter is missing or empty. At least one output column must be specified for the query.
Operation on line *number* of .IDA file *<file>* is invalid.	An unrecognized keyword was found in the .IDA file.
The query failed because the Web server is busy processing other requests.	The limit on the number of queries has been exceeded. To allow more queries to wait in the queue for processing, increase the value of the Registry key IsapiRequest QueueSize, and to allow more queries to be processed simultaneously, increase the value for the Registry key IsapiRequest ThresholdFactor.
Read error in file *<file>*.	I/O error occurred reading the file. Generally caused by hardware failure.
A restriction must be specified in the .IDQ file *<file>*.	The CiRestriction parameter is missing or empty. Every query must have a restriction. A restriction such as #vpath *.* will match all pages.

continues

Table 7.4 Continued

Message	Explanation
A scope must be specified in the .IDQ file *<file>*.	The `CiScope` parameter is missing or empty. Every query must have a scope. The scope / (for ward slash) will match every page in all virtual directories and the scope \ (backslash) will match every page on every physical path.
The template file cannot be found in the location specified by `'CiTemplate='` in file *<file>*	An attempt to open a .HTX file at the location specified by the `CiTemplate` parameter failed. The path may be invalid, it may specify a directory, or it may re solve to `NULL` after parameter replacement.
A template file must be specified in the .IDQ file *<file>*.	The `CiTemplate` parameter is missing or empty. Every query must have a template (.HTX) file.
Template for .IDA file *<file>* cannot have detail section.	A `<%BeginDetail%>` was found in the .IDA file. Please remove it and the entire detail section.
Unrecognized type.	Type specifed is not one of the valid types (DBTYPE_I4, DBTYPE_GUID, and so on).
You must specify `'MaxRecordsPerPage'` in the .IDQ file *<file>*.	The `CiMaxRecordsPerPage` parameter is missing or empty. Every query must specify the number of records per page.

Event Log Messages

Index Server system errors are reported in the application event log under the `Ci Filter Service` category. System errors reported here include page filtering (indexing) problems, out-of-resource conditions, index corruption, and so on.

The messages in Table 7.5 are written to the Windows NT application event log. This information comes from Microsoft's online documentation, file ixerrlog.htm.

Table 7.5

The ixerrlog.htm file.

Message	Explanation
Account *user-id* does not have interactive logon privileges on this computer. You can give *user-id* interactive logon privileges on this computer using the user manager administrative tool.	The specified *user-id* does not have interactive logon privileges on the computer running Index Server. Give the *user-id* interactive logon privileges through the User Manager for Domains.
The CI filter daemon has prematurely stopped and will be subsequently restarted.	The filter daemon (Cidaemon.exe) stopped unexpectedly. It will be automatically restarted. This can be caused by poorly written filters, or experimentation with the Windows NT Task Manager.
CI has started on *<catalog>*.	An informational message logged when Index Server is started successfully.
Class for extension *<extension>* unknown. Sample file: *<file>*	This is a warning that files with the specified extension are being filtered with the default (text) filter. This can lead to the addition of unnecessary data in the index. Consider turning off filtering for this extension. The full physical path of a representative file is included in the message. Generation of this message can be disabled by turning on a special flag in `ContentIndex` Registry key.
Cleaning up corrupted content index metadata on *<catalog>*. Index will be automatically restored by refiltering all documents.	A catastrophic data corruption error was detected on the specified catalog. The catalog will be rebuilt. This is usually caused by hardware failure, but also can occur in rare circumstances because of abrupt shutdown or power failure. Recovery will occur automatically.

continues

Table 7.5 Continued

Message	Explanation
Content index on *<catalog>* could not be initialized. Error *<number>*.	Unknown, possibly catastrophic error. Please report the error number to Microsoft Technical Support. To recover, delete all files under *<catalog>* and re-index.
Content index on *<catalog>* is corrupted. Please shut down restart Web server.	A catastrophic data corruption error and was detected on the specified catalog. The catalog will be rebuilt. This is usually caused by hardware failure, but also can occur in rare circumstances because of abrupt shutdown or power failure. You must shut down and restart the Web server for recovery to occur.
Content index corruption detected in component *<component>*. Stack trace is *<stack>*.	The content index is corrupted. Delete the catalog and start over. If you keep getting this error, remove and reinstall Index Server.
Content index corruption detected in component *<component>* in catalog *<catalog>*. Stack trace is *<stack>*.	The content index is corrupt. Delete the catalog and start over. If you keep getting this error, remove and reinstall Index Server.
The content index could not filter file *<file>*. The filter operation was retried *<number>* times without success.	The specified document failed to successfully filter *<number>* times. This usually indicates a corrupted document or corrupted properties. In rare cases, filtering may fail because the document was in use for a long period of time.
Content index on drive is corrupted. Please shut down and restart the Content Index service (cisvc).	In the Windows NT Control Panel under Services, stop the Content Index service, and then restart it.

Message	Explanation
The content index filter for file "*<file>*" generated content data more than *<size>* times the file's size.	Filtering of the specified document generated more than the allowed maximum amount of output. This is usually caused by a poorly written filter, a corrupted document, or both.
The content index filter stopped while filtering "*<file>*". The CI daemon was restarted. Please check the validity of the filter for objects of this class.	Filtering of the specified document was started, but did not finish before the timeout period expired. This is usually caused by a poorly written filter, a corrupted document, or both.
A content scan has completed on *<catalog>*.	A content scan of the catalog has been completed successfully.
An error has been detected on *<catalog>* that requires a full content scan.	The catalog lost a change notification, usually due to lack of resources (disk space) or hardware failure. The complete scope of the catalog will be scanned, and all documents will be refiltered. This action is deferred until a suitable time.
An error has been detected in content index on *<catalog>*.	The content index is corrupted. Delete the catalog and start over. If you keep getting this error, remove and reinstall Index Server.
An error has been detected on *<catalog>* that requires a partial content scan.	The catalog lost a change notification, usually due to lack of resources (disk space) or hardware failure. A partial scope of the catalog will be scanned, and some documents will be refiltered. This action is deferred until a suitable time.
Error *<number>* detected in content index on *<catalog>*.	Unknown, possibly catastrophic error. Please report error number to Microsoft Techical Support. To recover, delete all files under *<catalog>* and start over.

continues

Table 7.5   Continued

Message	Explanation
File change notifications are turned off for scope "*<scope>*" because of error *<number>*. This scope will be periodically rescanned.	An error prevented reestablishing automatic change notifications for the specified directory scope. To determine documents that changed in the scope, periodic incremental scans will be done by Index Server. The rescan interval is specified in the registry.
File change notifications for scope "*<scope>*" are not enabled because of error *<number>*. This scope will be periodically rescanned.	An error prevented establishment of automatic change notifications for the specified directory scope. This usually happens with virtual roots that point to remote shares on file servers that do not support automatic change notifications. To determine which documents changed in the scope, periodic incremental scans will be done by Index Server. The rescan interval is specified in the registry.
The filter service could not run since file *<file>* could not be found on your system.	An executable or DLL required for filtering cannot be found, usually because Cidaemon.exe is not on the path.
A full content scan has started on *<catalog>*.	A complete rescan of the catalog has been initiated.
<number> inconsistencies were detected in PropertyStore during recovery of catalog *<catalog>*.	Corruption was detected in the property cache during startup. Recovery is automatically scheduled. Usually the result of hardware failure or abrupt shutdown.
Master merge cannot be restarted on *<catalog>* due to error *<number>*.	A master merge cannot be restarted on the specified catalog. The error code gives the reason.

Message	Explanation
Master merge cannot be started on <*catalog*> due to error <*number*>.	A master merge cannot be started on the specified catalog. The error code gives the reason.
Master merge has been paused on <*catalog*>. It will be rescheduled later.	A master merge has been temporarily halted on the specified catalog. Often occurs when a merge runs out of system resources (disk space, memory, and so on).
Master merge has completed on <*catalog*>.	A master merge has been completed on the specified catalog. This is an informational message.
Master merge has restarted on <*catalog*>.	A paused master merge has been restarted.
Master merge has started on <*catalog*>.	A master merge has been initiated on the specified catalog. This is an informational message.
Master merge was started on <*catalog*> because the amount of remaining disk space was less than <*number*>%.	A master merge was started because the amount of free space on the catalog volume dropped below a minimum threshold. The total free disk space should be increased after the master merge completes.
Master merge was started on <*catalog*> because more than <*number*> documents have changed since the last master merge.	A master merge was started because the number of documents changed since the last master merge exceeded the maximum thresh old.
Master merge was started on <*catalog*> because the size of the shadow indexes is more than <*number*>% the disk.	A master merge was started because the amount of data in shadow indexes exceeded the maximum threshold.

continues

Table 7.5 Continued

Message	Explanation
Notifications are not enabled on *<pathname>* because this is a DFS aware share. This scope will be periodically scanned.	If a virtual root points to a distributed file system (DFS) share, notifications are disabled for the entire DFS share because DFS does not support notifications.
One or more embeddings in file *<file>* could not be filtered.	The specified file was filtered correctly, but several of the embedded objects could not be filtered. This is usually caused by embedded objects without a registered filter. Text within unfiltered embedded objects is not searchable. Generation of this message can be disabled by turning on a special flag in key registry.
The path *<pathname>* is too long for Content Index.	The Content Index service detected a path that was longer than the maximum number of characters allowed for a path name as determined by the constant MAX_PATH (260 characters). As a result, no documents from that path will be returned or indexed.
Please check your system time. It might be set to an invalid value.	This event is generated when the system time is invalid, for example, when set to a date before January 1, 1980. When the system time is invalid, the date may appear as 2096.

Message	Explanation
<Process-Name> failed to logon *<UserId>* because of error *<number>*.	The specified process (Index Server SearchEngine or CiDaemon) failed to log on the specified user because of an error. The remote shares for which the UserId is used will not be filtered correctly. This can happen if either the password is wrong or the validity of the password could not be verified due to network errors.
PropertyStore inconsistency detected in catalog *<catalog>*.	Corruption was detected in the property cache. Recovery is automatically scheduled. Usually the result of hardware failure or abrupt shutdown.
Recovery is starting on PropertyStore in catalog *<catalog>*.	Corruption was detected in the property cache. Recovery is starting on the property cache. This can take a long time, depending upon the size of the property cache.
Recovery was performed successfully on PropertyStore in catalog *<catalog>*.	Corruption was detected in the property cache. The error has been fixed. Usually the result of hardware failure or abrupt shutdown.
Very low disk space was detected on drive *<drive>*. Please free up at least *<number>* MB of space for content index to continue.	Free space has fallen below the minimum threshold required for successful merge. This is just a warning, but no merges will be initiated until space is freed up. Filtering will also stop.

Virtual Roots

Table 7.6, which follows, is from the ixerrlog.htm as well, and it describes the error messages that occur when virtual root problems are the cause of the error.

Table 7.6

The virtual roots component of ixerrlog.htm.	
Message	Explanation
Added virtual root *<root>* to index.	The message "Mapped to *<path>*" is added to the event log when a virtual root is indexed.
Removed virtual root *<root>* from index.	This message is written to the event log when a virtual root is deleted from the index.
Added scope *<path>* to index.	This message is added to the event log when a new physical scope is indexed.
Removed scope *<path>* from index.	This message is written to the event log when a new physical scope is deleted from the index.

Other Index Server Issues

Other issues to be aware of with Index Server include the following:

▶ Index Server starting and stopping

▶ Word weighting

▶ Disk filling

Index Server Starting and Stopping

Index Server, by default, is set to automatically start when IIS does. If this is set to another value, such as manual, then IIS can be started from the Services icon in the Control Panel. This is the same utility that can be used to stop the Index Server service, although it automatically shuts down when IIS does.

If Index Server isn't running and a query comes in, Index Server automatically starts. Therefore, as an administrator, the starting of Index Server is not something you should ever need to do manually. The stopping of Index Server is something you should never need to do, either, but you can do it from the Services utility.

Word Weighting

Word weighting determines how words in the data are indexed. This process is done by the Waisindx.exe utility. It determines what to index, how much to weight words, how to optimize the server, and where to find the actual data. As a rule of thumb, seven indexes are created for each data file, with the combined size of the seven indexes being equal to 110% of the size of the data file.

The weighting factors that Waisindx.exe uses are as follows:

▶ **The actual weight of the word.** Whether it appears in a headline, capitalized, etc., or just in the body of the data.

▶ **The term of the weight.** How many times does it appear, and thus, how important is it to the data?

▶ **The proximity.** How close do multiple words always appear to each other? For example, computer publishing.

▶ **The density of the word.** This is computed by taking the number of times the word appears and dividing it by the total number of all words in the data.

When Waisindx.exe is run, it creates the indexes that are then used to locate the data. As you add new records to the data, the indexes are not updated, and you must rerun Waisindx.exe to create new indexes incorporating the new data.

Running Out of Disk Space

One of the most common problems with using Index Server is that of running out of disk space. If the drive fills, indexing is paused, and the only method of knowing this is by a message written to the event log. The event log should be monitored routinely by an administrator for this and similar occurrences.

Resolving Setup Issues When Installing IIS on a Windows NT Server 4.0 Computer

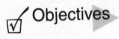 **Objectives**

Before you install IIS 4.0, you must remove any installations of a previous version of IIS, and disable other versions of FTP, Gopher, or World Wide Web services running under Windows NT Server 4.0.

You must be logged on to the Windows NT Server computer with Administrator privileges, and need to have the following software installed:

▶ Windows NT Server 4.0

▶ Service Pack 3 for Windows NT Server 4.0

▶ Internet Explorer (4.01 or higher)

If all of the above conditions have been met, and problems exist, then you should know where to turn for assistance. There are a number of places to find help, and they include the following:

▶ The Windows NT Resource Kit

▶ Online help in both Windows NT and IIS

▶ Microsoft Technet

▶ CompuServe

▶ The Microsoft Internet site

The Microsoft Windows NT Resource Kit includes three volumes of in-depth information and a CD of utilities. The Resource Kit utilities add a large number of troubleshooting utilities and can help you isolate problems much easier.

The online help in NT is available from the Start Menu, Help, or from almost anywhere else in the product by pressing F1. The IIS help is available at several locations, but most notably by selecting Product Documentation from the IIS section of the Programs menu.

Microsoft Technet is a monthly CD subscription that includes the latest service packs, drivers, and updates for all operating system products. Once installed, you can run it at any time by choosing Microsoft TechNet from the Programs menu.

The CompuServe forums are not as well supported as they once were and almost everything is shifting to the Web, but they are still a good location to find interaction among users experiencing similar problems. The easiest method to use to find a forum supporting the problem you're experiencing is to click the stoplight icon on the main CompuServe menu (or type GO at a command prompt) and enter NDEX. This brings up an index of all the forums currently available. You can select a choice from the list, or—depending upon your version of CompuServe—choose GO again, and enter the abbreviation for the forum you want.

The Microsoft Internet site at http://www.microsoft.com makes all software updates and patches available. It also serves as an entry point to the KnowledgeBase where you can find documentation on all known problems.

Use a WebMap to Find and Repair Broken Links, Hyperlink Texts, Headings, and Titles

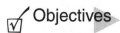

Content Analyzer's WebMaps can be used to administer Web site content to help you keep your Web site up-to-date and functioning correctly. You use the Link Info window, searches, and properties to help manage your site's content. In this section you are shown how to use the Link Info windows to find and repair the following:

- ▶ Broken links
- ▶ Hyperlink text
- ▶ Headings
- ▶ Titles

To show the Link Info window, create a WebMap of your Web site. Click the Object Links toolbar button, or right-click the page you want to view and select Links. The Link Info window is displayed (see Figure 7.7). In this window, you can display different types of links on a page.

Figure 7.7

The Link Info window.

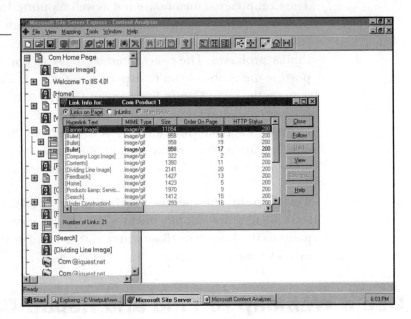

Click the Links on Page option to display all links on a selected page. This is handy if you want to review navigational paths on a page.

Click the InLinks option to display links that reference the page you are reviewing. These are called InLinks, and can be from pages on the same site as the page you're viewing or from another site.

When you click the Main Route option, the Link Info window displays all ancestor links from the main page to the selected page. If the page you're reviewing is your site's home page, for instance, you won't see any other ancestors. However, if the page is one level below the home page (that is, you can link to the page from the home page), you'll see the home page displayed when selecting the Main Route option. This is because the home page is the *parent* of the page you're reviewing. Pages one level below the child page are considered *grandchildren* to the home page, and so on. You'll find this option handy when you're viewing a page that is buried deep in the hierarchy and ancestry is not easy to discern.

Finally, to see the number of links for each type of link option you can display, look at the bottom of the Link Info window.

Fix Broken Links

As your Web site matures and content is upgraded, deleted, moved, and renamed, you'll need to update links on your pages. Over time, however, some of your page may contain broken links, those references that lead nowhere. You can use a WebMap to discover broken links and then launch your Web page editor to fix the link.

You can use two methods to search for broken objects in your pages. One way is to conduct a search for all links that are broken. Another way is to search for broken objects or for objects based on a specific HTTP status.

To search for broken links, use these steps:

1. Create a WebMap and select Tools, Custom Search (or click the Search toolbar button). The Search dialog box is displayed.

2. Configure the Search dialog box using the following parameters:

   ▶ Object Type set to Links

   ▶ Field set to Broken

   ▶ Modifiers set to Equals

   ▶ Value set to True

Note

There is also an option to select TOOLS, QUICK SEARCH, and BROKEN LINKS.

3. Click Search. The Search Results window displays all broken links, if any.

Note

Sometimes links are shown as broken (shown in red) but really aren't broken at all. A site may be unavailable because of repairs it is going through. Or there may be too much network traffic to enable you to connect to the server. You may need to try the site later to establish a connection to it.

To fix a broken link from the Search Results window, implement the following steps:

1. Select the link.

2. Select the parent page (the page that includes the broken link) of the page you just selected.

3. Select Tools, Launch Helper App.

Checking and Modifying Hyperlink Text

Text that is used to describe a link (that is, the text that is hyperlinked to another object) also can be viewed using the Content Analyzer. Many sites use consistent wording and spellings for hyperlink text pointing to the same object. You can check the In-Links text to a particular object quickly with Content Analyzer. Then, if necessary, launch your editor to modify this text.

To review the hyperlink text, perform the following steps:

1. Select the object that you want to see the InLinks text for.

2. Click the Object Links toolbar button. The Link Info window is displayed.

3. Click the InLinks option.

4. Scroll through the list of InLinks and view the hyperlink text in the Hyperlink Text column.

Note

If Hyperlink Text is not a column in the Links Info window, add it by right-clicking any column header in the Links Info window. Use the Configure Columns dialog box to add the Hyperlink Text column to the Links Info window. Click Done.

5. Select a link you want to change and click Follow. The page you want to change is displayed.

6. Right-click a page you want to modify and select Launch Helper App and the specific application to modify the page. Change the hyperlink text on that page.

Checking and Changing Headers

Content Analyzer can be used to check header information in pages. Headers are HTML tags used to set up sections in your Web pages.

To view headers on a page in Content Analyzer, implement the following steps:

1. Create a WebMap.

2. Right-click a page you want to check.

3. Select Properties to display the Properties dialog box.

4. Click the Page tab and review the Headings area.

5. Click OK to close the Properties dialog box.

If the page you just checked includes a header you want to change, or does not include headers but you want to add them to the page, right-click the page in the WebMap and select Launch Helper App. Select the helper application that enables you to edit the source code of the page. Modify the page to include headers.

Checking Page Titles

You can use Content Analyzer to check page titles. Page titles are referenced by many index servers, and also are used by some browsers (such as Internet Explorer) in bookmark lists.

You'll probably want to check page titles as your Web page content changes or evolves. To check page titles, implement the following steps:

1. Create a WebMap and perform a Custom Search for all pages.

2. Add the Title column to the Search Results window. This shows you the titles for each page displayed.

3. Double-click an object in the Search Results window. The associated browser launches, with the page displayed. Review the page to see if the title for it describes the content of the page. If a title is not shown, create a title for the page based on its content. You can then launch a helper application for editing Web pages to add or modify a page's title.

Resolving WWW Service Problems

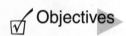 Objectives

HTTP is currently the most used protocol on the Internet. The default control port assignment is 80, and you can hide the service by moving it to any other available port above 1023.

By default, all configured IIS services (WWW, FTP, etc.) start automatically and stop automatically when IIS does. To start, stop, or pause the service manager by site, perform the following steps:

1. Start Internet Service Manager and select the site.

2. Right-click the mouse and choose which of the three options you want (Start, Stop, or Pause).

3. Alternatively, after selecting the site, you can choose the action to take from the toolbar.

If users experience problems viewing your Web site, it can be an indication of permission problems. Make certain that Read permission is assigned to all users for the directory containing the site.

The Anonymous Access and Authentication Control field of the site's property sheet enable you to choose among anonymous access, basic authentication permissions, or Windows NT Challenge/Response. Work backwards in selecting an option from the list until you hit the combination allowing all of your clients to connect to the site without difficulty.

Resolving FTP Service Problems

As discussed elsewhere in this book, you can install a Windows NT FTP server that can provide FTP file transfer services to other systems. This allows the server to serve clients in the same manner that has traditionally been done on UNIX machines. The FTP service is a component of IIS.

FTP, or file transfer protocol, provides a simple but robust mechanism for copying files to or from remote hosts using the connection-oriented services of TCP/IP. FTP is a component of the TCP/IP protocol, and is defined in RFC 959. To use FTP to send or receive files, the following requirements must be met:

▶ The client computer must have FTP client software, such as the FTP client included with Windows NT.

▶ The user must have a username and password on the remote system. In some cases, a username of *anonymous* with no password suffices.

▶ The remote system must be running an FTP daemon or service (depending upon whether it is UNIX or NT).

▶ Your system and the remote system must be running the TCP/IP protocol.

You can use FTP in either a command line mode or in a command interpreter mode. The following options are available from the command line:

```
C:\>ftp ?
Transfers files to and from a computer running an FTP server
              service (sometimes called a daemon). Ftp can be
              used interactively.

FTP [-v] [-d] [-i] [-n] [-g] [-s:filename] [-a] [-w:windowsize]
➥[host]

    -v           Suppresses display of remote server responses.
    -n           Suppresses auto-login upon initial connection.
    -i           Turns off interactive prompting during multiple
                 file transfers.
    -d           Enables debugging.
    -g           Disables filename globbing (see GLOB command).
    -s:filename  Specifies a text file containing FTP commands;
                 the commands will automatically run after FTP
                 starts.
    -a           Use any local interface when binding data
                 connection.
    -w:buffersize Overrides the default transfer buffer size of
                 4096.
    host         Specifies the host name or IP address of the
                 remote host to connect to.
```

If you use FTP in a command interpreter mode, some of the more frequently used options are as follows:

▶ open: Specifies the remote system to which you connect.

▶ close: Disconnects from a remote system. Bye or Quit work as well.

▶ ls: Obtains a directory listing on a remote system, much like the dir command in DOS. Note that the ls -l command provides file size and time stamps. In Windows NT you can use the old DOS DIR as well.

▶ cd: Changes directories on the remote system. This command functions in much the same way as the DOS cd command.

▶ lcd: Changes directories on the local system. This command also functions in much the same way as the DOS cd command.

▶ binary: Instructs FTP to treat all files transferred as binary.

▶ ascii: Instructs FTP to treat all files transferred as text. You need to choose a transfer type because certain files cannot be read correctly as binary, while ASCII is universally accepted.

▶ get: Copies a file from the remote host to your local computer.

▶ put: Copies a file from your local computer to the remote host.

▶ debug: Turns on debugging commands that can be useful in diagnosing problems.

Because remote host systems typically are based on UNIX, you will encounter a number of nuances relating to UNIX if you interact with these hosts in your FTP connections:

▶ The UNIX operating system uses the forward slash in path references, not the backward slash. In UNIX, the filename \WINNT40\README.TXT would be /WINNT40/ README.TXT.

▶ UNIX is case sensitive at all times—the command get MyFile and the command get MYFILE are not the same. Usernames and passwords also are case sensitive.

▶ UNIX treats wild card characters, such as the asterisk and the question mark, differently. The glob command within FTP changes how wild card characters in local filenames are treated.

The biggest problems with FTP typically involve permissions in uploading and downloading files. To upload files, a user (whether specified by name or anonymous) must have change permission to the directory. To download files, a user (again, either by name or anonymous) must have read permission. These represent the very bare bones permissions required to perform these operations. If an anonymous user cannot get connected, verify that the anonymous user password is the same in both User Manager for Domains and Internet Service Manager. These are distinct logons and passwords, and unified logons work only if their values are the same.

To prevent anonymous users from logging on to your site, you can take advantage of this information about FTP. When FTP is running on the server it constantly looks for activity on control port 21—its pre-assigned number. If you wish to offer the service, yet hide its availability, you can do so by changing the port assignment from 21 to any open number greater than 1023. Alternatively, or additionally, you can disable anonymous access by unchecking the Allow Anonymous Access checkbox in the Authentication Methods dialog box for each site.

FTP usage statistics can be gathered from Performance Monitor using the Connection Attempts and Logon Attempts counters. The former reports when a host attempts to connect to a target anonymously, while the latter indicates those times a connection other than anonymous was attempted.

Exercises

Exercise 7.1:   Examine your Windows 95 TCP/IP configuration

To become familiar with how TCP/IP is configured, examine your TCP/IP configuration information on a Windows 95 system and implement the following steps:

1. Choose Run from the Start menu.

2. Type WINIPCFG and press Enter.

3. Select the More Info >> button.

4. Note the Host and Adapter information that appears.

Exercise 7.2:   Examine your Windows NT TCP/IP configuration

To become more familiar with how TCP/IP is configured, examine your TCP/IP configuration information on a Windows NT Workstation or Server system that is manually configured. Implement the following steps:

1. Right-click Network Neighborhood and choose Properties.

2. Select the Protocols tab.

3. Highlight TCP/IP and choose Properties.

4. Note the configuration information presented.

Exercise 7.3:   Setting NTFS Permissions

To set the NTFS Permissions on a directory or file object, the following steps must be completed:

1. Right-click the NTFS Resource.

2. Select Properties from the pop-up menu for the object.

3. Switch to the Security Page of the object. This only appears if the resource is on an NTFS volume.

continues

Exercise 7.3: Continued

4. Click the Permissions button.

5. Click the Add Button to add new groups and users to assign NTFS permissions to the resource.

6. Click the local group or user that you want to assign permissions to and choose the NTFS permission you wish to assign from the bottom drop list.

7. Click the OK button to return to the Directory Permissions dialog box. From the top of the dialog box, choose whether you want to replace the permissions on all existing files in the directory and whether you want the changes to propagate to all subdirectories.

8. Click OK to make your changes to NTFS permissions effective.

9. Answer Yes to the dialog box that questions whether you want the change in security information to replace the existing security information on all files in all subdirectories.

10. Click OK to exit the Directory's properties dialog box.

Exercise 7.4: Using NBTSTAT to view the local NetBIOS name cache and add entries to the cache from an LMHOSTS file

You should have installed TCP/IP and have another Windows client with TCP/IP installed and file sharing enabled.

1. Use Notepad to open the file \WINNT\SYSTEM32\DRIVERS\ETC\LMHOSTS.SAM.

2. Add an entry to the bottom of the file for the other Windows client, specifying the NetBIOS name and the IP address of the Windows client. Make sure that there's not a comment (#) in front of this line.

3. Save the file in the same directory as LMHOSTS (without an extension).

4. From a command prompt on your NT computer, type `nbtstat -c`. This displays the local cache.

5. From a command prompt, type nbstat -R. This purges the cache and loads the contents of the LMHOSTS file into the local cache.

6. From a command prompt, type nbtstat -c to display the new contents of the local cache.

7. Using Windows NT Explorer, map a network drive to the other Windows client. The local cache was used to resolve the NetBIOS name for this connection.

8. From a command prompt, type nbtstat /? to see all the switches available with the NBTSTAT command.

Exercise 7.5: Examine your Windows NT TCP/IP configuration

To examine your TCP/IP configuration information on a Windows NT Workstation or Server system that is configured through static or dynamic IP addresses (DHCP), implement the following steps:

1. From the Start menu, select Programs, and then Command Prompt.

2. Type in IPCONFIG.

3. Note the information that appears. Now type IPCONFIG /ALL.

4. Note the information that appears.

Exercise 7.6: Examine your Windows NT configuration with the Resource Kit

To examine your TCP/IP configuration information if the Windows NT Resource Kit CD has been installed on your system, implement the following steps:

1. From the Start menu, Choose Programs, then Resource Kit 4.0.

2. Choose Internet Utils and then IP Configuration.

continues

Exercise 7.6: Continued

   3. Select the More Info >> button.

   4. Note the Host and Adapter information that appears.

Exercise 7.7: Correcting a network configuration error

Use this exercise to see the effects that an improperly configured network card has on other networking services and protocols. Before starting, make sure you have installed Windows NT Server with a computer that has a network adapter card and that TCP/IP has been installed.

1. Clear the System Log in Event Viewer.

2. From the desktop, right-click on Network Neighborhood and choose Properties from the resulting menu.

3. From the Network Properties dialog box, select the Adapters tab.

4. Select your adapter card from the list and choose Properties.

5. Note the correct setting as it is and change the .IRQ of your adapter card to an incorrect setting.

6. Close this dialog box and choose to reboot your computer when prompted.

7. When your computer reboots, note the message received after the Logon prompt is displayed. The message should indicate A Dependency Service Failed to Start.

8. Log on and open Event Viewer.

9. Note the error message generated from the adapter card. Note the other error messages generated after the adapter card error.

10. Clear the System Log in Event Viewer.

11. From the command prompt, type ping 127.0.0.1. This Ping fails because TCP/IP doesn't start if the adapter doesn't start.

12. From the Network Properties dialog box, change the .IRQ of your adapter card back to its proper setting and reboot.

13. Log on and check the System Log. There should be no adapter card errors or errors from networking services.

14. From the command prompt, type ping 127.0.0.1. This Ping succeeds because TCP/IP is started now.

Exercise 7.8:   Using Ping to test an IP configuration

This exercise uses Ping to verify a TCP/IP installation and configuration. You should have installed Windows NT Server and TCP/IP.

1. From the desktop, right-click on Network Neighborhood and choose Properties from the resulting menu.

2. From the Bindings tab, expand all the networking services.

3. Select TCP/IP and choose Disable.

4. Repeat Step 3 until you have disabled TCP/IP for all the listed networking services.

5. Close the dialog box and, when prompted, choose to reboot your computer.

6. When the computer reboots, log in.

7. From a command prompt, type ping 127.0.0.1. This Ping works because TCP/IP is installed.

8. From a command prompt, type ping x.x.x.x, where x.x.x.x is your default gateway address. This Ping fails because you have disabled TCP/IP from all the networking services. There isn't a way for TCP/IP packets to be sent on the network.

9. From the Bindings tab in Network Properties, enable TCP/IP for all the networking services.

10. Close the dialog box and, when prompted, choose to reboot your computer.

continues

Exercise 7.8: Continued

11. When the computer reboots, log in.

12. From a command prompt, ping your default gateway. The Ping works this time because a path now exists by which TCP/IP communications can reach the network.

Review Questions

1. Which of the following NTFS Directory permissions enables the user to view the contents of a directory and to navigate to its subdirectories?

   A. No Access

   B. List

   C. Read

   D. Add

   E. Change

2. Which of the following NTFS Directory permissions overrides all other permissions?

   A. No Access

   B. List

   C. Read

   D. Add

   E. Change

3. Which of the following NTFS Directory permissions enables the user to do the most data manipulation?

   A. No Access

   B. List

   C. Read

   D. Add

   E. Change

4. Which of the following NTFS Directory permissions enables the user to navigate the entire directory structure, view the contents of the directory, view the contents of any files in the directory, and execute programs?

   A. No Access

   B. List

   C. Read

   D. Add

   E. Change

5. Which of the following NTFS Directory permissions enables the user to add new subdirectories and files to the directory, but not to access files within the directory?

   A. No Access

   B. List

   C. Read

   D. Add

   E. Change

6. Which set of permissions enable a user to add new files to the directory structure and, once the files have been added, ensures that the user has read-only access to the files?

   A. No Access

   B. List

   C. Read

   D. Add

   E. Change

7. HOSTS file entries are limited to how many characters?

   A. 8

   B. 255

   C. 500

   D. unlimited

8. The number of entries in the HOSTS file is limited to

   A. 8

   B. 255

   C. 500

   D. unlimited

9. Which of the following files are case sensitive on NT 3.5 systems?

   A. HOSTS

   B. LMHOSTS

   C. ARP

   D. FQDN

10. Which of the following files is used for NetBIOS name resolution?

    A. HOSTS

    B. LMHOSTS

    C. ARP

    D. FQDN

11. Index Server error messages can be viewed with

    A. Server Manager

    B. User Manager for Domains

    C. Event Viewer

    D. Disk Administrator

12. Index Server error messages are written to what log file?

    A. System

    B. Server

    C. Security

    D. Application

13. To run IIS 4.0 on NT, which Service Pack must be installed?

    A. none

    B. 1

    C. 2

    D. 3

14. What version of Internet Explorer is required on the IIS Server for IIS version 4.0?

    A. 2.0

    B. 3.0

    C. 3.01

    D. 4.01

15. Which of the following server services operates, by default, at control port 80:

    A. WWW

    B. FTP

    C. Gopher

    D. Index Server

Review Answers

1. **B**. List enables the user to view the contents of a directory and to navigate to its subdirectories.

2. **A**. No Access overrides all other permissions.

3. **E**. Change enables the user to do the most data manipulation.

4. **C**. Read enables the user to navigate the entire directory structure, view the contents of the directory, view the contents of any files in the directory, and execute programs.

5. **D**. Add enables the user to add new subdirectories and files to the directory, but not to access files within the directory.

6. **C, D**. Read and Add enable a user to add new files to the directory structure and, once the files have been added, the user then has only read-only access to the files.

7. **B**. HOSTS file lines are limited to 255 characters in length.

8. **D**. The HOSTS file can be an unlimited number of lines long.

9. **A**. The HOSTS file, prior to NT 4.0, was case sensitive and remains so on non-NT systems.

10. **B**. LMHOSTS is the static file used for NetBIOS name resolution.

11. **C**. Index Server system errors can be viewed with Event Viewer.

12. **D**. Index Server error messages are written to the application log.

13. **D**. To run IIS 4.0 on NT, Service Pack 3 must be installed.

14. **D**. Internet Explorer 4.01 or greater is required on the IIS Server for IIS version 4.0.

15. **A**. The WWW server services operates, by default, at control port 80.

Answers to Test Yourself Questions at Beginning of Chapter

1. The IP address, the subnet mask, and the default gateway are the three values that must be entered at each host to configure TCP/IP. See "Resolving IIS Configuration Problems."

2. With the Read permission, users can view any documents that are stored in the share, but they cannot make any changes to the documents. See "Resolving Security Problems."

3. IPCONFIG/ALL shows the DHCP server as well as all IP configuration information. See "Resolving Resource Access Problems."

4. By default, Index Server starts when IIS starts. If, for some reason, it has not started, Index Server starts with the first query. See "Resolving Index Server Query Problems."

5. To upgrade IIS 3.0 to IIS 4.0, you must first delete all traces of the IIS 3.0 operating files before installing 4.0. See "Resolving Setup Issues When Installing IIS on a Windows NT Server 4.0 Computer."

6. Content Analyzer's WebMap can be used to administer site content. It is new to IIS 4.0 and can help you keep your site up-to-date and functioning correctly. See "Use a WebMap to Find and Repair Broken Links, Hyperlink Texts, Headings, and Titles."

7. The default TCP control port for the WWW service is 80. See "Resolving WWW Service Problems."

8. The default TCP control port for the FTP service is 21. See "Resolving FTP Service Problems."

Appendix

Modifying IIS 4 with the Registry

Many of the customization choices available to you with IIS 4.0 can be made from the Internet Service Manager. However, you also can make changes directly in the Windows NT Registry that affect IIS 4.0 performance.

Note

Don't make any Registry changes until you've made a backup. You can learn how to do this and more about the Registry in general by reading *Windows NT Registry Troubleshooting*, published by New Riders.

Table A.1 lists and describes some of the common Registry changes you can make to the Web service settings that appear under the following Registry path:

`HKEY_LOCAL_MACHINE\SYSTEM\CurrentControlSet\Services\W3SVC\Paramters`

Table A.1

Registry entries for the Web service.

Property	Data Type	Default Setting	Range Value	Description
AcceptByte Ranges	REG_DWORD	1 (enabled)	1, 0	When enabled, the Web server sends the Accept-Range:bytes header field to accept range requests.

continues

Table A.1 Continued

Property	Data Type	Default Setting	Range Value	Description
AllowGuest Access	REG_DWORD	1 (enabled)	1, 0	Enables guest services on the service. This entry is available for the FTP service (MSFTPSVC) as well. Change this entry to 0 to disable guest access on your server.
AllowSpecial CharsInShell	REG_DWORD	0 (disabled)	1, 0	Enables batch files (.BAT and .CMD) to use special characters, including ;, ,, |, (, %, and <>. Keep this setting to 0 to reduce the threat of hackers using these characters to hack into your site. If you enable this setting, users can pass these characters (except | and <>) to CGI scripts. When disabled, however, users cannot send these characters to CGI scripts.

Property	Data Type	Default Setting	Range Value	Description
DLCCookie NameString	REG_STRING	none	string	Denotes the cookie string that is sent to downlevel clients.
DLCHost NameString	REG_STRING	none	string	Specifies the Web site name where the downlevel host menu document is stored. You can find the downlevel host menu name by looking at the DLCCookieMenu DocumentString Registry entry.
DLCCookie MenuDocument String	REG_STRING	none	string	Indicates the host menu file name for clients that do not support HOST header but that support cookies.
DLCMunge MenuDocument String	REG_STRING	none	string	Indicates the host menu filename for clients that do not support cookies.
DLCMenu String	REG_STRING	none	string	Specifies the special prefix of URLs requested by downlevel clients.

continues

Table A.1 Continued

Property	Data Type	Default Setting	Range Value	Description
DLCSupport	REG_DWORD	0 (disabled)	1, 0	Enables downlevel client support.
EnableSvc Loc	REG_DWORD	1 (enabled)	1, 0	Registers IIS services so the Internet Service Manager can locate the service. This entry is supported by the FTP service as well.
Language Engines*	REG_STRING	none	string	Specifies a scripting language that does not support the Active Server Pages Object Method syntax.
LogError Requests	REG_DWORD	1 (enabled)	1, 0	Enables or disables error logging.
LogSuccess Requests	REG_DWORD	1 (enabled)	1, 0	Enables or disables the logging of successful activities.
SSIEnable CmdDirective	REG_DWORD	1 (enabled)	1, 0	Setting this value to 0 increases security for sites wanting to disable the #exec cmd directive of server-side includes when shell commands are executed.

Property	Data Type	Default Setting	Range Value	Description
TryExcept Disable	REG_DWORD	0 (disabled)	1, 0	When ISAPI applications run, this setting enables or disables exception caching when Http Extensionproc() is called. Set this entry to 1 when you want to perform JIT debugging. Otherwise, set it to 0 so ISAPI applications do not bring the server down in the event of an error in the ISAPI application.
UploadRead Ahead	REG_DWORD	48KB	0-0x80000000	Specifies the default amount of data posted by a client that the server reads before passing control to the application. Higher values require more server RAM.

*To use the LanguageEngines entry, you must create the following key under the W3SVC key:

\ASP\LanguageEntries*Name_of_Language*.

Appendix

Background on Subnets

B

An *internet* or *internetwork* is a group of computers linked together using TCP/IP technology. An internet can be either a portion of the *Internet* (the worldwide network of publicly interconnected TCP/IP networks) or a private corporate or enterprise internetwork. Such private internetworks are usually called *intranets* to show that they are internal to an enterprise and not part of the Internet.

Communication in a TCP/IP network is based on sending messages back and forth between computers and network devices. The messages contain sender and recipient addresses, known as *IP addresses*. The IP addresses are in an octet-based (coming from eight binary numbers) form, such as 100.34.192.212. The first octet (you learn about the others later) dictates the *class* of network that is being referred to, and as such, there are three classes:

01–126	Class A
128–191	Class B
192–223	Class C

Thus, an address of 100.34.192.212 is clearly a class A address, and one of 220.34.192.212 is a class C address. The class is important, because it indicates the maximum number of hosts that a network can have. The breakout of numbers of host looks like this:

Class A	16,777,214
Class B	65,534
Class C	254

Although the existing shortage of addresses has made it impossible to obtain a class A address for some time, imagine the difficulties inherent in trying to network 16 million hosts at a single site—it is virtually impossible. At the same time, networking 254 hosts, although not impossible, is rarely done at a single site either. Typically, hosts are spread out across several physical locations, often within the same building, campus, or other geographical area.

For that reason, and to make routing practical, subnets are used to divide the network (and network numbers) into smaller portions. This appendix assumes some familiarity with the basics of TCP/IP and addressing and concentrates on *subnetting*—one of the most misunderstood components of addressing.

Simply put, subnetting is a mechanism for using some bits in the host ID octets as a subnet ID. Without subnetting, an IP address is interpreted as two fields:

netid + hostid

With subnetting, an IP address is interpreted as three fields:

netid + subnetid + hostid

This topic is examined thoroughly in the following sections:

▶ Subnet masks, host IDs, and network IDs

▶ Purpose of subnet masks

▶ Default subnet masks

▶ Subdividing a network

Subnet Masks, Host IDs, and Network IDs

Subnets are created in a TCP/IP internetwork by choosing the IP addresses and subnet masks used, a process known as *subnet addressing* or *subnetting*. The term *network* is used when it is not necessary to distinguish between individual subnets and internet-works. A *subnet* is simply a subdivision of a network. The term *sub-networking* or *subnetting* is used when a single network ID is subdivided into multiple network IDs by applying a custom subnet mask.

> **Note**
>
> An analogy for a subnet is a phone number. The area code equates to a network, the prefix equates to a subnet, and the last four digits equate to the actual host.

The *subnet mask*, like the IP address, is a 32-bit number, often shown in dotted decimal notation. When shown in binary notation, the subnet mask has a 1 bit for each bit corresponding to the position of the network ID in the IP address and a 0 bit for each bit corresponding to the position of the host ID in the IP address (in binary notation). An example of a subnet mask is

11111111111111111100000000000000

or 255.255.0.0 in dotted decimal notation.

> **Note**
>
> A binary number is made up of bits. A bit can be either a 1 or a 0, where 1 represents TRUE and 0 represents FALSE. All computer operations are performed using binary numbers, because the bits are easily represented by electrical charges. Huge binary numbers are usually fairly meaningless to the average person, so the computer converts them to more human-friendly states, such as decimal numbers and characters.
>
> Any decimal number is represented in binary notation, using 1s and 0s. Each bit with a 1 represents 2 raised to the power of $n-1$ ($2^{(n-1)}$), in which n is the position of the bit from the right. Each bit with a 0 represents a 0 in decimal notation as well. The decimal number results from adding together all the 1 bits after converting each to $2^{(n-1)}$.
>
> For example, the binary number 100 is 2^2, which means the decimal equivalent is 4.
>
> *continues*

The binary number 101 is 2^2+0+2^0, or 5 in decimal notation.

With TCP/IP, you often use 8-bit binary numbers, also called octets or bytes in IP addresses. An example is

11111111

Each bit in position n from the right gives a value of $2^{(n-1)}$. Therefore the first bit represents a 1, the second bit a 2, the third a 4, the fourth an 8, and so forth, so that you have the following:

1 1 1 1 1 1 1 1   (binary)

128+64+32+16+8+4+2+1 = 255   (decimal)

Keep in mind that any 0 bits do not add to the total, so the following are equal:

1 1 0 0 1 0 0 1 (binary)

128+64+0 +0 +8+0+0+1 = 201   (decimal)

Memorizing the decimal equivalent number of each character in the 8-bit number, as in the following:

Decimal to Binary

1	1	1	1	1	1	1	1
128	64	32	16	8	4	2	1

makes it extremely easy to convert between binary and decimal quickly. For example, the number

01111111

should be easily recognized as 127, by taking the maximum value (255) and subtracting the missing digit (128). Likewise, the following:

11011111

is quickly converted to 223 by subtracting the value of the missing digit (32) from the maximum value (255).

The 0 bits of the subnet mask essentially mask out, or cover up, the host ID portion of an IP address. Thus, the subnet mask is used to determine on which network or subnet the address being referred to is found. When one host sends a message to another host, the TCP/IP protocol must determine whether the hosts are on the same subnet and can communicate by broadcasts, or whether they are on different subnets and the message should be sent via a router to the other subnet. It is impossible to determine whether two IP addresses are on the same subnet just by looking at the IP addresses without the subnet mask. For example, if the host at 192.20.1.5 sends a message to the host at 192.20.6.8, should it be sent by broadcast or to a router connecting to another subnet?

The answer depends on the subnet mask being used on the network. If the subnet mask was 255.255.255.0, the network ID of the first host would be 192.20.1, and the network ID of the second host would be 192.20.6. The hosts would be on different subnets, and therefore they must communicate via a router. On the other hand, if the subnet mask was 255.255.0.0, both hosts would be on subnet 192.20 and could communicate by using local broadcasts and local address resolution.

When the subnet mask is one of 255.0.0.0, 255.255.0.0, or 255.255.255.0, it is fairly obvious which part of the IP address is the network ID (these are the defaults for class A, B, and C networks, respectively). Yet, it becomes less apparent which part of the IP address is the network when other subnet masks are used (such as 255.255.248.0). In this case, if both the IP address and subnet mask are converted to binary, it becomes more apparent (the 1 bits of the subnet mask correspond to the network ID in the IP address).

By figuring out what subnet a host is on from the IP address and subnet mask, it becomes easier to route a packet to the proper destination. Fortunately, all you have to do is supply the proper IP addresses with one subnet mask for the entire internetwork, and the software determines which subnet the destination is on. If the destination address is on a different subnet than the sender, it is on a remote network and the packet is routed appropriately, usually by being sent to the default gateway.

If a network has a small number of hosts, all on the same segment without any routers, they are likely given the same network ID (the network portion of an IP address). If the network is larger, however, with remote segments connected by routers (an internetwork), each individual subnet needs a different network ID. Therefore, when assigning IP addresses and subnet masks, the network administrator must know how many subnets are required and the maximum number of hosts that are on each subnet.

Depending on the subnet mask chosen, the internetwork can have either a lot of different network IDs with a smaller number of hosts on each subnet or a smaller number of network IDs with a larger number of hosts on each subnet. It will become clearer why the results are the way they are as you read further; Table B.1 shows the maximum number of hosts and subnets available per the number of bits used.

Table B.1

Hosts and subnets.

Subnet Address	Additional Bits Required	Maximum Number of Subnets	Maximum Number of Hosts— C Network	Maximum number of Hosts— B Network	Maximum number of Hosts— A Network
0	0	0	254	65,534	16,777,214
192	2	2	62	16,382	4,194,302
224	3	6	30	8,190	2,097,150
240	4	14	14	4,094	1,048,574
248	5	30	6	2,046	524,286
252	6	62	2	1,022	262,142
254	7	126	invalid	510	131,070
255	8	254	invalid	254	65,534

Purpose of Subnet Masks

By specifying the correct subnet mask for addresses, you are letting the TCP/IP software know which part of the address refers to the host and which part refers to the specific subnet the host is located on. As mentioned previously, the IP address and subnet mask are made up of four 8-bit octets that are most often shown in decimal rather than binary format for ease of reading. As an example, an IP address and subnet mask in binary format could be

```
IP Address:     11001000 00010100 00010000 00000101
Subnet Mask:    11111111 11111111 11111111 00000000
Network ID:     11001000 00010100 00010000 00000000
Host ID:        00000000 00000000 00000000 00000101
```

Notice that the network ID is the portion of the IP address corresponding to a bit value of 1 in the subnet mask.

In the preceding example, you could have a maximum of 254 different hosts on the network 192.20.16 (192.20.16.1 through 192.20.16.254). If you want to have more hosts on one network, you have to use a different addressing scheme. For example, using a subnet mask of 255.255.0.0 gives the following results:

```
IP Address      192.20.16.5
Subnet Mask     255.255.0.0
Network ID      192.20
Host ID         16.5
```

Note

It is common in TCP/IP to omit the trailing zero octets in a network ID and the leading zero octets in a host ID. Therefore, the network ID 192.20 really represents 192.20.0.0, and the host ID 16.5 really represents 0.0.16.5.

Because the host ID in this example is a 16-bit value, it allows you to have (256×256)−2 hosts on the network 192.20. The two addresses that must be subtracted from the possibilities are 0 (consisting of all 0s) and 255 (consisting of all 1s)—both reserved addresses. 0 is used to define the network, and 255 is a broadcast address for all computers in the network.

A host ID cannot have all bits set to either 1 or 0 because these addresses would be interpreted to mean a broadcast address or "this network only," respectively. Thus, the number of valid addresses is $(2^n)-2$, where n is the number of bits used for the host ID.

Common law dictates that address bits cannot be all 1s or 0s. In reality, if—and *only* if—the routers on the network support extended prefixing addressing, it is possible to have addresses of all 1s or 0s. Both the software and the routers must support RIP V2, and you must disallow the possibility of traffic over any older—noncompatible—routers.

Cisco routers, NetWare 4.*x*, and Windows NT all support the extended prefixing address (though they often call it a *zero network*). Although going against the principles of RFC 950, they permit the use of the all-0s and all-1s subnets. Just one NetWare 3.*x* system anywhere on your network, or any older router, means that the zero-network option cannot be used. For all practical purposes, however, you should consider 0s and 1s off limits.

You may also notice that the second scheme allows fewer combinations of network IDs than the first scheme. Although the second sample scenario might seem preferable for most networks, you often may not have the freedom to use such a scheme. For example, if the hosts are on the Internet, you must assign a certain set of IP addresses by the Internet address assignment authority, InterNIC (the Internet Network Information Center). Because the number of IP addresses available today is limited, you usually do not have the luxury of choosing a scheme that gives so many combinations of available host addresses. Suppose you are assigned the network ID 192.20.5 and have a total of 1,000 hosts on three remote networks. A class C network using the default subnet mask of 255.255.255.0 has only one network (192.20.5) and 254 hosts (192.20.5.1 through 192.20.5.254).

Now look at how a subnet mask is used to determine which part of the IP address is the network ID and which part is the host ID. TCP/IP does a binary calculation using the IP address and the subnet mask to determine the network ID portion of the IP address.

The computation TCP/IP performs is a logical bitwise AND of the IP address and the subnet mask. The calculation sounds complicated, but all it means is that the octets are converted to binary numbers, and a logical AND is performed whose result is the network ID. To make it simpler, recall that in the preceding example, the network ID is the portion of the IP address corresponding to a bit value of 1 in the subnet mask.

Performing a bitwise AND on 2 bits results in 1 (or TRUE) if the two values are both 1. If either or both of the values are not 1, the result is 0 (or FALSE).

Any logical AND with a 0 results in 0. For example:

1 AND 1 results in 1.

1 AND 0 results in 0.

0 AND 1 results in 0.

0 AND 0 results in 0.

In the first example of this section, the IP address 192.20.16.5 is ANDed with the subnet mask 255.255.255.0 to give a network ID of 192.20.16. The calculation that is performed is illustrated in Table B.2.

Table B.2

Example of a bitwise AND operation.

	Decimal Notation	Binary Notation
IP address	192.20.16.5	11000000.00010100. 00010000.00000101
Subnet mask	255.255.255.0	11111111.11111111. 11111111.00000000
IP address AND subnet mask	192.20.16.0	11000000.00010100. 00010000.00000000

Determining the network ID is very easy if the subnet mask is made up of only 255 and 0 values. Simply "mask" or cover up the part of the IP address corresponding to the 0 octet of the subnet mask. For example, if the IP address is 15.6.100.1 and the subnet mask is 255.255.0.0, the resulting network ID is 15.6. You are not able to use a subnet mask with only 255 and 0 values if you need to subdivide your network ID into individual subnets.

Default Subnet Masks

There are default masks, usually assigned by the vendor, based upon the class of network in question. Table B.3 shows the subnet mask that appears in the subnet mask field when an IP address is selected.

Table B.3

Default subnet masks.

Class	IP Address	Default Subnet Mask
A	001.y.z.w to 126.y.z.w	255.0.0.0
B	128.y.z.w to 191.y.z.w	255.255.0.0
C	192.y.z.w to 223.y.z.w	255.255.255.0

Thus, using the default mask, the emphasis is on the number of hosts available and nothing more, as Table B.4 illustrates.

Table B.4

Maximum number of networks and hosts per network in TCP/IP.

Class Hosts	Using Default Subnet Mask	Number of Networks	Number of per Network
A	255.0.0.0	126	16,777,216
B	255.255.0.0	16,384	65,534
C	255.255.255.0	2,097,152	254

If the hosts on your internetwork are not directly on the Internet, you are free to choose the network IDs that you use. For the hosts and subnets that are a part of the Internet, however, the network IDs you use must be assigned by InterNIC.

It must be noted that if you are using network IDs assigned by InterNIC, you do not have the choice of choosing the address class you use (and you can bet you will be given class C addresses). In this case, the number of subnets you use is normally limited by the number of network IDs assigned by InterNIC, and the number of hosts per subnet is determined by the class of address. Fortunately, by choosing the proper subnet mask, you can subdivide your network into a greater number of subnets with fewer possible hosts per subnet.

Today, many companies with Internet requirements are avoiding the addressing constraints and security risks of having hosts directly on the Internet by setting up private networks with gateway access to the Internet. Having a private network means that only the Internet gateway host needs to have an Internet address. For security, a firewall can be set up to prevent Internet hosts from directly accessing the company's network.

Subdividing a Network

Internetworks are networks comprised of individual segments connected by routers. The reasons for having distinct segments are

- ▶ They permit physically remote local networks to be connected.

- ▶ A mix of network technologies are connected, such as ethernet on one segment and token ring on another.

- ▶ They allow an unlimited number of hosts to communicate, whereas the number of hosts on each segment are limited by the type of network used.

- ▶ Network congestion is reduced as broadcasts and local network traffic are limited to the local segment.

Each segment is a subnet of the internetwork and requires a unique network ID. If you have only one network ID that is used—for example, if you have an InterNIC-assigned Internet network ID—you have to subdivide that network ID into subnets.

The steps involved in subnetting a network are

1. Determine the number of network IDs required for planning future growth needs.

2. Determine the maximum number of host addresses that are on each subnet, again allowing for future growth.

3. Define one subnet mask for the entire internetwork that gives the desired number of subnets and allows enough hosts per subnet.

4. Determine the resulting subnet network IDs that are used.

5. Determine the valid host IDs and assign IP addresses to the hosts.

For Further Information

The best possible sources of subnet information are two RFCs that define the concept:

▶ RFC 950—Internet Standard Subnetting Procedure

▶ RFC 1219—On the Assignment of Subnet Numbers

These can be found at a number of locations on the Internet.

Appendix

C

Passing the Internet Information Server 3.0 Exam

The Microsoft IIS 3.0 exam, "Implementing and Supporting Microsoft Internet Information Server 3.0 and Microsoft Index Server 1.1," is commonly referred to by its exam number, 70-77. This exam is still valid and offered by Microsoft as an elective in several tracks. As you look at the exam, you will see that 70-77 is really a subset of 70-87. The exam is much simpler because you need know only about Information Server and Index Server and nothing about the products that had not yet been added to IIS, such as SMTP, NNTP, Certificate Server, and so on.

The material presented here reveals the simplicity of the exam and the ease with which you can pass it if you are familiar with IIS (3.0 *or* 4.0). On exam 70-77, there are 49 questions asked, and a candidate has 90 minutes to answer them.

The exam is divided into seven objective categories: Planning, Installation and Configuration, Managing Resources, Connectivity, Running Applications, Monitoring and Optimization, and Troubleshooting. These categories are covered below in terms of the exam highlights.

Planning

The WWW service and FTP service are the services the exam primarily focuses on (and Index Server, of course). The WWW is the most popular service on the Internet, and FTP is mainly used for uploading and downloading files.

IIS automatically creates a user account upon installation with the username of IUSR_*computername*. This is the account used for anonymous access and is granted Log on Locally user rights by default. The account is necessary for anonymous logon access to your Web site, and permissions applied to it control the permissions for the anonymous user. You can ever go so far as to disable anonymous access if security is a concern (as in an intranet versus an Internet site).

For the WWW service, available authentication methods include the following:

▶ Allow Anonymous Access—Enables clients to connect to your Web site without requiring a username or password by using the default account of IUSR_*computername*.

▶ Basic Authentication—This method is used if you do not specify anonymous access and you want a client connecting to your Web site to enter a valid Windows NT username and password to log on. This sends a password in clear text format (the passwords are transmitted in an unencrypted format).

▶ Windows NT Challenge/Response—This setting is used if you want the Windows NT Challenge/Response feature to authenticate the client attempting to connect to your Web site. The only Web browsers that support this feature include Internet Explorer 2.0 and higher. During the challenge/response procedure, cryptographic information is exchanged between the client and server to authenticate the user.

For the FTP service, available authentication methods include the ability to specify that anonymous connections are allowed, that only anonymous connections are allowed, or the administrator can configure user and group accounts. On the exam, know that you cannot specify that only anonymous connections are allowed until you have first allowed anonymous connections.

Know the basics of TCP/IP (including what WINS and DNS are) and IP values, namely the number of hosts available per IP address class as recapped in Table C.1.

Table C.1

IP Address Classes

Class	Address	Number of Hosts Available	Default Subnet Mask
A	01-126	16,777,214	255.0.0.0
B	128-191	65,534	255.255.0.0
C	192-223	254	255.255.255.0

The WINS service is used for dynamic resolution of NetBIOS names to IP addresses, while DNS is used for dynamic resolution of host names to IP addresses. The static version of each is the LMHOSTS and HOSTS files, respectively.

Secure Sockets Layer—or SSL—enables you to protect communications over a network whether that network is an intranet or the Internet. It does so by establishing a private (and encrypted) communication link between the user and the server. SSL can be used not only to authenticate specific users, but anonymous users as well. If SSL is enabled and a user attempts anonymous access, the Web server looks for a valid certificate on the client and rejects those lacking such. To use SSL, you must obtain a digital certificate from an authentication authority and use Key Manager to generate keys. SSL URLs begin with `https://` instead of `http://`.

Installation and Configuration

For purposes of the exam, to install IIS 3.0 you must first remove any previous versions of IIS (2.0 came with Windows NT 4.0). During the installation you are prompted for the services you want to install and given the choice of installing Index Server as well. If you choose not to install a service at this time (including

Index Server), you can restart the installation routine and choose only the additional services you want to add.

Note

> The installation described is for the exam. In reality, you can install IIS 2.0 and then install Service Pack 3 to upgrade to IIS 3.0 and it works fine.

Port settings are used by clients to connect to your FTP or WWW site. By default, the Gopher server service is set to port 70, the FTP server is set up with a port setting of 21, and WWW is set to port 80 (server-side numbers only; client numbers are dynamically assigned). You can change the settings to unique TCP port numbers, but you must announce this setting to all clients who want to access your server.

An FTP directory listing style is the way in which your server will display a directory listing. The two choices are DOS (such as C:\folder\subfolder) and UNIX format (such as C:/directory/subdirectory/). Use UNIX format for the greatest compatibility on the Internet.

You can set IIS to display a default page when clients access your site without a specified document in the URL. From this default page (usually your home page or index page), you can direct users to other documents or resources on your site. Virtual servers (which exist only with WWW) must all use the same default page.

Managing Resources

The Internet Service Manager is the primary utility used for most tasks, including creating and sharing new directories or virtual directories (entities in WWW or FTP that do not exist, but give you the ability to reference relative file locations to make it appear as if they are in a directory). Access permissions for either include the following:

▶ Allow Read Access

▶ Allow Script Access

▶ Allow Execute Access

▶ Allow Write Access

▶ Allow Directory Browsing

The five rights that you can select for IIS access work in conjunction with all other rights. Like share rights, the IIS rights are *in addition to* NTFS rights, and of greatest value when you are using anonymous access. Allowing Read access lets a user view a file if his NTFS permissions also allow such. Taking away Read, however, prevents the user from viewing the file regardless of what his NTFS right may be.

The names of the rights are pretty self-explanatory as to what they offer. The only caveats to note are that Read and Script access are assigned by default, and Execute includes Script access.

With virtual directories (which must exist on servers all within the same NT domain) you can get around issues such as disk space, determining where best to store files, and so on. There are two downfalls to using virtual directories:

▶ There is a slight decrease in performance, as files must be retrieved from the LAN, rather than being centralized

▶ Virtual directories do not show up in WWW listings, and must be accessed through explicit links within HTML files

You also should have a Scripts directory under every virtual home directory to handle the executables there.

The HTML Administrator can let you manage the FTP and WWW services remotely (WWW must first be running in order to use it). From HTML Administrator, you can accomplish almost everything you can do remotely that you can do locally, with the exception of making MIME Registry changes or stopping and starting services (if you stopped WWW, you would be disconnected).

Connectivity

Such databases as Oracle and Microsoft SQL (Structured Query Language) Server can be used with IIS to supply the information to fulfill a query, update information, and add new data through the Web almost as easily as if a user were sitting on a local area network.

Open Database Connectivity (ODBC) is an API (Application Programming Interface) that provides a simple way to connect to an existing database (whether that database is SQL or any ODBC-compliant database). It was designed by Microsoft to address the issue of any number of applications needing to interface with SQL server. Authentication can be done by Windows NT or SQL. If SQL is chosen, it uses standard logon security, and an SQL Server user ID and password must be given for all connections. If you choose to use Windows NT authentication, the Windows NT user account is associated with a SQL Server user account, and integrated security is used to establish the connection regardless of the current security mode at the server.

The greatest advantage that ODBC offers is that it defines a clear distinction between the application and the database, and thus does not require any specific programming. To use it, you create a query and template for how the output is to look.

There are four major components to ODBC:

▶ .htm—The file containing the hyperlink for a query. The request comes from the browser and merely specifies the URL for the .idc (Internet Database Connector) file on IIS.

▶ .htx—The file of HTML extensions containing the template document with placeholders for the result. Database fields that it receives are known as containers, and are identified by field names surrounded by percents (%) and braces (<>). Thus the `employeeno` field that comes from the SQL database is known as `<%employeeno%>`. All processing is done in loops that start with `<%begindetail%>` and end with `<%enddetail%>`. Logic can be included with `<%if...%>` and `<%endif%>`, as well as `<%else%>` statements.

- ▶ .idc—The file containing the data source file information and SQL statement. Four required parameters are Data-source, Username, Template, and SQLStatement. The SQLStatement is the list of commands you want to execute. Parameter values can be used if they are enclosed in percents (%), and if multiple lines are required, then a plus sign (+) must be the first character on each line.

- ▶ Httpodbc.dll—The dynamic link library included with the server.

Index Server differs from the ODBC discussion in the files used to hold the queries. Rather than using the .IDC file, Index Server uses an .IDQ (Internet Data Query) file. The .IDQ file should always be placed in the Scripts directory, and it requires Execute or Script permission to function properly.

There are two sections to the file and it begins with a tag of [Query] (the first section) and is followed by the [Names] section. The Names section is purely optional, and not used most of the time. If it is used, it defines nonstandard column names that are referred to in a query. The Query section of the file is all that is required, and it can contain parameters, variables, and conditional expressions.

Restrictions are that lines must start with the variable you are trying to set, and only one variable can be set per line. Additionally, percents (%) are used to identify the variables and references.

The variables that can be used in .IDQ files are as follows:

- ▶ CiCatalog—Sets the location for the catalog. If the value is already set, the value here overrides that one.

- ▶ CiCodepage—Sets the server's code page. Again, if the value is already set, the entry here overrides the previous one.

- ▶ CiColumns—Defines a list of columns that will be used in the .HTX file.

- ▶ CiDeferNonIndexedTrimming—By default is not used, but can be set if the scope of the query must be limited.

▶ CiFlags—Query flags can be set to DEEP or SHALLOW to determine if only the directory listed in CiScope is searched or more.

▶ CiForceUseCi—By setting to TRUE, you can force the query to use the content index even if it's out of date.

▶ CiLocale—Specifies the locale used to issue the query.

▶ CiMaxRecordsInResultSet—Specifies the maximum number of results that can be returned from the query.

▶ CiMaxRecordsPerPage—Specifies the maximum number of records that can appear on a display page.

▶ CiRestriction—A restriction that you are placing on the query.

▶ CiScope—Specifies the starting directory for the search.

▶ CiSort—Specifies whether the results should be sorted in an ascending or descending order.

▶ CiTemplate—Specifies the full path of the .HTX file from the root. Index Server is bound by the Windows NT shell limit of 260 characters per path.

As with most script files, a pound sign (#) can be used to specify a comment. At whatever point the # sign is in the line, from there on the line will be ignored. The conditional expressions that can be used in .IDQ files are as follows:

▶ CONTAINS—Is true if any part of the first value is found in the second value

▶ EQ—Equal to

▶ GE—Greater than or equal to

▶ GT—Greater than

▶ ISEMPTY—Is true if the value is null

▶ LE—Less than or equal to

▶ LT—Less than

▶ NE—Not equal to

Running Applications

ISAPI—Internet Server API—can be used to write applications that Web users can activate by filling out an HTML form or clicking a link in an HTML page on your Web server. The user-supplied information can then be responded to and the results returned in an HTML page or posted to a database.

ISAPI was a Microsoft improvement over popular CGI (Common Gateway Interface) scripting, and offers much better performance over CGI because applications are loaded into memory at server runtime. This means that they require less overhead and each request does not start a separate process. Additionally, ISAPI applications are created as DLLs on the server, and allow preprocessing of requests and post-processing of responses, permitting site-specific handling of HTTP requests and responses.

ISAPI filters can be used for applications for such functions as customized authentication, access, or logging. You can create complex sites by combining ISAPI filters and applications.

ISAPI works with OLE connectivity and the Internet Database Connector. This allows ISAPI to be implemented as a DLL (in essence, an executable) or as a filter (translating another executable's output). If ISAPI is used as a filter, then it is not called when the browser accesses a URL, but is summoned by the server in response to an event (which could easily be a URL request). Common uses of ISAPI filters include the following:

▶ Tracking URL usage statistics

▶ Performing authentication

▶ Adding entries to log files

▶ Compression

You don't need to be an ISAPI programmer to pass the exam, but there are several things you need to know:

▶ ISAPI applications effectively extend server applications to the desktop

▶ ISAPI is similar to CGI but offers better performance; CGI needs a new process for every execution

▶ Although created by Microsoft, ISAPI is an open specification that third-parties can write to

▶ ISAPI filters can do pre- or post-processing

▶ Execute, but not necessarily Read, permission is required for CGI or ISAPI script execution

Monitoring and Optimization

With Performance Monitor you can monitor functions relating to HTTP and FTP sessions. Performance Monitor is used when you want to see trends and patterns in your site's usage. When you install IIS, new objects relating to Web and FTP services are added to Performance Monitor, along with specific counters for those services. Objects are individual occurrences of a system resource, such as Web Service, FTP Service, Active Server Pages, Browser, and other items. Counters, on the other hand, are statistics relating to the objects, such as Debugging Requests, Memory Allocated, and Request Wait Time (all of which relate to the Active Server Pages object).

Performance Monitor can be started from the Administrative Tools (Common) folder. To specify the object and counter(s) you want to track, select Edit, Add to Chart. The Add to Chart dialog box is then displayed.

Performance Monitor can be used to monitor functions relating to Web and FTP services. The most practical monitoring involves the following objects and counters:

► Web Services object with Anonymous User/sec, Bytes Sent/ sec/, and Maximum NonAnonymous Users counters selected

► FTP Server object with Bytes Total/sec, Current Anonymous Users, and Maximum Connections counters selected

Bottlenecks occur when one (or several) hardware resource is being used too much, usually resulting in the draining of another hardware resource. The result is a performance reduction over the entire network. A bottleneck may occur as a result of insufficient server memory or because of too little bandwidth available to the connected users.

Start looking for bottlenecks by running Performance Monitor to create a baseline of activities for your site. You also can use Event Viewer to record events and audit situations on your computer that may require your attention. Another useful tool to use to locate bottlenecks is Task Manager. Task Manager shows you all of the ongoing tasks and threads on your computer.

For medium to very busy sites, you can expect IIS to saturate a 10MB Ethernet network adapter. This will certainly cause network-related bottlenecks to occur. To check for network server saturation, check for CPU % Utilization on both the client and server. To prevent the server from becoming network bound, try one of the following solutions:

► Use multiple 10MB Ethernet cards

► Install a 100MB Ethernet or FDDI network card

You may encounter hard disk bottlenecks if you have a very large file set that is being accessed by clients in a random pattern. In Performance Monitor, the % Disk Time counter shows the percentage of elapsed time the disk is busy servicing read or write requests. If there is a bottleneck involving disk access, the PhysicalDisk % Disk Time counter will be high. This is because the percentage of the CPU being utilized will remain low and the network card will not be saturated. When you notice a disk-related bottleneck, you can improve performance by using a redundant array of inexpensive drives (RAID) and striped disk sets.

 Note

> For the real world, consider a busmastering controller card. It reduces CPU usage and produces better hard disk performance.

CPU bottlenecks can be identified by measuring the amount of the server CPU that is being utilized. If the CPU % Processor Time value is high, try the following remedies:

▶ Upgrade the CPU to a faster one.

▶ Add additional CPUs to your server.

▶ Move any CPU-intensive applications (such as database applications) you run on the Web server to another computer.

▶ Add more computers on which you replicate your site and then distribute traffic across them.

Another performance option you implement is Bandwidth Throttling, which enables you to set a bandwidth setting based on kilobytes per second (KB/s). The purpose of such a setting is to reduce the amount of traffic you are allowing on your site, and prevent it from interfering with traffic from the rest of your LAN.

Microsoft Index Server is used to index the contents and properties of Internet or intranet documents stored on an IIS server. It can be monitored through Performance Monitor or .IDA scripts.

One way to optimize its performance is to run it on a system with an optimum configuration. By and large, the basic Windows NT Server configuration is enough to install Index Server. Using Index Server to index the contents and properties of Internet or intranet documents is probably best suited, however, for a small organization, or for an Internet site that does not expect a large amount of daily traffic.

To optimize the performance of Index Server, you should first look at the configuration of the computer on which it resides. The following are the factors that you need to measure to set this configuration:

▶ Number of documents in the corpus, which is the collection of documents and HTML pages indexed by Index Server

▶ Corpus size

▶ Rate of search requests

▶ Kind of queries

You'll find that the amount of memory you have installed greatly affects the performance of Index Server. For sites that have fewer than 100,000 documents stored in the corpus, a minimum of 32MB is required and recommended. However, if you have over 100,000 up to 250,000 documents, the recommended amount of memory jumps to 64–128 MB, whereas the minimum required is still 32 MB. For sites with 250,000 to 500,000 documents, you need a minimum of 64 MB of RAM, but it is recommended that you have 128–256 MB. Finally, if you have over 500,000 documents, you must have 128 MB of RAM installed, but at least 256 MB is recommended.

Another system configuration setting you should pay attention to is the amount of free hard disk space where the Index Server catalog is stored. If less than 3 MB of free space is available on the index disk, indexing and filtering are temporarily paused until additional disk space is made available. The event log records a message that `Very low disk space was detected on drive <drive>.` `Please free up at least <number> MB of space for content index to` `continue.`

Troubleshooting

The three main parameters that specify how TCP/IP is configured are as follows:

▶ The IP address (the network address and host address of the computer)

▶ The subnet mask (specifies what portion of the IP address specifies the network address and what portion of the address specifies the host address)

▶ The default gateway (most commonly, the address of the router)

Using a DHCP server can greatly reduce TCP/IP configuration problems. Scopes are ranges of available addresses on a DHCP server. The most important part of the configuration is to make sure you don't have duplicate addresses in the different scopes.

Most troubleshooting/trouble correction is implemented automatically with Index Server. For example, if the cache becomes corrupted, Index Server begins a recovery operation, and no administrator interaction is required. In all events, messages are written to the event log indicating the actions taking place, and administrators can monitor their Index Server from there.

Other issues to be aware of with Index Server include the following:

▶ Index Server starting and stopping

▶ Word weighting

▶ Disk filling

Index Server, by default, is set to automatically start when IIS does. If this is set to another value, such as Manual, then IIS can be started from the Services icon in the Control Panel. This is the same utility that can be used to stop the Index Server service, although it automatically shuts down when IIS does.

If Index Server isn't running, and a query comes in, Index Server starts automatically. Therefore, as an administrator, the starting of Index Server isn't something you should ever need to do manually. As an administrator, the stopping of Index Server is something you should never need to do, either, but you can do it from the Services utility.

Word weighting determines how words in the data are indexed. This process is done by the Waisindx.exe utility. It determines what to index, how much to weight words, how to optimize the server, and where to find the actual data. As a rule of thumb, seven indexes are created for each data file, and the Index Server data is equal to 40 percent of the document (corpus) size.

The weighting factors that Waisindx.exe uses are as follows:

▶ The actual weight of the word as to whether it appears in a headline, capitalized, or just in the body of the data.

▶ The term of the weight—how many times does it appear, and thus, how important it is to the data.

▶ The proximity—how close do multiple words always appear to each other. For example, "computer publishing."

▶ The density of the word. This is computed by taking the number of times the word appears and dividing it by the total number of all words in the data.

When Waisindx.exe is run, it creates the indexes that are then used to locate the data. As you add new records to the data, the indexes are not updated, and you must rerun Waisindx.exe to create new indexes incorporating the new data.

One of the most common problems with using Index Server is that of running out of disk space. If the drive fills, indexing is paused, and the only way of knowing this is by a message written to the event log. The event log should be monitored routinely by an administrator for this and similar occurrences.

MIME mappings are in the Registry associate file types with extensions. Mappings are under INETINFO and can be added or changed with REGEDIT or REGEDT32.

Last-Minute Studying for the Internet Information Server 4.0 Exam

The seven chapters of this book have looked at objectives and components of the Microsoft IIS 4.0 exam. After reading all of that, what is it that you must really know? What should you read as you sit and wait in the parking lot of the testing center—right up until the hour before going in to gamble your $100 and pride?

The following material covers the salient points of the previous seven chapters and the points that make excellent test fodder. Although there is no substitute for real-world, hands-on experience, knowing what to expect on the exam can be equally meaningful. The information that follows is equivalent to *Cliffs Notes*, providing the information you must know in each of the seven sections to pass the exam. Don't just memorize the concepts given; attempt to understand the reason why they are so, and you will have no difficulties ace-ing the exam.

Planning

As with previous IIS exams, the WWW service and FTP service are the core ones the exam focuses on. IIS can be installed on a stand-alone machine or in almost any other configuration. It can be installed on a workstation or server, but a workstation should be used only as a test environment and is not suitable for most purposes.

Remember that IIS automatically creates a user account upon installation, with the username of IUSR_*computername*. This is the account used for anonymous access and granted Log on Locally user rights by default. The account is necessary for anonymous logon access to your Web site, and permissions applied to it control the permissions for the anonymous user. You even can go so far as to disable anonymous access if security is a concern.

For the WWW service, available authentication methods are

> ▶ **Allow Anonymous Access**. Enables clients to connect to your Web site without requiring a username or password by using the default account of IUSR_*computername.*

> ▶ **Basic Authentication**. This method is used if you do not specify anonymous access and you want a client connecting to your Web site to enter a valid Windows NT username and password to log on. This sends a password in clear text format, with the passwords being transmitted in an unencrypted format.

> ▶ **Windows NT Challenge/Response.** This setting is used if you want the Windows NT Challenge/Response feature to authenticate the client attempting to connect to your Web site. The only Web browsers that support this feature include Internet Explorer 2.0 and higher. During the challenge/response procedure, cryptographic information is exchanged between the client and server to authenticate the user.

For the FTP service, available authentication methods include the ability to specify that anonymous connections are allowed or only anonymous connections are allowed, or the administrator can configure user and group accounts. Although it makes perfect sense, you cannot specify on the exam that only anonymous connections are allowed until you have first allowed anonymous connections.

Know the basics of TCP/IP (including what WINS and DNS are) and IP values, namely the number of hosts available per IP address class, as recapped in Table D.1.

Table D.1

Address classes.

Class	Address	Number of Hosts Available	Default Subnet Mask
A	01–126	16,777,214	255.0.0.0
B	128–191	65,534	255.255.0.0
C	192–223	254	255.255.255.0

The WINS service is used for dynamic resolution of NetBIOS names to IP addresses, and DNS is used for dynamic resolution of hostnames to IP addresses. The static versions of each are the LMHOSTS and HOSTS files, respectively.

The Secure Sockets Layer (SSL) enables you to protect communications over a network, whether that network be an intranet or the Internet. It does so by establishing a private (and encrypted) communication link between the user and the server. SSL can be used not only to authenticate specific users, but also the anonymous user. If SSL is enabled and a user attempts anonymous access, the Web server will look for a valid certificate on the client and reject those lacking one. To use SSL, you must obtain a digital certificate from an authentication authority and use Key Manager to generate keys. SSL URLs begin with https:// instead of http://

Memorize the table of subnets and the number of hosts that using each makes available on a C-level network:

Last Digits of Subnet Address	Number of Addresses in Range
128	128
192	64
224	32
240	16
248	8

continues

Last Digits of subnet Address	Number of Addresses in Range
252	4
254	2
255	1 (not used)

Installation and Configuration

To install IIS 4.0, you must first remove any previous versions of IIS (IIS 3.0, or version 2.0 that came with Windows NT 4.0). During the installation of it, you are prompted to select the services you want to install. IIS 4.0 includes the features listed in Table D.2.

Table D.2

IIS 4.0 services and features.

Component	Subcomponents	Description
Certificate Server	Certificate Server Certificate Authority	Enables you to create Certificate Authority on the IIS server to issue digital certificates to users accessing your web.
	Certificate Server Documentation	Documents to help you install and configure Certificate Authorities.
	Certificate Server Web Client	Enables you to post Web pages on your server to submit requests and retrieve certificates from a Certificate Authority.
FrontPage 98 Server Extensions	FrontPage Server Extensions files	Enables you to author Web pages and administer Web sites using Microsoft FrontPage and Visual InterDev.

Component	Subcomponents	Description
Internet Information Server (IIS)	Common Program Files	Files used by several IIS components.
	Documentation	Product documentation for IIS.
	File Transfer Protocol (FTP) Server	Provides FTP support to set up an FTP site to allow users to upload and download files from your site.
	Internet News Server	Installs the Microsoft Internet News Server for NNTP news.
	Internet Service Manager	Provides a snap-in for the Microsoft Management Console (MMC) to administer IIS.
	Internet Service Manager (HTML)	Provides an HTML-based administrative tool for IIS. You use IE 4 with this manager to administer IIS.
	SMTP Server	Installs the SMTP (Simple Mail Transfer Protocol) Server for email.
	World Wide Web samples	Installs sample IIS Web sites and other samples.
	World Wide Web Server	Installs the Web server so clients can access your Web site.
Microsoft Data Access Components 1.5	Data Sources	Installs the drivers and providers to access common data sources, including Jet and Access (ODBC), Oracle, and SQL Server data sources.

continues

Table D.2   Continued

Component	Subcomponents	Description
	MDAC, ADO, ODBC, and OLE	Installs the ActiveX Data Objects and other OLE DB and ODBC files.
	Remote Data Service 1.5 (RDS/ADC)	Installs Remote Data Service. Click the Show Subcomponents button to see options for this subcomponent.
Microsoft Index	Index Server System Files	Installs Server the files for the Index Server system.
	Language Resources	Installs Index Server language resources. Click the Show Subcomponents button to see a list of these languages. US English Language is the default setting.
	Online Documentation	Installs Index Server documentation.
	Sample Files	Installs sample files on how to use the Index Server.
Microsoft Management Console (MMC)	Management Console	Allows management of the IIS Services through the new console.
Microsoft Message (MSMQ)	HTML Documentation	Installs the MSMQ Queue Administration Guide.
	Administration Tools	Enables you to control and monitor your message queuing enterprise.

Component	Subcomponents	Description
	Microsoft Message Queue (Core)	Installs the required MSMQ files.
	Software Development Kit	Installs the MSMQ SDK for creating MSMQ applications with C or C++ APIs, or with ActiveX components.
Microsoft Script Debugger	Microsoft Script Debugger	Installs the Microsoft Script Debugger to debug Active Server Pages scripts and applications.
Microsoft Site Server Express 2.0	Analysis—Content	Enables you to analyze your site with content, site visualization, link management, and reporting tool.
	Analysis—Usage	Enables you to analyze your site usage.
	Publishing—Posting Acceptor 1.01	Enables IIS to receive files uploaded to it using the HTTP POST protocol.
	Publishing—Web Publishing Wizard 1.52	Automatically uploads new or revised content to Web servers.
Remote Access Services	Connection Manager Administration Kit	Sets up dial-up profiles in Connection Manager.
	Connection Point Services	Provides administration and services to phone books.
	Internet Authentication Services	Installs the Internet Authentication Service.

continues

Table D.2 Continued

Component	Subcomponents	Description
	Product Documentation	Installs documentation for Remote Access Services.
Transaction Server	Microsoft Management Console	Installs MMC, which is an interface for systems management applications.
	Transaction Server (MTS) Core Components	Installs MTS files.
	Transaction Server Core Documentation	Installs MTS product documentation.
	Transaction Server Deployment	Installs headers, libraries, and samples to help you create transaction components.
Visual InterDev RAD	Visual InterDev RAD Remote Deployment Support	Enables you to deploy applications remotely on the Web server.
Windows Scripting Host	Windows Scripting Host Files	Installs executable files for the Windows Scripting Host.
NT Option Pack Common Files		Files shared by all components of the NT Option Pack.

If you choose not to install a service at this time, you can restart the installation routine at any time and choose only the additional services you want to add. IIS 4.0 hardware requirements for an Intel system are

Hardware Device	Requirements
CPU	Minimum of a 90MHz 486 processor. For better performance, you need a Pentium 33-or-higher processor.

Hardware Device	Requirements
Hard disk space	Minimum of 50MB, but it is recommended you have at least 120MB. This does not include storage needed for files you plan to distribute via IIS.
Memory	Minimum of 32MB. For a Web site on which you will store multimedia files or expect a great deal of traffic, 48MB is the recommended minimum.
Monitor	Super VGA monitor with 800×600 resolution.

TCP Port settings are used by clients to connect to your FTP or WWW site. Memorize the default port settings:

Service	Port
FTP	21
SMTP	25
WWW	80
NNTP	119
SSL	443
NNTP with SSL	563

You can change the settings to unique TCP port numbers, but you must announce this setting to all clients who want to access your server.

An FTP directory listing style is the way in which your server will display a directory listing. The two choices are DOS (such as C:\folder\subfolder) and UNIX format (such as C:/directory/subdirectory/). Use UNIX format for the greatest compatibility on the Internet.

Limiting bandwidth is known as *throttling bandwidth,* and it limits only the bandwidth used by the Web service. IIS 4.0 provides support for HTTP 1.1 Host Headers in order to allow multiple hostnames to be associated with one IP address. With this feature, a separate IP address is not needed for every virtual server you support. Microsoft Internet Explorer 3.0-and-later and Netscape Navigator 2.0-and-later support this feature, but many other browsers do not.

IIS 4.0's Keep-Alive feature enables clients to maintain open connections. This way, a client does not need to re-establish connections for each request. By enabling Keep-Alives, you decrease the amount of time a client waits to connect to another document or application on your site. But you also increase the amount of resources devoted to this client.

Configuring and Managing Resource Access

The Microsoft Management Console is the primary utility used for most tasks. Accessed by choosing Internet Service Manager from the Programs menu, it is used for almost everything, including creating and sharing new directories or virtual directories, or servers. If there is only one thing you need to learn for the exam, it is everything you possibly can about MMC.

Access permissions for directories include

- ▶ Allow Read Access
- ▶ Allow Script Access
- ▶ Allow Execute Access
- ▶ Allow Write Access
- ▶ Allow Directory Browsing

The five rights that you can select for IIS access work in conjunction with all other rights. Like share rights, the IIS rights are *in addition to* NTFS rights and of greatest value when you are using anonymous access. Allowing Read access lets users view a file if their NTFS permissions also allow it. Taking away Read, however, prevents users from viewing the file, regardless of what the NTFS permissions may be.

The names of the rights are pretty self-explanatory as to what they offer. The only caveats to note are that Read and Script access are assigned by default, and Execute is a superset of Script access.

With virtual directories (which must exist on servers all within the same NT domain) you can get around issues such as disk space, determining where best to store files, and so forth. There are two downfalls to using virtual directories:

▶ A slight decrease in performance, because files must be retrieved from the LAN rather than being centralized

▶ Virtual directories do not show up in WWW listings and must be accessed through explicit links within HTML files or in the URL itself, such as http://www.microsoft.com/ train_cert.

You should also have a scripts directory under every virtual home directory to handle the executables there.

The Internet Service Manager (HTML) can enable you to manage the FTP and WWW service remotely (WWW must first be running in order to use it). Remotely, you can do almost everything you can locally, with the exception of making MIME Registry changes or stopping and starting services (if you stopped WWW, you would be disconnected).

MIME is used to define the type of file sent to the browser based upon the extension. If your server is supplying files in multiple formats, it must have a MIME mapping for each file type, or browsers will most likely be unable to retrieve the file. Mappings can be added or changed with REGEDIT or REGEDT32.

Integration and Interoperability

Databases such as Oracle or Microsoft SQL (Structured Query Language) Server can be used with IIS to supply the information to fulfill a query, update information, and add new data through the Web almost as easily as if a user were sitting on a Local Area Network.

Open Database Connectivity (ODBC) is an API (Application Programming Interface) that provides a simple way to connect to an existing database (whether that database is by SQL or is any ODBC-compliant database). It was designed by Microsoft to address the issue of any number of applications needing to interface with SQL server. Authentication can be done by NT or SQL. If SQL is chosen, it uses standard logon security, and a SQL Server user ID and password must be given for all connections. If you choose to use Windows NT authentication, the Windows NT user account is associated with a SQL Server user account, and integrated security is used to establish the connection, regardless of the current security mode at the server.

The greatest advantage that ODBC offers is that it defines a clear distinction between the application and the database, and thus does not require any specific programming. To use it, you create a query and template for how the output is to look.

There are four major components to IIS's implementation of ODBC:

> ▶ .htm—The file containing the hyperlink for a query. The request comes from the browser and merely specifies the URL for the .idc (Internet Database Connector) file on IIS.

> ▶ .htx—A file of HTML extensions containing the template document with placeholders for the result. Database fields that it receives are known as containers and are identified by field names surrounded by percent signs (%) and braces (<>). Thus the employeeno field that comes from the SQL database

is known as `<%employeeno%>` here. All processing is done in loops that start with `<%begindetail%>` and end with `<%enddetail%>`. Logic can be included with `<%if…%>` and `<%endif%>`, as well as `<%else%>` statements.

▶ .idc—The file containing the data source file information and SQL statement. Four required parameters are `Datasource`, `Username`, `Template`, and `SQLStatement`. `SQLStatement` is the list of commands you want to execute. Parameter values can be used if they are enclosed in percent signs (`%`); if multiple lines are required, a plus sign (+) must be the first character on each line.

▶ Httpodbc.dll—The dynamic link library included with the server.

Index Server differs from the ODBC discussion in the files used to hold the queries. Rather than using the .IDC file, Index Server uses an .IDQ (Internet Data Query) file. The .IDQ file should always be placed in the Scripts directory, and it requires Execute or Script permission to function properly.

There are two sections to the file: It begins with a tag of `[Query]` (the first section), followed by the `[Names]` section. The Names section is purely optional and not used most of the time. If it is used, it defines nonstandard column names that are referred to in a query. The Query section of the file is all that is required, and it can contain parameters, variables, and conditional expressions.

Restrictions are that lines must start with the variable you are trying to set, and only one variable can be set per line. Additionally, percent signs (%) are used to identify the variables and references.

The variables that can be used in .IDQ files are as follows:

▶ `CiCatalog`—Sets the location for the catalog. If the value is already set, the value here overrides that one.

▶ `CiCodepage`—Sets the server's code page. Again, if the value is already set, the entry here overrides the previous one.

- ▶ CiColumns—Defines a list of columns that will be used in the .HTX file.

- ▶ CiDeferNonIndexedTrimming—By default, is not used, but can be set if the scope of the query must be limited.

- ▶ CiFlags—Query flags can be set to DEEP or SHALLOW to determine whether only the directory listed in *CiScope* is searched or more.

- ▶ CiForceUseCi—By setting to TRUE, you can force the query to use the content index even if it is out of date.

- ▶ CiLocale—Specifies the locale used to issue the query.

- ▶ CiMaxRecordsInResultSet—Specifies the maximum number of results that can be returned from the query.

- ▶ CiMaxRecordsPerPage—Specifies the maximum number of records that can appear on a display page.

- ▶ CiRestriction—A restriction that you are placing on the query.

- ▶ CiScope—Specifies the starting directory for the search.

- ▶ CiSort—Specifies whether the results should be sorted in ascending or descending order.

- ▶ CiTemplate—Specifies the full path of the .HTX file from the root. Index Server is bound by the Windows NT shell limit of 260 characters per path.

As with most script files, a pound sign (#) can be used to specify a comment. At whatever point the # is in the line, from there on the line will be ignored. The conditional expressions that can be used in .IDQ files are the following:

- ▶ CONTAINS—Is true if any part of the first value is found in the second value

- ▶ EQ—Equal to

- ▶ GE—Greater than or equal to

- ▶ GT—Greater than

- ISEMPTY—Is true if the value is null

- LE—Less than or equal to

- LT—Less than

- NE—Not equal to

Running Applications

ISAPI (Internet Server Application Programming Interface) can be used to write applications that Web users can activate by filling out an HTML form or clicking a link in an HTML page on your Web server. The user-supplied information can then be responded to and the results returned in an HTML page or posted to a database.

ISAPI was a Microsoft improvement over popular CGI (Common Gateway Interface) scripting and offers much better performance over CGI because applications are loaded into memory at server runtime. This means that they require less overhead and each request does not start a separate process. Additionally, ISAPI applications are created as DLLs on the server and allow preprocessing of requests and post-processing of responses, permitting site-specific handling of HTTP requests and responses.

ISAPI filters can be used for applications for such functions as customized authentication, access, or logging. You can create complex sites by combining ISAPI filters and applications.

ISAPI works with OLE connectivity and the Internet Database Connector. This allows ISAPI to be implemented as a DLL (in essence, an executable) or as a filter (translating another executable's output). If ISAPI is used as a filter, it is not called by the browser's accessing an URL, but rather summoned by the server in response to an event (which could easily be an URL request). Common uses of ISAPI filters include

- Tracking URL usage statistics

- Performing authentication

▶ Adding entries to log files

▶ Compression

You don't need to be an ISAPI programmer to pass the exam, but there are several things you need to know:

▶ ISAPI applications effectively extend server applications to the desktop.

▶ ISAPI is similar to CGI but offers better performance; CGI needs a new process for every execution.

▶ Although created by Microsoft, ISAPI is an open specification that third parties can write to.

▶ ISAPI filters can do pre- or post-processing.

▶ Execute, but not necessarily read, permission is required for CGI or ISAPI script execution.

Monitoring and Optimization

The Active Log Format drop-down list enables you to select the type of log format you want to create. The following are the supported log file formats:

▶ **Microsoft IIS Log Format.** This is a fixed ASCII format that records basic logging items, including username, request date, request time, client IP address, number of bytes received, HTTP status code, and other items. This is a comma-delimited log file, making it easier to parse than other ASCII formats.

▶ **NCSA Common Log File Format.** This is a fixed ASCII format endorsed by the National Center for Supercomputing Applications (NCSA). The data it logs includes remote hostname, username, HTTP status code, request type, and the number of bytes received by the server. Spaces separate different items logged.

▶ **ODBC Logging.** This is a fixed format that is logged to a database. This log includes client IP address, username, request date, request time, HTTP status code, bytes received, bytes sent, action carried out, and the target. When you choose this option, you must specify the database for the file to be logged to. In addition, you must set up the database to receive that log data.

▶ **W3C Extended Log File Format.** This is a customizable ASCII format endorsed by the World Wide Web Consortium (W3C). This is the default setting. You can set this log format to record a number of different settings, such as request date, request time, client IP address, server IP address, server port, HTTP status code, and more. Data is separated by spaces in this format. Details of this format are presented in Table D.3.

Table D.3

W3C extended log file format logging options.

Option	Description
Date	Date the activity occurred
Time	Time the activity occurred
Client IP Address	IP address of the client attaching to your server
User Name	Username of the user who accessed your server
Service Name	Client computer's Internet service
Server Name	Server name where the log entry was created
Server IP	Server IP address where the log entry was created
Server Port	Port number to which the client is connected
Method	Action the client was performing

continues

Table D.3   Continued

Option	Description
URI Stem	Logs the resource the client was accessing on your server, such as an HTML page, CGI program, and so on
URI Query	Logs the search string the client was trying to match
HTTP Status	Status (in HTTP terms) of the client action
Win32 Status	Status (in Windows NT terms) of the client action
Bytes Sent	Number of bytes sent by the server
Bytes Received	Number of bytes received by the server
Time Taken	Amount of time to execute the action requested by the client
User Agent	Browser used by the client
Cookie	Content of any cookies sent or received by the server
Referrer	URL of the site from where the user clicked on to get to your site

In the New Log Time Period section of the site's configuration, you set when you want IIS to create a new log file for the selected Web site. The default is Daily, but you can select Weekly, Monthly, Unlimited File Size, or When File Size Reaches. If you select the last option, you need to set a maximum file size the log file can reach before a new file is created. The default is 19MB. The default directory in which you store log files is %WinDir\System32\LogFiles.

The Report Writer and Usage Import Database help you analyze and create reports based on logs created by IIS. The main difference between Report Writer and Usage Import is that Report Writer creates analysis reports based on the log file data. Usage Import, on the other hand, reads the log files and places the data into a relational database.

Performance Monitor is used when you want to see trends and patterns of your site's usage. When you install IIS, new objects relating to Web and FTP services are added to Performance Monitor along with specific counters for those services. Objects are individual occurrences of a system resource, such as Web Service, FTP Service, Active Server Pages, Browser, and other items. Counters, on the other hand, are statistics relating to the objects, such as Debugging Requests, Memory Allocated, and Request Wait Time (all of which relate to the Active Server Pages object).

Bottlenecks occur when one (or several) hardware resource(s) is being used too much, usually resulting in the draining of another hardware resource. The result is a performance reduction over the entire network. A bottleneck may occur as a result of insufficient server memory or because of too little bandwidth available to the connected users.

Start looking for bottlenecks by running Performance Monitor to create a baseline of activities for your site. You also can use Event Viewer to record events and audit situations on your computer that may require your attention. Another useful tool to use to locate bottlenecks is Task Manager. Task Manager shows you all the ongoing tasks and threads on your computer.

For medium–to–very busy sites, you can expect IIS to saturate a 10MB Ethernet network adapter. This will certainly cause bottlenecks to occur that are network-related. To check for network saturation, check for CPU % Utilization on both the client and server. To prevent the server from becoming network-bound, try one of the following solutions:

▶ Use multiple 10MB ethernet cards.

▶ Install a 100MB ethernet or FDDI network card.

CPU bottlenecks can be identified by measuring the amount of the server CPU that is being utilized. If the CPU % Processor Time value is high, try the following remedies:

▶ Upgrade the CPU to a faster one.

▶ Add additional CPUs to your server.

- ▶ Move any CPU-intensive applications (such as database applications) you run on the Web server to another computer.

- ▶ Add more computers on which you replicate your site and then distribute traffic across them.

To optimize the performance of Index Server, you should start by looking at the configuration of the computer on which it resides. The following are the factors that you need to measure to set this configuration:

- ▶ Number of documents in the corpus, which is the collection of documents and HTML pages indexed by Index Server

- ▶ Corpus size

- ▶ Rate of search requests

- ▶ Kind of queries

You'll find that the amount of memory you have installed will greatly affect the performance of Index Server. For sites that have fewer than 100,000 documents stored in the corpus, a minimum of 32MB is required and recommended. However, if you have over 100,000 up to 250,000 documents, the recommended amount of memory jumps to 64–128MB, whereas the minimum required still is 32MB. For sites with 250,000 to 500,000 documents, you need a minimum of 64MB of RAM, but it is recommended that you have 128–256MB. Finally, if you have over 500,000 documents, you must have 128MB of RAM installed, but at least 256MB is recommended.

Troubleshooting

Content Analyzer's WebMaps can be used to administer Web site content to help you keep your Web site up-to-date and functioning correctly. You use the Link Info window, searches, and properties to help you manage your site's content.

The three main parameters that specify how TCP/IP is configured are

▶ The IP address (the network address and host address of the computer)

▶ The subnet mask (specifies what portion of the IP address specifies the network address and what portion of the address specifies the host address)

▶ The default gateway (most commonly, the address of the router)

Using a DHCP server can greatly reduce TCP/IP configuration problems. Scopes are ranges of available addresses on a DHCP server. The most important part of the configuration is to make sure you don't have duplicate addresses in the different scopes.

Most Index Server troubleshooting and correction is implemented automatically without administrator interaction.

If Index Server is not running and a query comes in, Index Server will automatically start. Therefore, as an administrator, the starting of Index Server is not something you should ever need to do manually. As an administrator, the stopping of Index Server is something you should never need to do either, but you can do it from the Services utility.

One of the most common problems with using Index Server is running out of disk space. If the drive fills, indexing is paused, and the only way of knowing this is by a message written to the event log. The event log should be monitored routinely by an administrator for this and similar occurrences.

Appendix

Annotated Practice Exam

E

This appendix consists of 70 questions that are representative of what you should expect on the actual exam. There are figures (exhibits) and multiple-choice questions. The answers are at the end of the appendix. It is strongly suggested that when you take this exam, you treat it just as you would the actual exam at the test center. Time yourself, read carefully, and answer all the questions as best you can.

Some of the questions are vague and require deduction on your part to come up with the best answer from the possibilities given. Many of them are verbose, requiring you to read a lot before you come to an actual question. These are skills you should acquire before attempting the actual exam. Run through the test, and if you score less than 750 (missing more than 17), try rereading the chapters containing information where you were weak (use the index to find keywords to point you to the appropriate locations).

Exam Questions

The next three questions refers to Figure E.1.

Figure E.1

Questions 1, 2, and 3 refer to this figure.

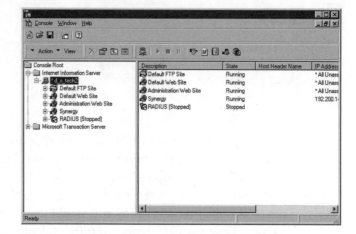

1. The utility shown in Figure E.1 is known as

    A. Internet Service Manager

    B. Internet Service Console

    C. Microsoft Console Manager

    D. Microsoft Management Console

2. It is the goal of all the Microsoft BackOffice products to use the management utility shown in Figure E.1. The ability to plug and unplug "interfaces" is provided by

    A. Plug-ins

    B. Snap-ins

    C. Add-ons

    D. ADO

3. Several icons are shown in the utility's main menu (see Figure E.1) representing links to other utilities available in NT. On the far right, there is one representing a globe with people in front of it. This is a link to

   A. Server Manager

   B. User Manager for Domains

   C. Performance Monitor

   D. Key Manager

4. Evan is asking Spencer about a Web site he has stumbled across. The last three letters of the Web site's FQDN are *mil.* Spencer informs Evan that this signifies

   A. A unique entity

   B. A militia group

   C. A military site

   D. A network

5. Evan asks Spencer a follow-up question regarding the use of the DNS database. He realizes that one server cannot possibly answer every request that is made, so the DNS database is obviously broken into smaller entities. Spencer confirms Evan's synopsis and informs him that the smaller increments are known as

   A. Servers

   B. Zones

   C. Regions

   D. Links

The next three questions refers to Figure E.2.

Figure E.2

Questions 6, 7, and 8 refer to this figure.

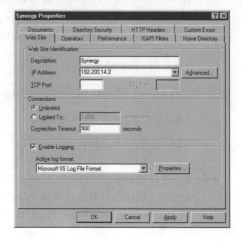

6. The TCP port shown for Synergy in Figure E.2 is blank. By default, this value should be

    A. 21

    B. 25

    C. 80

    D. 110

7. To make the Synergy site, shown in Figure E.2, hidden, which of the following TCP ports should be considered?

    A. 80

    B. 100

    C. 1000

    D. 5000

8. Kristin needs to implement bandwidth throttling to provide some bandwidth to her users and stop the Web service from taking it all. Which of the following tabs shown in Figure E.2 should she select to enable bandwidth throttling?

   A. Performance

   B. Directory Security

   C. Custom Errors

   D. Home Directory

9. Kristin and Karen are attempting to implement security on their intranet Web site. They have decided to use session keys between the clients and the server to encrypt and decrypt the transmissions. Session keys are typically how long in length?

   A. 16-bit

   B. 32-bit

   C. 40-bit

   D. 128-bit

10. With public-key encryption, how many keys are involved?

   A. 1

   B. 2

   C. 3

   D. 4

The next four questions refers to Figure E.3.

Figure E.3

*Questions 11, 12,
13, and 14 refer
to this figure.*

11. Figure E.3 shows the properties for a Web site log file. The log file the administrator has chosen to create in order to get to these properties must be

    A. SQL Logging

    B. ODBC Logging

    C. W3C Extended Log File Format

    D. NCSA Common Log File Format

    E. Microsoft IIS Log File Format

12. Which of the following items, which can be checked in Figure E.3, would add to the log file the site from which the user is coming?

    A. URI Stem

    B. Referrer

    C. Client IP Address

    D. User Agent

    E. Method

13. Which of the following items, which can be checked in Figure E.3, would add to the log file the action the client was performing?

    A. URI Stem

    B. Referrer

    C. Client IP Address

    D. User Agent

    E. Method

14. Which of the following items, which can be checked in Figure E.3, would add to the log file the resource the user is accessing on your server?

    A. URI Stem

    B. Referrer

    C. Client IP Address

    D. User Agent

    E. Method

15. Allan and Donna work in a static environment, with very few machines (clients or servers) on their network. They add a new database server, and Allan tells Donna that she must update the file so the other hosts will know the TCP/IP address of the new server. What file is he most likely referring to?

    A. HOSTS

    B. HOSTNAME

    C. SERVERS

    D. NETWORK

The next question refers to Figure E.4.

Figure E.4

Question 16 refers to this figure.

16. On the Operators tab of the Web site's properties (shown in Figure E.4), there is one group of operators added by default during creation of the site. That group is

    A. Users

    B. IUSR_*computername*

    C. Administrators

    D. Guests

17. Jerry and Jennifer have finished installing IIS 4. Jennifer needs to verify some information about the installation. Jerry tells her that there is a hierarchical database that stores the IIS 4 settings. In that database, there are keys that correspond to IIS elements, and each key has properties that affect the configuration of the element. This database is known as

    A. Bindery

    B. NDS

    C. Registry

    D. Metabase

18. Austin needs to install IIS 4. After probing about in the local computer store and on the Web, he finds that it is available only on

    A. The NT Server Web CD

    B. The NT Server Service Pack 3 CD

    C. The NT Server Option Pack CD

    D. The NT Server IIS CD

19. In reference to question 18, to install IIS 4, Austin must first install what Service Pack?

    A. NT Server Service Pack 4

    B. NT Server Service Pack 3

    C. NT Server Service Pack 2

    D. No Service Pack install is needed

20. What version of Microsoft Internet Explorer must Austin be running before he can truly begin the IIS 4 installation process?

    A. 2.0

    B. 3.0

    C. 4.0

    D. 4.01

The next four questions refer to Figure E.5.

Figure E.5

Questions 21, 22, 23, and 24 refer to this figure.

21. In Figure E.5, not everyone is allowed access to this site. Web site access has been denied to

    A. All IP addresses except 193.100.100.1

    B. Only the IP address 193.100.100.1

    C. A number of IP addresses beginning with 193.100.100.1

    D. All IP addresses except a small set of those beginning with 193.100.100.1

22. The significance of the subnet mask shown in Figure E.5 is that the number of sites affected is

    A. 1

    B. 8

    C. 16

    D. 32

    E. 64

23. To change the subnet mask shown in Figure E.5 to effectively remove subnetting, the new value would be

    A. 0.0.0.0

    B. 1.1.1.1

    C. 255.255.255.255

    D. 255.255.255.0

24. To change the subnet mask shown in Figure E.5 to make 128 sites affected, the new value would be

    A. 255.255.255.128

    B. 255.255.255.224

    C. 255.255.255.240

    D. 255.255.255.248

    E. 255.255.255.255

25. Amy is installing NT Server 4.0 on a new server, and the option appears to install IIS. If she selects that she wants it to be installed, what version of IIS will be installed on her server:

    A. No version of IIS is included on the NT 4.0 CD

    B. 2.0

    C. 3.0

    D. 4.0

26. In reference to question 25, if Amy chooses to install IIS during the installation of Windows NT Server, which of the following user accounts will be created on her server:

    A. Administrator

    B. Guest

    C. IUSR_*computername*

    D. IIS

27. Joseph wants to install IIS 4 on an Intel server that has been sitting dormant for some time, and he wants to verify that the equipment is sufficient. The minimum CPU is

    A. 50 MHz

    B. 90 MHz

    C. 133 MHz

    D. 150 MHz

28. Lori is planning on running IIS on an intranet and wants to ease the configuration of TCP/IP on her client machines. She should consider implementing

    A. DNS

    B. WINS

    C. DHCP

    D. HOSTS

29. One of the requirements Lori will have on her intranet server is file-level security. In order to obtain this, she will need to convert to

    A. FAT

    B. NTFS

    C. DNS

    D. CDFS

The next three questions refer to Figure E.6.

Figure E.6

Questions 30, 31, and 32 refer to this figure.

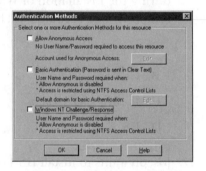

30. Figure E.6 shows the Authentication Methods available at a Web site. This box is obtained by selecting which tab from the Web site's properties?

    A. Web Site

    B. Operators

    C. Home Directory

    D. Directory Security

    E. Documents

31. In reference to Figure E.6, if the Allow Anonymous Access check box is checked, what account is used on a server named Synergy for the anonymous account?

    A. Synergy

    B. Synergy_anonymous

    C. Anoymous_Synergy

    D. IUSR_Synergy

32. Connie selects Windows NT Challenge/Response for the authentication method to be used at her site (as shown in Figure E.6). She must now make certain that all her users' Internet Explorer browsers are at least what version?

    A. 1.0

    B. 2.0

    C. 3.0

    D. 4.0

    E. 4.01

33. After installing IIS 4, three services are automatically set to start when you start Windows NT Server. The three services are

    A. World Wide Web Publishing Service

    B. Index Server Service

    C. FTP Publishing Service

    D. IIS Administration Service

34. Which standard NT utility includes 75 counters and can be used to track IIS services?

    A. User Manager for Domains

    B. Server Manager

    C. Performance Monitor

    D. Task Manager

35. When using the FTP Service, if users type in only a slash (/) as an URL, to what directory do they default?

    A. C:\

    B. C:\inetpub\Ftproot

    C. C:\Ftproot\Inetpub

    D. C:\Winnt\System32

The next three questions refer to Figure E.7.

Figure E.7

Questions 36, 37, and 38 refer to this figure.

36. Mike has chosen to deny access to a group of computers in order to keep the sales staff from accessing the human resources intranet. In Figure E.7, he has entered a starting IP address and now must enter the corresponding subnet. What value should he enter if he wishes to keep 16 hosts out?

    A. 255.255.255.240

    B. 255.255.255.224

    C. 255.255.255.248

    D. 255.255.255.252

37. In reference to question 35 and Figure E.7, what should the subnet value be if he wishes to keep 8 hosts out?

    A. 255.255.255.240

    B. 255.255.255.224

    C. 255.255.255.248

    D. 255.255.255.252

38. In reference to question 35 and Figure E.7, what should the subnet value be if he wishes to keep 32 hosts out?

    A. 255.255.255.240

    B. 255.255.255.224

    C. 255.255.255.248

    D. 255.255.255.252

39. Pat must use Bandwidth Throttling and enable it today or lose her comfortable administrator's position. She quickly figures up the amount of total available bandwidth and the amount she wishes to restrict the Web site to. The Web site restriction must be expressed in what type of measurement?

    A. BPS

    B. KB/S

    C. MB/S

    D. GB/S

40. Jodi has a number of users coming to her Web site without specifying a URL to a document. She, therefore, decides to implement default document pages. When specifying more than one default page, which one will the user see?

    A. The topmost document in the list

    B. The bottom-most document in the list

    C. The one specific to his or her IP Address

    D. The one specific to his or her referring Web site

The next three questions refer to Figure E.8.

Figure E.8

Questions 41, 42, and 43 refer to this figure.

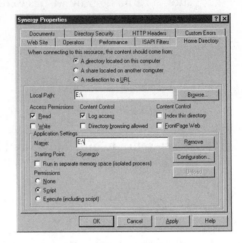

41. There are a number of action buttons displayed on the Home Directory tab shown in Figure E.8. One of those buttons, when pressed, will change its text to Create. That button is

    A. Browse

    B. Remove

    C. Configuration

    D. Unload

42. If the home directory depicted in Figure E.8 is changed to be a share located on another computer, which of the following is a valid choice for the path specification?

    A. E:\

    B. \\synergy\website

    C. http://www.synergy.com

    D. 192.5.6.7

43. Which access permission is required to see the parent directory of whatever subdirectory you may begin in?

    A. Read

    B. Write

    C. Directory browsing allowed

    D. None

44. Multiple hostnames can be associated with a single IP address through the use of

    A. Multi-homed hosts

    B. HTTP 1.1 host headers

    C. HTTP Keep-Alives

    D. Virtual directories

45. If you employ the use of virtual servers, what version of Internet Explorer should be considered the minimum requirement for your users' machines?

    A. 1.0

    B. 2.0

    C. 3.0

    D. 4.0

    E. 4.01

46. Clients may maintain open connections to reduce the amount of time re-establishing connections for requests taken through the use of

    A. Multi-homed hosts

    B. HTTP 1.1 host headers

    C. HTTP Keep-Alives

    D. Virtual directories

The next three questions refer to Figure E.9.

Figure E.9

Questions 47, 48, and 49 refer to this figure.

47. The properties shown in Figure E.9 are for what type of site:

   A. WWW

   B. FTP

   C. NNTP

   D. Gopher

48. The default TCP Port that should be in the field shown in Figure E.9 is

   A. 21

   B. 25

   C. 80

   D. 110

49. To make the site shown in Figure E.9 hidden, which of the following TCP ports should be considered?

   A. 80

   B. 100

   C. 1000

   D. 5000

50. Scott is setting up an FTP server for authors to upload their files to. A directory will be created for each book the publishing company is working on, and the authors will log in using anonymous access. What permission should be given under these circumstances?

    A. Read

    B. Write

    C. Read and Write

    D. Execute

51. Ann and Joyce are setting up the SMTP service and need to complete reams of paperwork to document the process and keep their ISO certification. In the paperwork, they need to detail what TCP port the service is using. If defaults are used, the answer is

    A. 21

    B. 25

    C. 80

    D. 110

52. By default, the FTP service is limited to how many connections?

    A. Unlimited

    B. 900

    C. 10,000

    D. 100,000

53. By default, the connection timeout for the FTP service is set to how many seconds?

    A. Unlimited

    B. 900

    C. 10,000

    D. 100,000

The next three questions refer to Figure E.10.

Figure E.10

Questions 54, 55, and 56 refer to this figure.

54. The FTP service can be configured to display three messages based upon events that occur. Refer to Figure E.10; the message that would be entered at the location marked C: would display

    A. On welcome

    B. On exit

    C. On error

    D. On maximum connections reached

55. Referring to Figure E.10, the message that would be entered at the location marked A: would display

    A. On welcome

    B. On exit

    C. On error

    D. On maximum connections reached

56. Referring to Figure E.10, the message that would be entered at the location marked B: would display

    A. On welcome

    B. On exit

    C. On error

    D. On maximum connections reached

57. If Loraine decides to use daily log files to keep track of the activity on her FTP site, the log filename syntax will be

    A. inetsv#.log

    B. inyymmdd.log

    C. inyymmdd.txt

    D. yymmddlog.txt

The next three questions refer to Figure E.11.

Figure E.11

Questions 58, 59, and 60 refer to this figure.

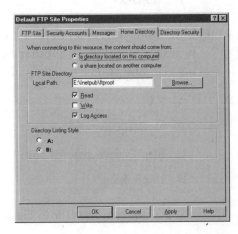

58. There are two possible directory listing styles available to a Web site, as shown by the markings A: and B: in Figure E.11. The two styles are

    A. LFN

    B. UNIX

    C. NTFS

    D. FAT

    E. MS-DOS

59. In reference to question 58 and Figure E.11, the default style is

    A. LFN

    B. UNIX

    C. NTFS

    D. FAT

    E. MS-DOS

60. If the home directory depicted in Figure E.11 is changed to be a share located on another computer, which of the following is a valid choice for the path specification

    A. E:\

    B. \\synergy\website

    C. http://www.synergy.com

    D. 192.5.6.7

The next four questions refer to Figure E.12.

Figure E.12

Questions 61, 62, 63, and 64 refer to this figure.

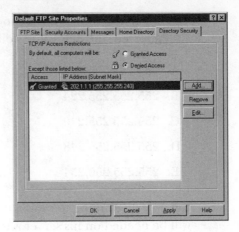

61. Refer to Figure E.12. Not everyone is allowed access to this site. FTP site access has been denied to

A. All IP addresses except 202.1.1.1

B. Only the IP address 202.1.1.1

C. A number of IP addresses beginning with 202.1.1.1

D. All IP addresses except a small set of those beginning with 202.1.1.1

62. The significance of the subnet mask shown in Figure E.12 means that the number of sites affected is

A. 1

B. 8

C. 16

D. 32

E. 64

63. To change the subnet mask shown in Figure E.12 to make 2 sites affected, the new value would be

    A. 255.255.255.128

    B. 255.255.255.224

    C. 255.255.255.240

    D. 255.255.255.248

    E. 255.255.255.254

64. Kenaz is attempting to estimate how much hard disk space will be needed on his server after the implementation of Index Server. In all cases, the size of the Index Server data is approximately what percentage of the size of the corpus?

    A. 40

    B. 30

    C. 20

    D. 10

65. If the hard drive space available to Index Server drops below a certain amount, Index Server will stop operating. That amount is

    A. 100MB

    B. 30MB

    C. 10MB

    D. 3MB

66. Sven is adding comments to a number of files and scripts so that the person who inherits his job will be able to understand the flow of data. The comment character(s) Sven should use in all cases is

    A. %

    B. @

    C. #

    D. \\

67. When working with IIS's implementation of ODBC, what file extension is necessary to stipulate how data is presented?

    A. HTX

    B. HTM

    C. IDC

    D. IDQ

68. When working with IIS's implementation of ODBC, what file extension is necessary to stipulate how data is accessed?

    A. HTX

    B. HTM

    C. IDC

    D. IDQ

69. How is ISAPI implemented in IIS?

    A. As a plug-in

    B. As a snap-in

    C. As an add-on

    D. As a dynamic link library

70. With Index Server, what is the minimum amount of RAM you should have on the server if you are indexing over 600,000 documents?

   A. 128MB

   B. 256MB

   C. 512MB

   D. GB

Exam Answers

1. **D**. The utility shown in Figure E.1 is the Microsoft Management Console.

2. **B**. Interfaces are loaded and unloaded in MMC through the use of snap-ins.

3. **B**. User Manager for Domains is depicted by the icon of the globe with users in front of it.

4. **C**. A domain ending with *mil* represents a military site.

5. **B**. The DNS database is divided into zones.

6. **C**. The default port for WWW sites is 80.

7. **D**. To make a Web site hidden, its TCP port should be changed to a value greater than the known ports (approximately 1023).

8. **A**. Bandwidth Throttling is enabled on the Performance tab of the site's properties.

9. **C**. Sessions employ 40-bit encryption. 128-bit keys are also an option when both parties are in the US.

10. **B**. With public-key encryption two keys are used—one public and one private.

11. **C**. The extended properties are available with W3C Extended Log File Format.

12. **B**. The Referrer option will denote the Web site the user is coming from.

13. **E**. The Method option will denote the action the client was performing.

14. **A**. URI Stem will denote the resource the user is accessing on your server.

15. **A**. The HOSTS file is used for static hostname–to–IP address resolution.

16. **C**. The administrators group is added by default to the Operators tab.

17. **D**. The metabase stores values and variables unique to IIS 4.

18. **C**. The NT Option Pack CD is needed to install IIS 4.

19. **B**. Before IIS can be installed, NT Service Pack 3 must be installed.

20. **D**. Internet Explorer 4.01 is required for IIS 4 installation.

21. **C**. Site access is denied to a number of computers beginning with 193.100.100.1.

22. **E**. A subnet mask of 192 denotes that 64 hosts are denied access to the site.

23. **D**. The default subnet mask for a Class C network is 255.255.255.0.

24. **A**. To deny access to 128 sites, the subnet mask used must be 255.255.255.128.

25. **B**. IIS 2.0 was included with NT Server 4.0.

26. **A**, **B**, **C**. Administrator and Guest accounts are always created during NT installation. `IUSR_computername` is created if IIS is installed as well.

27. **B**. The minimum CPU requirement on an Intel machine is 90 MHz.

28. **C**. DHCP (Dynamic Host Configuration Protocol) will ease the burden of TCP/IP implementation and administration.

29. **B**. NTFS partitions are required on a server for file-level security.

30. **D**. Authentication Methods is accessed through the Directory Security tab.

31. **D**. IUSR_Synergy is the account created for anonymous user access.

32. **B**. NT Challenge/Response requires Internet Explorer browsers of version 2.0 or greater.

33. **A, C, D**. The three services that automatically start after IIS installation are World Wide Web Publishing Service, FTP Publishing Service, and IIS Administration Service.

34. **C**. Performance Monitor includes over 75 counters and can be used to track IIS services.

35. **B**. When the slash (/) is used as an URL with FTP, the directory defaulted to is C:\Inetpub\Ftproot.

36. **A**. A subnet value of 255.255.255.240 is required to deny access to 16 hosts.

37. **C**. A subnet value of 255.255.255.248 is required to deny access to 8 hosts.

38. **B**. A subnet value of 255.255.255.224 is required to deny access to 32 hosts.

39. **B**. Bandwidth throttling is measured in terms of KB/S.

40. **A.** With multiple default documents, the topmost one of the list is used unless it is unavailable, and then the next one in the list is used.

41. **B.** The Remove button changes to Create after it is pressed.

42. **B.** Share names are always given as \\server\share.

43. **C.** Directory browsing allowed is needed to see parent directories and other directories.

44. **B.** Multiple hostnames can be associated with a single IP address (virtual servers) through HTTP 1.1 host headers.

45. **C.** To employ virtual servers, your users need IE 3.0 or higher.

46. **C.** HTTP Keep-Alives maintain open connections to reduce the time used for re-establishing connections.

47. **B.** The properties shown in Figure E.9 are for an FTP site.

48. **A.** The default TCP port for an FTP site is 21.

49. **D.** To hide the site, its TCP port should be changed to one above the known ports (approximately 1023).

50. **B.** Write permission best fits the scenario, letting authors upload files but not see other files or download.

51. **B.** SMTP's default TCP port is 25.

52. **D.** By default, FTP is limited to 100,000 connections.

53. **B.** By default, FTP connections timeout after 900 seconds.

54. **D.** The C: location in Figure E.10 is used for messages when maximum connections are reached.

55. **A.** The A: location in Figure E.10 is used for messages upon welcome.

56. **B.** The B: location in Figure E.10 is used for messages upon exit.

57. **B.** The syntax for daily logs is inyymmdd.log.

58. **B, E.** The two possible FTP listing styles are UNIX and MS-DOS.

59. **E.** MS-DOS is the default FTP listing style used.

60. **B.** Share names are always given as \\server\share.

61. **D.** In Figure E.12, all hosts are denied access to the site except a small group of those beginning with IP address 202.1.1.1.

62. **C.** The subnet value 255.255.255.240 limits the number of hosts to 16.

63. **E.** Changing the subnet value to 255.255.255.254 limits the number of hosts that can access the site to 2.

64. **A.** The Index Server data is approximately 40 percent of the corpus.

65. **D.** Below 3MB of free space, Index Server stops indexing (and functioning).

66. **C.** The pound sign (#) is used to denote comments.

67. **A.** HTX files are used for data presentation.

68. **C.** IDC files are used to define data access.

69. **D.** ISAPI is implemented in IIS as a DLL (Dynamic Link Library).

70. **A.** With 600,000 documents, Index Server *needs* 128MB of RAM. 256MB of RAM, however, is highly recommended and should be considered.

Appendix

Overview of the Certification Process

F

You must pass rigorous certification exams to become a Microsoft Certified Professional. These certification exams provide a valid and reliable measure of your technical proficiency and expertise. The closed-book exams are developed in consultation with computer industry professionals who have on-the-job experience with Microsoft products in the workplace. These exams are conducted by an independent organization—Sylvan Prometric—at more than 1,200 Authorized Prometric Testing Centers around the world.

Currently Microsoft offers six types of certification, based on specific areas of expertise:

▶ **Microsoft Certified Professional (MCP).** Holders of this certification are qualified to provide installation, configuration, and support for users of at least one Microsoft desktop operating system, such as Windows NT Workstation. In addition, candidates can take elective exams to develop areas of specialization. MCP is considered the first level of expertise leading to a premium certification.

▶ **Microsoft Certified Professional—+Internet (MCP+Internet).** Holders of this certification are qualified to plan security, install and configure server products, manage server resources, extend service to run CGI scripts or ISAPI scripts, monitor and analyze performance, and troubleshoot problems.

▶ **Microsoft Certified Systems Engineer (MCSE).** Holders of this certification are qualified to effectively plan, implement, maintain, and support information systems with Microsoft Windows NT and other Microsoft advanced systems and workgroup products, such as Microsoft Office and Microsoft BackOffice. MCSE is a second level of expertise.

▶ **Microsoft Certified Systems Engineer—+Internet (MCSE+Internet).** Holders of this certification are qualified in the core MCSE areas, and also are qualified to enhance, deploy, and manage sophisticated intranet and Internet solutions that include a browser, proxy server, host servers, database, and messaging and commerce components. In addition, an MCSE+Internet-certified professional is able to manage and analyze Web sites.

▶ **Microsoft Certified Solution Developer (MCSD).** Holders of this certification are qualified to design and develop custom business solutions by using Microsoft development tools, technologies, and platforms, including Microsoft Office and Microsoft BackOffice. MCSD is a second level of expertise.

▶ **Microsoft Certified Trainer (MCT).** Holders of this certification are instructionally and technically qualified by Microsoft to deliver Microsoft Education courses at Microsoft-authorized sites. An MCT must be employed by a Microsoft Solution Provider Authorized Technical Education Center or a Microsoft Authorized Academic Training site.

Note

For up-to-date information about each type of certification, visit the Microsoft Training and Certification World Wide Web site at `http://www.microsoft.com/train_cert`. You must have an Internet account and a WWW browser to access this information. You also can call the following sources:

▶ Microsoft Certified Professional Program: 800-636-7544

▶ Sylvan Prometric Testing Centers: 800-755-EXAM

▶ Microsoft Online Institute (MOLI): 800-449-9333

How to Become a Microsoft Certified Professional (MCP)

Becoming an MCP requires you to pass one operating system exam. The following list shows the names and exam numbers of all the operating systems from which you can choose to qualify for your MCP certification. Each test's identification number is listed after its title:

- ▶ Implementing and Supporting Microsoft Windows 95, #70-063*

- ▶ Implementing and Supporting Microsoft Windows 95, #70-064

- ▶ Implementing and Supporting Microsoft Windows NT Workstation 4.02, #70-073

- ▶ Implementing and Supporting Microsoft Windows NT Workstation 3.51, #70-042

- ▶ Implementing and Supporting Microsoft Windows NT Server 4.0, #70-067

- ▶ Implementing and Supporting Microsoft Windows NT Server 3.51, #70-043

- ▶ Microsoft Windows for Workgroups 3.11-Desktop, #70-048*

- ▶ Microsoft Windows 3.1, #70-030*

- ▶ Microsoft Windows Architecture I, #70-160

- ▶ Microsoft Windows Architecture II, #70-161

* Exams marked with an asterisk are scheduled to be retired. Check the Microsoft Training and Certification World Wide Web site at http://www.microsoft.com/ train_cert for details.

How to Become a Microsoft Certified Professional—+Internet (MCP+Internet)

Becoming an MCP with a specialty in Internet technology requires you to pass the following three exams. Each test's identification number is listed after its title:

▶ Internetworking Microsoft TCP/IP on Microsoft Windows NT 4.0, #70-059

▶ Implementing and Supporting Microsoft Windows NT Server 4.0, #70-067

▶ Implementing and Supporting Microsoft Internet Information Server 3.0 and Microsoft Index Server 1.1, #70-077

OR, Implementing and Supporting Microsoft Internet Information Server 4.0, #70-087

How to Become a Microsoft Certified Systems Engineer (MCSE)

MCSE candidates must pass four operating system exams and two elective exams. The MCSE certification path is divided into two tracks: the Windows NT 3.51 track and the Windows NT 4.0 track.

Note

> The exams included in this software product span the core requirements for the Windows NT 4.0 track only.

The following lists show the core requirements (four operating system exams) for both the Windows NT 3.51 and 4.0 tracks, and the elective courses (two exams) you can choose from for either track.

The four Windows NT 3.51 Track Core Requirements for MCSE certification are as follows. Each test's identification number is listed after its title:

- ▶ Implementing and Supporting Microsoft Windows NT Server 3.51, #70-043

- ▶ Implementing and Supporting Microsoft Windows NT Workstation 3.51, #70-042

- ▶ Networking Essentials, #70-058

- ▶ Microsoft Windows 3.1, #70-030*

   OR Microsoft Windows for Workgroups 3.11, #70-048*

   OR Implementing and Supporting Microsoft Windows 95, #70-063*

   OR Implementing and Supporting Microsoft Windows 95, #70-064

The four Windows NT 4.0 Track Core Requirements for MCSE certification are as follows. Each test's identification number is listed after its title:

- ▶ Implementing and Supporting Microsoft Windows NT Server 4.0, #70-067

- ▶ Implementing and Supporting Microsoft Windows NT Server 4.0 in the Enterprise, #70-068

- ▶ Networking Essentials, #70-058

- ▶ Microsoft Windows 3.1, #70-030*

   OR Microsoft Windows for Workgroups 3.11, #70-048*

   OR Implementing and Supporting Microsoft Windows 95, #70-063*

OR Implementing and Supporting Microsoft Windows 95, #70-064

OR Implementing and Supporting Microsoft Windows NT Workstation 4.0, #70-073

For either the Windows NT 3.51 and or the 4.0 track, you must pass two of the following elective exams for MCSE certification:

▶ Implementing and Supporting Microsoft SNA Server 3.0, #70-013

OR Implementing and Supporting Microsoft SNA Server 4.0, #70-085

▶ Implementing and Supporting Microsoft Systems Management Server 1.0, #70-014*

OR Implementing and Supporting Microsoft Systems Management Server 1.2, #70-018

OR Implementing and Supporting Microsoft Systems Management Server 1.2, #70-086

▶ Microsoft SQL Server 4.2 Database Implementation, #70-021

OR Implementing a Database Design on Microsoft SQL Server 6.5, #70-027

OR Implementing a Database Design on Microsoft SQL Server 7.0, #70-029

▶ Microsoft SQL Server 4.2 Database Administration for Microsoft Windows NT, #70-022

OR System Administration for Microsoft SQL Server 6.5, #70-026

OR System Administration for Microsoft SQL Server 7.0, #70-028

▶ Microsoft Mail for PC Networks 3.2-Enterprise, #70-037

- ▶ Internetworking with Microsoft TCP/IP on Microsoft Windows NT (3.5-3.51), #70-053

  OR Internetworking with Microsoft TCP/IP on Microsoft Windows NT 4.0, #70-059

- ▶ Implementing and Supporting Microsoft Exchange Server 4.0, #70-075*

  OR Implementing and Supporting Microsoft Exchange Server 5.0, #70-076

  OR Implementing and Supporting Microsoft Exchange Server 5.5, #70-081

- ▶ Implementing and Supporting Microsoft Internet Information Server 3.0 and Microsoft Index Server 1.1, #70-077

  OR Implementing and Supporting Microsoft Internet Information Server 4.0, #70-087

- ▶ Implementing and Supporting Microsoft Internet Explorer 4.0 by Using the Internet Explorer Resource Kit, #70-079

How to Become a Microsoft Certified Systems Engineer—+Internet (MCSE+ Internet)

MCSE+Internet candidates must pass seven operating system exams and two elective exams.

The following lists show the core requirements and the elective courses (two exams). The seven MCSE+Internet core exams required for certification are as follows. Each test's identification number is listed after its title:

- ▶ Networking Essentials, #70-058

- ▶ Internetworking with Microsoft TCP/IP on Microsoft Windows NT 4.0, #70-059

▶ Implementing and Supporting Microsoft Windows 95, #70-063

OR Implementing and Supporting Microsoft Windows NT Workstation 4.0, #70-073

▶ Implementing and Supporting Microsoft Windows NT Server 4.0, #70-067

▶ Implementing and Supporting Microsoft Windows NT Server 4.0 in the Enterprise, #70-068

▶ Implementing and Supporting Microsoft Internet Information Server 3.0 and Microsoft Index Server 1.1, #70-077

OR Implementing and Supporting Microsoft Internet Information Server 4.0, #70-087

▶ Implementing and Supporting Microsoft Internet Explorer 4.0 by Using the Internet Explorer Resource Kit, #70-079

You must also pass two of the following elective exams:

▶ System Administration for Microsoft SQL Server 6.5, #70-026

▶ Implementing a Database Design on Microsoft SQL Server 6.5, #70-027

▶ Implementing and Supporting Microsoft Exchange Server 5.0, #70-076

OR Implementing and Supporting Microsoft Exchange Server 5.5, #70-081

▶ Implementing and Supporting Microsoft Proxy Server 1.0, #70-078

OR Implementing and Supporting Microsoft Proxy Server 2.0, #70-088

How to Become a Microsoft Certified Solution Developer (MCSD)

MCSD candidates must pass two core technology exams and two elective exams. The following lists show the required technology exams, as well as the elective exams that apply toward obtaining the MCSD.

You must pass the following two core technology exams to qualify for MCSD certification. Each test's identification number is listed after its title:

▶ Microsoft Windows Architecture I, #70-160

▶ Microsoft Windows Architecture II, #70-161

You also must pass two of the following elective exams to become an MSCD:

▶ Microsoft SQL Server 4.2 Database Implementation, #70-021

   OR Implementing a Database Design on Microsoft SQL Server 6.5, #70-027

   OR Implementing a Database Design on Microsoft SQL Server 7.0, #70-029

▶ Developing Applications with C++ Using the Microsoft Foundation Class Library, #70-024

▶ Microsoft Visual Basic 3.0 for Windows-Application Development, #70-050

   OR Programming with Microsoft Visual Basic 4.0, #70-065

   OR Developing Applications with Microsoft Visual Basic 5.0, #70-165

- Microsoft Access 2.0 for Windows-Application Development, #70-051

  OR Microsoft Access for Windows 95 and the Microsoft Access Development Toolkit, #70-069

- Developing Applications with Microsoft Excel 5.0 Using Visual Basic for Applications, #70-052

- Programming in Microsoft Visual FoxPro 3.0 for Windows, #70-054

- Implementing OLE in Microsoft Foundation Class Applications, #70-025

Becoming a Microsoft Certified Trainer (MCT)

To understand the requirements and process for becoming a Microsoft Certified Trainer (MCT), you must obtain the Microsoft Certified Trainer Guide document (MCTGUIDE.DOC) from the following WWW site:

```
http://www.microsoft.com/train_cert/download.htm
```

On this page, click the hyperlink MCT GUIDE (mctguide.doc) (117k). If your WWW browser can display DOC files (Word for Windows native file format), the MCT Guide appears in the browser window. Otherwise, you need to download it and open it in Word for Windows or Windows 95 WordPad. The MCT Guide explains in detail the following four-step process for becoming an MCT:

1. Complete and mail a Microsoft Certified Trainer application to Microsoft. You must include proof of your skills for presenting instructional material. The options for doing so are described in the MCT Guide.

2. Obtain and study the Microsoft Trainer Kit for the Microsoft Official Curricula (MOC) course(s) for which you want to be certified. Microsoft Trainer Kits can be ordered by calling 800-688-0496 in North America. Other regions should review the MCT Guide for information about how to order a Trainer Kit.

3. Pass the Microsoft certification exam for the product for which you want to be certified to teach.

4. Attend the Microsoft Official Curriculum (MOC) course for the course for which you want to be certified. This must be done so you can understand how the course is structured, how labs are completed, and how the course flows.

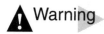 **Warning**

You should consider the preceding steps as a general overview of the MCT certification process. The precise steps that you need to take are described in detail in the MCTGUIDE.DOC file on the WWW site mentioned earlier. Do not misconstrue the preceding steps for the actual process.

If you are interested in becoming an MCT, you can receive more information by visiting the Microsoft Certified Training (MCT) WWW site at http://www.microsoft.com/train_cert/mctint.htm; or you can call 800-688-0496.

Appendix

Study Tips

G

Before you begin to study for a certification exam, you should know exactly what Microsoft expects you to learn.

Pay close attention to the objectives posted for the exam. The entire set of objectives is listed in the introduction to this book, and the relevant subset of objectives appears at the beginning of each chapter. The objectives can always be found on the WWW site at `http://www.microsoft.com/train_cert`. You also can make use of the handy tear-out card at the front of this book—its objective matrix lists all objectives and the page you can turn to for information on that objective.

Humans vary in their learning styles. Some people are visual learners, others are textual, and still others learn best from aural sources. However, there are some basic principles of learning that apply to everyone. For example, students who take notes on lectures have better recall on exam day—even if they did not study the notes later. Because they encoded the information as well as decoded it, they processed it in a deeper, more active fashion than those who simply listened to the lecture.

Hence, use the study techniques that you know work for you, but also take advantage of more general principles of learning. For example, if you are a visual learner, pay special attention to the figures provided in this book. Create your own visual cues by doing such things as diagramming processes and relationships.

Take advantage of a general principle of learning and study the organization and the details of information separately. Cognitive learning research has demonstrated that if you attempt to focus on learning just the organization of the information, followed by a focus on just learning the specific details, you retain the information better than if you attempt to take in all of the information at once.

Use your study materials to prepare a detailed outline of the material on the exam. Study it first by learning the organization of the material. Then, in your next pass through the outline, focus on memorizing and understanding the detail. Trying to do both at once only leads to the two types of information interfering with your overall learning.

Finally, follow common-sense practices in your studying as well. Basic studying strategies are detailed in the following list:

▶ Study in bright light to reduce fatigue and depression.

▶ Establish a regular study schedule and stick as close to it as possible.

▶ Turn off all forms of distraction, including radios and televisions; or try studying in a quiet room.

▶ Always study in the same place so your materials are readily at hand.

▶ Take short (approximately 15-minute) breaks every two to three hours or so. Studies have proven that your brain assimilates information better when these rest periods are taken.

Testing Yourself

Before taking the actual exam, verify that you are ready to do so by testing yourself many times in a variety of ways. Within this book there are questions at the beginning and end of each chapter. On the accompanying CD-ROM there is an electronic test engine that emulates the actual Microsoft exam and enables you to test your knowledge of the subject areas. Use this repeatedly until you are consistently scoring in the 90 percent range (or better).

Note

This means, of course, that you can't start studying five days before the exam begins. You need to give yourself plenty of time to read, practice, and test yourself several times.

We believe that the New Riders' TestPrep electronic testing engine is the best test preparation tool on the market. TestPrep is described in detail in Appendix I, "All About TestPrep."

Hints and Tips for Doing Your Best on the Tests

When you go to take the actual exam, be prepared. Arrive early and be ready to show two forms of identification. Expect wordy questions. However, if you have taken Microsoft certification exams before, expect fewer questions with the new Computer Assisted Testing (CAT) method. Instead of receiving a fixed number of questions in a fixed time period, you will take an exam that is more individually tailored to you and your responses. All test-takers start with an easy-to-moderate question; if you answer the question correctly you get a more difficult follow-up question. If you answer correctly, the difficulty of following questions also increases. On the other hand, if you answer the second question incorrectly, the following questions will be easier. This process continues only until the test determines your ability level. Thus there is no fixed number of questions you will receive. The good news is that these tests are no harder than traditional exams and take considerably less time! Prepare for them like you would any other exam.

These exams also include simulation questions. These questions display the windows and dialog boxes of an interface in order to imitate IIS functions and tasks. You are given a scenario and one or more tasks to complete in the simulation. In order to prepare for these questions, make sure you study the figures in this book and complete all the exercises at the ends of the chapters.

Things to Watch For

When you take the exam, read very carefully! Make sure that you understand just what the question requires, and take notice of the number of correct choices you need to make. Remember that some questions require that you select a single correct answer; other questions have more than one correct answer. Radial buttons next to the answer choices indicate that the answers are mutually exclusive—there is but one correct answer. On the other hand, checkboxes indicate that the answers are not mutually exclusive and there are multiple correct answers.

Again, read the questions fully. With lengthy questions, the last sentence often dramatically changes the scenario. When taking the exam, you are given pencils and two sheets of paper. If you are uncertain of what the question requires, map out the scenario on the paper until you have it clear in your mind. You must turn in the scrap paper at the end of the exam.

Changing Answers

The rule of thumb here is *don't*! If you have read the question carefully and completely, and you felt like you knew the right answer, you probably did. Don't second-guess yourself! If, as you check your answers, one stands out as clearly marked incorrectly, of course you should change it. But if you are at all unsure, go with your first impression.

Attaching Notes to Test Questions

At the conclusion of the exam, before the grading takes place, you are given the opportunity to attach a message to any question. If you feel that a question was too ambiguous, or tested knowledge you don't need to have to work with the product, take this opportunity to state your case. It's unheard of for Microsoft to change a test score as a result of an attached message, but it never hurts to try—and it helps to vent your frustration before blowing the proverbial 50-amp fuse.

Good luck!

Appendix H

What's on the CD-ROM

This appendix is a brief rundown of what you'll find on the CD-ROM that comes with this book. For a more detailed description of the newly developed TestPrep test engine, exclusive to Macmillan Computer Publishing, please see Appendix I, "All About TestPrep."

TestPrep

TestPrep is a new test engine developed exclusively for Macmillan Computer Publishing. It is, we believe, the best test engine available because it closely emulates the actual Microsoft exam and enables you to check your score by category, which helps you determine what topics you need to study further. Before running the TestPrep software, be sure to read CDROM.hlp (in the root directory of the CD-ROM) for late-breaking news on TestPrep features. For a complete description of the benefits of TestPrep, please see Appendix I.

Exclusive Electronic Version of Text

Also contained on the CD-ROM is the electronic version of this book. You can use this to help you search for terms or areas that you need to study. The electronic version comes complete with all figures as they appear in the book.

IIS 4 MMC Simulator

Finally, the CD-ROM includes a demonstration version of IIS 4 MMC Simulator. This test engine prepares you for the simulation or performance side of the exam. It prompts you to perform tasks related to the WWW service as you would in the actual management console. While this version is limited to the WWW service, it will provide you with the experience of answering simulation-based test questions and further prepare you for questions concerning the WWW service.

Copyright Information and Disclaimer

Macmillan Computer Publishing's TestPrep test engine: Copyright 1997 New Riders Publishing. All rights reserved. Made in U.S.A.

Appendix

All About TestPrep

The TestPrep software included on the CD-ROM accompanying this book enables you to test your Systems Management Server knowledge in a manner similar to that employed by the actual Microsoft exam. There are actually three applications included: Practice Exams, Study Cards, and Flash Cards. Practice Exams provide you with simulated multiple-choice tests. Study Cards provide the same sorts of questions (but enable you to control the number and types of questions) and provide immediate feedback to you. This format enables you to learn from your testing and control the topics on which you want to be tested. Flash Cards provide this same sort of feedback and allow the same sort of control, but require short answer or essay answers to questions; you are not prompted with multiple choice selections or given a cue as to the number of correct answers to provide.

Although it is possible to maximize the TestPrep applications, the default is for them to run in smaller mode so you can refer to your Internet Information Server 4 desktop while answering questions. TestPrep uses a unique randomization process to ensure that each time you run the programs, you are presented with a different sequence of questions—this enhances your learning and helps prevent you from merely memorizing the expected answers over time without reading the question each and every time.

Question Presentation

TestPrep Practice Exams and Study Cards emulate the actual Microsoft "Implementing and Supporting Microsoft Internet Information Server 4.0" exam (#70-018), in that radial (circle) buttons are used to signify only one correct choice, and check boxes (squares) are used to indicate multiple correct answers. When more than one answer is correct, the number you should select is given in the wording of the question.

Scoring

The TestPrep Practice Exam Score Report uses actual numbers from the "Implementing and Supporting Microsoft Internet Information Server 4.0" exam. For that exam, we expect the number of questions to be 49, and that the time limit will be about 90 minutes.

I n d e x

Symbols

* (asterisk), 225
//? parameter, 186
(pound sign), script files, 370

A

aa\ÄPROGRAM.DOC-1126, 393
aa\ÄPROGRAM.DOC-1127, 393
About tab (ODBC Data Source
  Administrator dialog box), 153
AcceptByte (Registry parameter), 343
access
  anonymous, 18-23
    IUSR_computername account, 364
  Certificate Server, configuring, 123-124
  Content Analyzer, 120
  DHCP address problems, resolving with
    IPCONFIG, 290-291
  directories, changing, 112-113
  files, changing, 113-114
  Index Server, configuring, 124
  IP configuration, troubleshooting
    utilities, 291-295
  MIME (Multipurpose Internet Mail
    Extension), 125
  names, troubleshooting resolution
    problems, 296-303
  NNTP (Network News Transport
    Protocol), configuring, 122-123
  permissions, 366
  resources
    configuration, 388-389
    problems, resolving, 290-303
  rights, 112, 367
  scripts, writing, 119-120
  security, troubleshooting problems, 289

SMTP (Simple Mail Transfer Protocol),
  121-122
web sites, denying, 25
WWW (World Wide Web), limiting with
  NTFS, 23
Access 7.0 (Microsoft), 91
accounts, IUSR_computername
  (anonymous access), 364
Action menu commands, New, 118
Active Server Pages, see ASP
ActiveX components, 63
ActiveX Data Objects, see ADO
Add Default Document dialog box, 82
Add to Chart dialog box, 233, 372
addresses
  client, pinging local addresses, 293
  IP (Internet Protocol), 349-350
    assigning, 118
    classes, 365
    dynamic resolution of NetBIOS
      names, 365
    in form of binary numbers, 355
    subnet masks, 350-358
    local, pinging, 293
    loopback, pinging, 292-293
Adjust requests timestamps to option
  (Usage Import Options dialog box
  Import tab), 222
administration
  IIS 4.0 installation, 87
  Windows NT Server tools, 87
Administrator option (Security Accounts
  tab), 71
Administrator property (anonymous user
  account), 20
ADO (ActiveX Data Objects)
  commands, 192
  configuring IIS 4.0 to support, 190-192

M

Q